TEXTS, TRADITIONS, AND SACREDNESS

This book presents a critical reading of *Kristapurāṇa*, the first South Asian retelling of the Bible. In 1579, Thomas Stephens (1549–1619), a young Jesuit priest, arrived in Goa with the aim of preaching Christianity to the local subjects of the Portuguese colony. *Kristapurāṇa* (1616), a sweeping narrative with 10,962 verses, is his epic poetic retelling of the Christian Bible in the Marathi language. This fascinating text, which first appeared in Roman script, is also one of the earliest printed works in the subcontinent. *Kristapurāṇa* translated the entire biblical narrative into Marathi a century before Bible translation into South Asian languages began in earnest in Protestant missions.

This book contributes to an understanding of translation as it was practiced in South Asia through its study of genre, landscapes, and cultural translation in *Kristapurāṇa*, while also retelling a history of sacred texts and biblical narratives in the region. It examines this under-studied masterpiece of Christian writing from Goa in the early era of Catholic missions and examines themes such as the complexities of the colonial machinery, religious encounters, textual traditions, and multilingualism, providing insight into the Portuguese Goa of the sixteenth and seventeenth centuries.

The first of its kind, the book makes significant interventions into the current discourse on cultural translation and brings to the fore a hitherto-understudied text. It will be an indispensable resource for students and researchers of translation studies, comparative literature, religious studies, biblical studies, English literature, cultural studies, literary history, postcolonial studies, and South Asian studies.

Annie Rachel Royson holds a PhD in Translation Studies and Comparative Literature from the Indian Institute of Technology Gandhinagar, India. She currently teaches literature and language at the School of Liberal Studies, Pandit Deendayal Energy University. Her research interests include Translation Studies, Comparative Literature, Travel Writings, Religious Studies, and Christian Writings in South Asia. She is currently working on the idea of cultural translation, genre, and, landscapes through a study of South Asian Christian texts. Her research on *Kristapurāṇa* and translation has been presented at Indian and international academic conferences and published in journals such as *Church History and Religious Culture, Asia Pacific Translation and Intercultural Studies, South Asia Multidiscipinary Academic Journal* (SAMAJ), *Nidan: International Journal of Indian Studies*, and *Translation Studies*. She was an Associate at the Nida School of Translation Studies 2016, a Sahapedia-UNESCO Fellow 2018, and a recipient of the Scientific and Solidarity Bursary of the International Association for Translation and Intercultural Studies in the year 2021. She has recently been awarded the India Fellowship (2022) from the Lakshmi Mittal and Family South Asia Institute, Harvard University.

TEXTS, TRADITIONS, AND SACREDNESS

Cultural Translation in *Kristapurāṇa*

Annie Rachel Royson

 Routledge
Taylor & Francis Group

LONDON AND NEW YORK

Designed cover image: © Aeduard / Getty Images

First published 2023
by Routledge
4 Park Square, Milton Park, Abingdon, Oxon OX14 4RN

and by Routledge
605 Third Avenue, New York, NY 10158

Routledge is an imprint of the Taylor & Francis Group, an informa business

© 2023 Annie Rachel Royson

British Library Cataloguing-in-Publication Data
A catalogue record for this book is available from the British Library

ISBN: 978-0-367-64158-0 (hbk)
ISBN: 978-0-367-70473-5 (pbk)
ISBN: 978-1-003-14654-4 (ebk)

DOI: 10.4324/9781003146544

Typeset in Bembo
by SPi Technologies India Pvt Ltd (Straive)

For Edward and Johan

CONTENTS

Preface   *viii*

Acknowledgements   *xi*

Note on Transliteration   *xiv*

Translator's Note   *xv*

    Introduction: Cultures, Scriptures, and Translation   1

1 Texts, Travels, and Christianities in South Asia   28

2 Into the Languages of this Land   60

3 Genre, Novelization, and Translatability in *Kristapurāṇa*   84

4 (Re)Painting Landscapes, (Re)Inventing Tradition   115

5 Speaking After   142

Bibliography   *151*

Index   *170*

PREFACE

This book grapples with themes of travel, sacredness, translation theory and practice, landscapes, and genre through a study of one text – *Kristapurāṇa* (1616) – a Marathi poetic work composed by the English Jesuit Thomas Stephens (1549–1619) in seventeenth-century Goa.

It is the outcome of a long-standing fascination with languages, translation, and sacred texts. Translation was an everyday reality in the multilingual atmosphere in which I grew up. Many years later, a formal training in literature and translation would turn this childhood fascination into a calling and become the motivation for this research. My encounter with *Kristapurāṇa* provided the spaces for exploring these crucial ties between translation and sacred texts.

The purpose of this book is to explore the complexities of sacred texts using translation as a critical lens. The translation of sacred texts in an activity fraught with the dangers of heresy and "faithfulness" and provide fault lines which afford fascinating insights into the ideas of translation, sacredness, genre, and geography. The religious texts of South Asia are a significant corpus waiting to be explored fully by scholars interested in the literary-cultural fabric of the region. This book is a modest attempt to delve into this area of sacred texts and uncover the complex networks of travel, textual production, and power that informed the early modern period in the subcontinent. Geography and place/space are also major preoccupations of the discussions in this volume. Physical landscapes and travel run as significant threads through the narrative.

In addition to being an academic inquiry into the text, this volume is also a collection of stories, and journeys, that weave through the narrative. The journey which is at the centre of this narrative is Stephens's historical journey from England to Rome and from Rome to Goa on whose shores he landed in the year 1579. Goa would become the place where Stephens lived and worked and eventually died in 1619, exactly forty years after his arrival.

In many ways this book is also the outcome of my own journeys that I undertook in pursuit of *Kristapurāṇa* and its composer, Stephens. Various sites in Goa became critical stops in my travels and form the background of this volume.

One of the most significant sites along this trail is the Rachol Seminary in Raia village, Goa. The Patriarchal Seminary of Rachol was built during Stephens' times. Stephens himself was the Rector of the college from 1609. *Kristapurāṇa* was printed at the printing press at Rachol, as is clear from the licences in the handwritten manuscripts. The buildings of the Rachol Seminary stand in their original form, as they were in Stephens' times. New buildings have been added to surround the original structure. However, there is a strange invisibility of Stephens himself in the Seminary. No printed copy of *Kristapurāṇa* from the seventeenth century is known to exist. The picture of Stephens framed in the library is from a recent reproduction a modern artist. There is no record of where Stephens has been buried, either, despite the fact that Goa has very well-preserved Christian structures and records from Stephens' era. This "invisibility and fragmentation" (Xavier and Županov 2015, 288) strikes one repeatedly while on the trail of *Kristapurāṇa* and its author Thomas Stephens.

The museum at the Pilar Monastery has on display one of the manuscripts of *Kristapurāṇa*. Several Avaswaru in this manuscript are illegible or missing due to damage. The museum is managed by historian and priest Father Jose Cosme Costa. The manuscript is especially dear to him as it was Father Costa who, as a young novice priest, salvaged the manuscript and preserved it for years before it was displayed in the museum. Father Costa argues that this manuscript was copied by more than one person as the handwriting seems to change after every few Avaswaru. He also believes that some portions of the manuscript may have been written by Stephens himself, as in place of 'Khrista' the Greek characters Chi Ro '☧', an acronym for Christ, is used. According to him, local scribes would not have been aware of this alphabet and only Stephens could have done it. There is no way of verifying this claim, as of today. This manuscript is undated.

Another symbolic site is the Thomas Stephens Konknni Kendr, a Jesuit institution set up to promote the usage and growth of the Konkani language. The Kendr possesses a handwritten version of the entire text. This manuscript reproduces all the licences of the editions of *Kristapurāṇa*. This manuscript is also undated. It holds special significance as it is housed in an institution named after Thomas Stephens in honour of his *Arte da Lingoa Canarim*, which is considered the first grammar of the Konkani language.

The Goa University Library houses the Bhaugun Kamat Wagh collection, which contains a handwritten manuscript of *Kristapurāṇa*. This is an incomplete version and is undated. The Pissurlencar collection of this library has important secondary material on *Kristapurāṇa* and on language and culture in Goa during the seventeenth century, when Stephens was writing his Purāṇa.

The Krishnadas Shama State Central Library houses a handwritten manuscript copied by Manuel Rebello in the year 1767. This manuscript is well preserved and is available for viewing and reading at the library. The library also holds scanned copies of the Marsden Purāṇas, the Pilar manuscript, and copies of all the modern editions of Kristapurāṇa. It is an excellent place for a comparative reading of the various editions of *Kristapurāṇa*.

ACKNOWLEDGEMENTS

This book was made possible with the support of nothing less than a village of people.

The research presented in this book is a culmination of my doctoral research completed at the Indian Institute of Technology Gandhinagar in the year 2018 under the supervision of Dr. Arnapurna Rath. As such, Dr. Rath remains an integral part of the narrative of this book. Many of the ideas explored in this work were refined in endless discussions with her during my doctoral research. She accepted my fascination with a seventeenth-century text without question, and gave me room to explore my ideas, which was invaluable in the early days of my research. My heartfelt thanks to her for her guidance.

Professor Milind Malshe's insights and motivation in this work have been invaluable. He very kindly took time out to patiently listen to my queries and provide feedback on my work at several stages. I am especially grateful to his family for sharing the late Professor S.G. Malshe's doctoral thesis with me. This is a resource that many researchers before me did not have the good fortune to access. I am especially grateful to Prof. S.G. Malshe's wife, the late Mrs. Malini Malshe and his daughter, Dr Sushama Powdwal, for graciously sharing a treasured family possession with me and trusting me to do good work with it. I would also like to thank Professor B. N. Patnaik for the enlightening conversations on Purāṇas.

Two scholarly figures I met in Goa have been important in this journey. Shri Suresh Amonkar (1935–2019) kindly shared the manuscripts of his Konkani translation of *Kristapurāṇa*, even while the book was in press. The conversations I had with him have been invaluable in my research. I will forever be indebted to his brilliant scholarship and generous spirit. Father Jose Cosme Costa of the Pilar Seminary museum took time out to meet me in spite of his ill health and showed me the Pilar manuscript. I am grateful to him. Special thanks to Father Glen D'Silva SFX, for agreeing to discuss his musical interpretations of *Kristapurāṇa* with me.

Professor Ines G. Županov, Professor David Bellos, and Professor Amith Kumar P.V provided valuable feedback and encouragement on my doctoral thesis. I am grateful for their insights which helped me revise this work for publication. My thanks to Professor Sudhir K. Jain for his mentorship, Professor Hephzibah Israel for her support and insight into my research from time to time, Father Nelson Falcao SDB for his research and support, and Professor Francis X. Clooney S.J., Harvard Divinity School, for his generous encouragement in this project.

I visited several libraries during the course of this research. I am grateful for the support of Dr. T.S. Kumbar, Librarian, Central Library, IIT Gandhinagar, from time to time in my work. The Inter-Library Loan facility provided by the library has been an important way of procuring out-of-print volumes for my research. My thanks to all the excellent library staff, especially Ms. Panna Chaudhari and Mr. Tapas Das for their assistance in procuring material for this research.

I am grateful to Dr. Carlos Fernandes, former Curator, Krishnadas Shama Goa State Central Library. He was extremely helpful throughout the duration of my doctoral research. I would also like to express my gratitude to Marianita Dias and Sneha Malkarnekar, librarians, for always being willing to help. Ms. Dias has been especially supportive in helping me procure the necessary permissions from the library for this book. The many mornings I spent reading at this library and discussing *Kristapurāṇa* with scholars from Goa was crucial to the shaping of my work. The librarian of Central Library, Goa University, Dr. Gopakumar V., was kind to me during my visit to the library and made it easy for me to access some important texts while I was there. I am grateful to Rev. M. Mani Chacko, General Secretary of the Bible Society of India, for facilitating my research at their Archives. Mr. Binu Aby Mathew, who was in charge of the Archives, was of great assistance in finding the material I needed. I am also grateful to all the library staff at Rachol Seminary for facilitating my visits.

The late Professor Aniket Jaaware taught me at the University of Pune (now Savitribai Phule Pune University). The first time I laid eyes on *Kristapurāṇa* was when he handed me his personal copy one morning, after listening to me present in class on Bible translation. His classes on Translation Studies were pure delight. I will forever be grateful for his teaching and for his foresight. Dr. Chandrani Chatterjee was one of the teachers who taught me Translation Studies at Pune. She has been a teacher, guide, and friend to me. It was a "word spoken in season" by her that led me to take up research after a break from academics. It is impossible to put in words how much I am indebted to her mentorship.

My editor at Routledge, Shoma Choudhury, helped me come this far in this book project with her patient guidance and support. This project would not have been possible without her. For her and for the help provided by Ms. Anvitaa Bajaj, Editorial Assistant, I am grateful.

Special thanks to my colleagues at Pandit Deendayal Energy University for their support, especially those at the School of Liberal Studies. My thanks to Dr. Leena Santosh for her friendship and support. My dear friend and colleague, Dr. Niyati Shah, was a pillar of strength to me and supported me in every way possible. My gratefulness and admiration for her strength and kindness cannot be described in words.

I am indebted to Pastor Jinu and his wife, Mini, for their generosity and the help they provided during my stay in Goa. I must also express my gratitude to the large network of friends and family without whom this journey would have been impossible: Shivani, Mahesh, Bejini and Sajan, my large family in Ahmedabad who pitched in with everything from prayers to babysitting, Benson and Shilna, my brother, Stanley, my mainstay in an ever-changing world, and Shalini, for just being who she is, the only completely kind and graceful person I know. Heartfelt thanks to each of them.

I will forever be indebted to the love and care that my parents-in-law have shown to me. Without my father this book probably would never have been conceived. He sowed in me the first seeds of my love for languages and literature. My mother's prayers were my stronghold. I am thankful for them.

My children have been doing a brilliant job of growing up while their mother was wrapped up in writing. They endured travel and short periods of separation and adjusted to unusual circumstances with much grace. Their little prayers for me have been rays of hope on dark days. My husband, Royson, walked by me every step of the way, and held me up whenever I faltered. I am grateful for this circle of strength and support around me.

NOTE ON TRANSLITERATION

Terms from *Kristapurāṇa* are transliterated according to the 1907 edition of the text by J.L. Saldanha. Terms such as "Puranna" and "Vaicunttha" have been transliterated according to the Saldanha edition in order to maintain consistency throughout the book. The spelling of the word Purāṇa varies in this book: "Purāṇa" has been used wherever a general reference is made to the genre, and "Puranna" is used when the reference is from within *Kristapurāṇa*. Any specific nuance in transliteration has been explained in endnotes. In case of quotes, the transliteration adopted by the respective authors is used. No diacritics have been used for commonly accepted spellings such as "Vishnu" and "shastra". Non-English words are italicized in the first instance of their usage and used without italics in other places.

Verses quoted from *Kristapurāṇa* have been cited with verse numbers, and not page numbers. This system of numbering shows the the chapter of *Kristapurāṇa* from which the quote is taken. For instance, the notation "1.2.40" shows that the verse is from the First Puranna, Avaswaru (Canto) two, and verse number forty.

TRANSLATOR'S NOTE

One of the ways in which I critically engage with *Kristapurāṇa* in this book is by translating select verses from the text into English. This translation enabled a closer reading of the text in my attempt to appreciate its nuances. I have attempted to retain the poetic structure of the text in my translation. A few recurring themes on translation are clarified in this section.

In the translation of verses from *Kristapurāṇa*, the aim was to familiarize readers of this book to the creative way in which the biblical narrative was shaped by Stephens. The experiences in translating verses from *Kristapurāṇa* are significant to the arguments put forth in this book. For example, it is Stephens' conscious use of the terms "shastra" and "puranna" to speak of "holy books" or "scriptures" at different places in the text which brought to light the significance of generic features of purāṇic tradition in which *Kristapurāṇa* was composed. These nuances were noticed while translating verses from the text for the book. Translation has been an important way of reading the text and has shaped the development of arguments in this book.

The verses in *Kristapurāṇa* do not use punctuation marks. This was in the style of the poetry of the period. The translations in this book, however, use commas and question marks to indicate the sense pauses and make for easy reading. No other punctuation marks have been used. Words such as "Puranna" and "Vaicunttha" are untranslated and retained as in the source text. The reason for this is that these words have been used as conceptual terms to formulate the arguments of this book. In some cases these words (eg. *Koel, Ganga*) are retained to underline Stephens's ingenious use of local markers from Goa to compose his biblical narrative. Translated passages which could not be incorporated into the main text of the chapters have been included in the Appendixes of this book. All translations from secondary sources written in Marathi are mine, unless otherwise stated.

Molesworth's Marathi–English Dictionary (1996) and *A Dictionary of Old Marathi* (1999) by S.G. Tulpule and Anne Feldhaus were referred to while translating Stephens' Marathi into English.

This journey into the world of *Kristapurāṇa* was in equal parts delightful and intimidating. The sheer pleasure of reading Stephens' verse was a rewarding experience. At the same time, negotiating the multiple intricacies of cultural translation present in the text raised anxieties about the approach to be taken while studying it. The volume of the text and its fragile nature in terms of the problems of sacred-text translation revealed in it was difficult to negotiate as a researcher. As a translator, the attempt was to unravel at least a few of these complexities while displaying the literary refinement of the text. While these translations are pale in comparison with Stephens' poetic genius, the hope is that this attempt at translation will lead to future translations of this text for a larger readership.

INTRODUCTION

Cultures, Scriptures, and Translation

> They seem to ask us: "Should we not make new for ourselves what is old and find ourselves in it? Should we not have the right to breathe our own soul into this dead body? … Indeed, translation was a form of conquest.
>
> *(Nietzsche, "Translation as Conquest")*[1]

This book studies the seventeenth-century poetic work, *Kristapurāṇa* (1616), a Marathi retelling of the Bible, through the critical lens of translation. Textual practices, travel, sacredness, genre, and geography in early-modern South Asia emerge as central threads in this narrative. This book may be described as a literary journey through Western India of the sixteenth and seventeenth centuries, through the paths carved out by *Kristapurāṇa* and the life of its author, Thomas Stephens S.J. (1549–1619).

There are two major intertwining strands of this book: (a) a critical reading of *Kristapurāṇa* as a work of cultural translation is undertaken through a study of Stephens' transformation into a Marathi-speaking poet-priest-translator, an analysis of generic nuances in the text, a study of landscapes, and translation practices specific to South Asia, and (b) translation of select passages of *Kristapurāṇa* into English is undertaken with a view to augment the critical arguments made in this book. After locating *Kristapurāṇa* as a work of translation, select passages from *Kristapurāṇa* are analyzed to understand the complexities that accompany sacred-text translations and Stephens' creative interventions as a translator. Some amount of archival research was conducted to trace the beginnings of the text in Goa and its reception in the centuries that followed its publication.

This book argues that *Kristapurāṇa* is distinctive among Christian writings as it is one of the earliest retellings of the Bible in South Asian language available today. It is also one of the first printed books in India, a Marathi narrative printed in Roman script. Stephens was an Englishman and Jesuit who travelled to India in the sixteenth

DOI: 10.4324/9781003146544-1

century, learnt Marathi and its contemporary literary styles, and composed a work of literary beauty. Cultural translation is the process through which Stephens mediated these spaces between texts and traditions. The following chapters explore the intersections between aspects of translation and culture(s) and locates *Kristapurāṇa* as a cultural translation in this rich framework of literary encounters.

The life and times of Stephens is one important theme that weaves in and out of the terrain of this book. It explores the thrill of reading a Marathi composition by possibly the only Englishman in the Portuguese mission at the time, in addition to his transformation into a poet-priest of the Marathi language. The book follows Stephens on his journey as a Jesuit missionary in seventeenth-century Goa in an attempt to repaint the landscapes which both served as the backdrop and became a central aspect of Stephens' epic narrative.

In understanding the epic genre of *Kristapurāṇa*, it is essential to analyse the writing practices that existed in pre-colonial Goa, as well as the writing strategies adopted by early Catholic and Protestant missionaries in the subcontinent. The writing practices that existed in Western India at the time were reflections of the socio-cultural changes that were sweeping the subcontinent. The development of religious sects within Hinduism, the evolution various regional languages of the subcontinent as literary languages, the arrival of Catholicism, and later Protestantism, were few of the critical factors that influenced writing in this period.

The shaping of the biblical narrative into a Purāṇa is of interest to the scholar of translation, and is one of the focal points of this work. The text deals primarily with two major traditions – the biblical and the purāṇic. Both traditions are laden with sacred value for different cultures. The generic features of both these traditions and the sacredness inherent in them are brought together in *Kristapurāṇa*, sometimes blending harmoniously, often clashing, to reveal the anxieties and unequal cultural politics of colonial-religious encounters. In addition to this, the intricacies of the geographical setting of Goa are incorporated into the text, lending novelty to the biblical narrative. A comparative study of these textual traditions is undertaken at several points in this book in order to bring out the literary nuances of the text.

In this context, the geographical landscape and cultural translation in *Kristapurāṇa* are explored as important threads. The creative ways in which religious translation was approached by missionaries is significant in the context of the text. In addition to this, Stephens' transformation to a Marathi poet, the generic features of Purāṇa, and the landscape writing in the text are the foci through which cultural translation in *Kristapurāṇa* is analysed in this book. The mapping of the cultural contexts and the routes of knowledge production which shaped the composition of this work is another significant aspect of this book.

The multilingual realities of South Asia have provided ample spaces for textual translations. Translated works from the various colonial periods of South Asia (Portuguese and British, among others) have been the subject of comparative reading by literary scholars and scholars of Translation Studies. These colonial periods also witnessed numerous Bible translations, with individual figures such as William Carey (1761–1834) being associated with translations of the Bible into as many as thirty languages of South Asia. Sacred-text translations have received limited attention from literary scholars, probably because of the evangelistic *telos* and the perceived "unscientific" nature of missionary texts. These biblical texts, however, are significant threads in the literary fabric of South Asia. In the context of the "sacredness" attributed to them, translation of biblical texts open up spaces for reading into the complexities of cultural translation and have a potential for contributing valuable knowledge to the existing epistemology of South Asian literature.

The biblical Tower of Babel, as described in the book of *Genesis*, has been used in the European tradition as a symbol of translation.[2] The scattering of languages that took place at Babel was a punishment and translation, the constant endeavour to reach back to a lost "one language". This view of translation, though, has shifted over time to more nuanced understandings of the act of translation, where translation is not necessarily viewed as a punishment for the aspiration of the builders of Babel. Over the last two decades, Translation Studies has begun to acknowledge the presence of "non-Western" approaches to translation. This book is also an attempt to underline the act of translation as it was practised in sixteenth- and seventeenth-century South Asia, through a reading of *Kristapurāṇa*. *Kristapurāṇa*, being a retelling of the biblical narrative in Marathi, lies at the intersection of scriptural translation, cross-cultural encounters, and regional translation practices.

This introductory chapter sets out the terms of the discussion in this book. A historical survey of the field of Translation Studies which forms the theoretical bedrock of this volume is discussed in the next few sections. Key concepts that are critical to the arguments developed in this book are discussed in some detail here. The focus of this chapter is twofold: (a) defining critical moments in Translation Studies, while mapping "cultural translation" as a ground within the larger discipline; and (b) understanding the various aspects and problems of cultural translation to explore a locale for the present research.

1.1 On Translation

Translation is the channel through which texts move across linguistic and cultural boundaries. Religious texts and ideas of the sacred have been disseminated for centuries through their translations. The history of scriptural translation in any religion is marked by a belief that the sacred is inherently untranslatable while at the same time the need for scripture translation was seen in every age (Long 2005, 7). Scriptures from various religions are translated today, for inter-faith understanding and academic debate, if not for evangelization. As such, these debates on whether the sacred can be translated and how it should be translated remain relevant in present times.

Translation practices and the discourse surrounding it have existed for over two millennia now.[3] The word "translation", derived from Latin "translatio", has the same etymology as the word "transfer", which means "to carry over". In textual translation "meaning" or "sense" is carried across from one language to another. The term "translation" was also used to signify the travelling of a saint's relics (or knowledge and power) from one location to another (Tymoczko 2015, 443). In this sense, the word invokes an image of travel, dislocation, and relocation. In the present age, the meaning of the word translation has evolved from the "figurative literary meaning of an interlingual transaction, to its etymological physical meaning of locational disrupture" (Bassnett and Trivedi 1999, 13). Travel, dislocation, and relocation are significant themes in this understanding of the term "translation".[4] The understanding that translation is not merely a linguistic activity and that it is necessary to study the cultural and political complexities that accompany any work of translation forms the core of the "cultural turn" in Translation Studies.

Translation Studies as a discipline has come a long way from translations being labelled as second-rate works of little literary value, as "poor copies" of the original to translation being viewed as an innovative activity that produces a new text in the target language. These discussions on various aspects of translation have thrown light on the fact that translation is not merely the linguistic transfer of a text from one language to another but also a dynamic grid of complex relationships between languages and cultures.

According to the *Routledge Encyclopedia of Translation Studies* (2009), one of the earliest instances of translation may be found in the Old Testament, when the Levites, the priests, read out the "Law" to the Jews and translated it for them (Baker and Saldanha 2009, 21). The Jews had returned after seventy years of captivity in Babylon (c.445 BC), and many of them could not understand the Hebrew language of the Law:

> The Levites ... instructed the people in the Law while the people were standing there. They read from the Book of the Law of God, making it clear (translating it) and giving the meaning so that the people understood what was being read.
>
> *(Nehemiah 5: 7, 8)*

According to the story recorded in the Old Testament, Nehemiah (c.445 BC) was a Jewish captive in Babylon. He gathered the captive Jews of his time and motivated them to rebuild the walls of Jerusalem. He gathered the Levites (the priestly tribe) to read out the laws of Moses to the people who had lived in foreign captivity for many years. This reading of the Book of Law was meant for the purpose of explicating the Law to the Jews who no longer spoke Hebrew. This early instance of translation is an oral interpretation of the law for people who could not understand the language in which it was written.

The need for translating the Bible and other scriptures was felt by different people at different times in history and the practice and study of translation as it is understood today can be said to have begun from this need. For instance, the Protestants in fourteenth-century Europe felt the need to bring back what they called the "original spirit of Christianity" and hence made their own translations of the Bible in languages that common people could read (Bassnett 1980, 45–50). In fact, the Septuagint Bible (c.300 BC) is often quoted as the first example of a translated work (Robinson D. 2002, 10). Translation began to acquire new meaning and significance when studied in the light of Scripture translation (Bassnett 1980, 45). The need to disseminate the Christian gospel gave rise to a massive volume of translations of Christian texts, especially since the beginning of the colonial period. On the one hand, there was the understanding that the "Word of God" was pure and powerful; hence the danger of heresy in translation. On the other hand, there was the overwhelming need for large-scale translation, especially since the beginning of colonial missions, to evangelize, and to negotiate the cultural complexities of faraway colonies. Translation itself was seen as a form of heresy. Through translation a text could be "subverted" and meaning unintended by the original begin to surface. This process of translation would mean destabilizing cultural and religious codes.

Early translators of the Bible faced persecution and even death on charges of heresy. Nevertheless, translators took up the challenge of translating the Bible, as it was important that the people should be able to read the Bible in their own language (Bassnett 1980, 45). Any "misrepresentation" in translation could be interpreted as heresy and a translator could be tried and condemned by the church for it. This mistrust of translation continued in later centuries and is evident in the events surrounding early translations of the Bible into English. Early translators, like William Tyndale (1494–1536), were tried on the charge of heresy and publicly executed for translating the Bible. Even a century after this, when the English Bible was authorized and published by King James in 1611, there was criticism that the Word of God was being defiled by putting it in the hands of common, English-speaking people. The translator was dangerous because she/he was seen "as the 'one who knows' both the codes; the one who has the power to 'do justice', 'be faithful', yet also to 'capture', deceive, betray one side to the other, or betray both to a third" (Pratt 1992, 96).[5] A reading of *Kristapurāṇa* as a translation provides critical insight into ways in which missionaries worked within the edicts of the Church, and found ways of surpassing the Church's suspicion of the act of translation, while composing texts that were rooted in the literary traditions of the target audiences.

In the preface to the King James Bible (1611) titled "From the translators to the Reader", the translators expound their philosophy of translation:

> Translation it is that openeth the window, to let in the light; that breaketh the shell, that we may eat the kernel; that putteth aside the curtaine, that we may looke into the most Holy place; that remooveth the cover of the well, that wee may come by the water, even as *Jacob* rolled away the stone from the mouth of the well, by which meanes the flockes of *Laban* were watered. Indeede without translation into the vulgar tongue, the unlearned are but like children at *Jacobs* well (which was deepe) without a bucket or some thing to draw with: or as that person mentioned by *Esau*, to whom when a sealed booke was delivered, with this motion, *Reade this, I pray thee*, hee was faine to make this answere, *I cannot, for it is sealed.*
>
> *(KJV, Introduction)*

For the translators of the KJV, it was translation that "let in the light" of the Word of God into the English language for the first time. This is one of the primary functions of translation, as a means of opening the window and "letting in the light", of enabling cross-cultural communication. In addition to exploring this role of translation as a channel for communication, this book also questions this image of the "unlearned" recipient of the translation, as helpless, mute participants to the process that brings the translated work to them, and locates them as active participants in the process of translation, specifically in sites of colonial encounter such as Goa.

Eugene Nida's (1914–2011) work was especially significant in the context of Bible translations. Nida introduced the terms "formal equivalence" and "dynamic equivalence" as to possible ways of translating the Bible. Of these two, Nida considered the "dynamic equivalence" method to be better suited to translating the Bible: "The dynamic equivalence approach adapts the translation to the realities of the target language and culture, so that the meaning of the source text can be clearly understood" (Baker and Saldanha 2009, 25). Nida argued that the translator should not attempt to merely transmit the source message into the target language, but attempt to produce an "equivalent effect" in the target reader.

> In such a translation one is not so concerned with matching the receptor-language message with the source-language message, but with the dynamic relationship, that the relationship between receptor and message should be substantially the same as that which existed between the original receptors and the message.
>
> (Nida, "Principles of Correspondence", 144)

"Dynamic Equivalence" proposes translation based on "equivalent effect" in the receiving culture, rather than linguistic faithfulness to the source language. Culture, thus, was a subject in the discussions on translation in this period. Nida proposes the idea that the message should be adapted to recreate the same "effect" on the target readers as on the source readers. For Nida, a text is "culturally translated" when it is adapted to the needs of the target audience. Colonial ventures into new lands, and the attendant need to translate the Bible into new languages, adapted for new cultures, highlighted the need for culture-sensitive translation. This transformation of the Bible into new cultural forms was meant to transform individuals of the target culture into Christians. A translator of the Bible was required to have sufficient "cultural information" (Venuti 111) while undertaking this task, which implied not just a knowledge of the languages involved in translation, but an understanding of the cultural nuances inherent in those languages.

The hermeneutic approach to translation by George Steiner (b. 1929) was another important thread in the understanding of translation. In *After Babel: Aspects of Language and Translation* (1975), Steiner puts forth the hermeneutic motion, which is fourfold: It involves an act of "trust" in the text, the violence of extracting meaning, the incorporation of the text, and, finally, the act of "restitution" or reparation (Steiner 182). This understanding of translation is in opposition to the linguistic model, which views translation largely as a communicative act between languages. Steiner summarizes the entirety of his thoughts on the fundamental nature of translation in linguistic communication in one line in the chapter "Understanding as Translation" in *After Babel*: "In short: inside or between languages, human communication equals translation" (49). For Steiner, every understanding even within the same language involves active interpretation because languages rarely have perfect synonyms for every word. However, for Steiner, translation is not limited to this communicative aspect, but constitutes a larger interpretative movement between texts and languages.

Another major rethinking of the complexities of translation took place with the opening up of the concept of "deconstruction" by Jacques Derrida (1930–2004). Derrida complicated the traditional understanding of translation when he displaced the original from its sacrosanct position. Translation was no longer viewed as a process that takes place between two languages, but as a process that was constantly at work even within individual languages. Translation serves to bring to light the "différance"[6] in a text, the meanings that are between the lines in a book (Derrida, *Of Grammatology*, 60). Derrida went back to Walter Benjamin's idea of "afterlife" to question the existence of the original text. In "Des Tours de babel" (1985), he argues that Benjamin's idea of afterlife is not merely a survival, but a "sur-vival" where the text lives "longer, it lives more and better, beyond the means of the author" (179). He elaborates on this in a later commentary in 1988:

> … the structure of an original is survival, what he calls 'Überleben'. A text is an original insofar as it is a thing, not to be confused with an organic or physical body, but a thing, let us say, of the mind, meant to survive the death of the author or the signatory, and to be above or beyond the physical corpus of the text, and so on.
>
> *(Derrida, "Roundtable on Translation", 121)*

As such, the translation is not secondary to its "original"; it is one of the readings of the text. The original is transformed by its translation, just as much as a translation is shaped by its reading of the 'original'. Thus, the original and its translation are mutually dependant.[7]

A study of scriptural translation also brings to light another question with which Translation Studies has grappled: how much can a translator "change" in a text? The lines between "translation" and "adaptation" have not always been clear. Beginning from Cicero and Horace who attempted to differentiate between "word-for-word" and "sense-for-sense" translation, the debate has continued. Adaptation was seen as loose and "free" translations, where a foreign text is modified to suit the tastes of target cultures (Bastin 3). The term "adaptation" was used in a negative sense, as a work which "distorted" the source text (Bastin 4). However, adaptation may also be seen as one of the strategies used during translation. When a reference in the source text cannot be found in the target culture, an equivalent term must be found from the target culture. According to Georges Bastin, in his article "Adaptation"

(2009), this understanding of adaptation as a translation strategy "views adaptation as a local rather than global strategy, employed to achieve an equivalence of situations wherever cultural mismatches are encountered" (Bastin 2009, 4). Scholars such as Christiane Nord have argued that there is no need to use two separate terms, "translation" and "adaptation", as the concept of translation may be used to cover all types of transformation or intervention in texts as long as "the target effect corresponds to the intended target functions" (Nord 1997, 93). To take this argument further, Yves Gambier warns against the "fetishization" of the original (Bastin 2009, 6). The translator is supposed to intervene actively, or adapt, in order to convey a text to a target audience.[8] The lines between translation and adaptation come under scrutiny specifically in instances of scriptural translation. The high reverence that is accorded to scriptures makes adaptation in scripture translation a sensitive issue.

The strict reverence for the source text is also problematic when the aspect of "orality" is taken into perspective. In traditions where classical texts were largely transmitted orally, the multiple "originals" that may exist of a source text problematizes the idea of translation. A.K. Ramanujan, for example, prefers the term "telling" rather than "versions" while referring to Indian epics such as the Ramayana (Ramanujan 1991, 24). This emphasizes the idea that each of these tellings from different places and languages has its place in the narrative traditions of the region. Translations, then, become "retellings" or a "speaking after" of the source text. These complexities of translation are brought out in the present reading of *Kristapurāṇa* as a work of translation.

Michael Cronin states that "… translation is above all an initiation into unsuspected complexity" (Cronin, in Buden et al. 2009, 218). Far from being a text that reflects any kind of inter-religious harmony, this work reads *Kristapurāṇa* as a site which opens up all the complexities associated with the idea of cultures and translation.

I.2 Poetry, Accuracy, and the Role of the Translator

The introduction of the "cultural" aspect into the study of translation has moved the focus away from linguistic studies of translation and has led to clearer understandings of the complex network of transactions that are at play in any act of translation. The use of the term "cultural translation" signifies that translation may no longer be viewed as an "innocent" (Bassnett and Trivedi 1999, 2) activity, but rather as an activity which is in constant interaction with the cultural context in which it takes place. The idea of "cultural translation" also serves to highlight the idea that translation is not merely an "aesthetic activity", but an activity that grapples with significant cultural and ideological problems (Bassnett and Trivedi 1999, 6).

In Avaswaru 2 of the "Dussarem Puranna" of *Kristapurāṇa*, the narrator, Padreguru, describes a moving scene from heaven, Vaicunttha. The listeners intervene in the narrative to ask the Padre-guru rather direct questions about his process of translation while composing the *Puranna*:

Tãua yecu vipru utthila suzannu
Padry sauẽ adharila prusttnu
Mhanne Limbaloquinchẽ vartamana
Zẽ sanguitalẽ tuuã

Then a wise Brahmin rose up,
And questioned the Padre,
And said, the news of Limbo
That you told us about

Anny suarguĩ deuadutanthẽ
Zi gostti quely vaincuntthanathẽ
Ti caissy zannaualy amanthẽ
Sanguitalẽ cauannẽ

And the things that the lord of Vaicunttha
Told the angels,
How was it made known to us?
Who reported it?

Qui tumĩ apule matipracassĩ
Cauitua srungharu chaddauila cathessi
Aissẽ hoe tari granthassi
Caissa ure visuassu

Or is it that you adorned the story poetically
With your own imagination?
If that is the case
How can we trust this book?

Vartalẽ nahĩ tẽ vartalẽ mhannatã
Tẽ lattiquẽ disse aicatã
Cauanna tẽ satia assatia
Zannize caissẽ

You say it has happened, when it has not
And it sounds false to us,
How will we know
What is true and what is false?

Maga Padri mhanne tẽ aicunu
Tuuã quela baraua prusttnu
Tari sangaina aica chita deunu
Srute tumĩ

On hearing this the Padre said,
You have asked a good question
I will answer it, listen carefully,
O Listeners

Hẽ amanchẽ utama xastra
Saruã tthaĩ satia anny pauitra
Ya mazi quinchita matra
Lattiquẽ nahĩ

Our excellent scriptures
Are true and holy above all
There is not a speck
Of falsehood in it

Gentiyanche cauy zaisse
Apule grantha carity bhalataisse
Amancheni nacarauẽ teyã sarissẽ
Sate xastra mithe hoila

The poets of the gentiles
Compose their books waywardly,
We cannot be like them
And make a true shastra false

Zaissẽ amruta ghatta bhituri
Vissa naghalauẽ themba bhari
Tennẽ auaghẽ amruta vissa sary
Hoila zanna

If in a pot of nectar,
A single drop of poison is added
Know this,
That all of the nectar will turn into poison

Taissy yecadi lattiquy matu
Missallitã ya xastra antu
Nassaila auagha granthu
Hoila sateassi hanni

If any false idea
Is mixed in this shastra,
The whole book will be spoilt,
And truth will be marred

(*Kristapurāṇa* 2.2.80–87)

It is significant to note Stephens' self-reflexive commentary on the "faithfulness" of his translation in an age long before translations began to receive scholarly attention. The dilemmas of a missionary working with poetic genre, while being expected to preserve the "truth" of the Bible unmarred, is clear from these verses. Through the Padre-guru's answer, Stephens defends his use of poetic imagery to narrate the Bible to the people of Goa. The Brahmin asked the Padre-guru how he got to know of the conversation between God (Vaicuntthanath) and the angels in Vaicunttha. They wanted to know whether he painted it in his own imagination (2.2.83). The Padre-guru hastened to explain that he would never change the narrative of the holy book and add the "poison" of falsehood to the "nectar" of the scriptures (*Kristapurāṇa* 2.2.85, 86). He had retained the "sasari" or the essence of the biblical narrative but had adorned it with poetic devices to make it interesting for his readers.

From the verses given above, it seems acceptable to Stephens that poetic devices may be used to beautify the narrative while translating biblical episodes. It is unacceptable, however, to mix "falsehood" into the scriptures. The line between "beautifying" and falsehood seems to be a thin one here. The narrator goes on to explain that as long as the truth of the scriptures is not marred, it is permissible to use poetic devices in translation, in order to engage listeners in the narrative. The process of translation pictured here is distinct from the traditional image of translation as a linear movement from the "original"[9] text to the "translated" text. It is a more iterative process, where the target audience of the translated work mediate and contribute to the way in which the work is finally shaped.

The quoted passage evokes two key aspects that highlight the complexities of translation, and are crucial to the present reading of *Kristapurāṇa*: (a) poetry and translation of sacred texts, and (b) the limitations imposed on "imagination" in the context of sacred-text translation. In scriptural translation, the complexities of translation are magnified, due to the reverence attached to the source text and the power centres that authorize and shape such translations. Even after the translation of the Bible became permissible, creative license was not encouraged in its translation. In the verses quoted above, the narrator's quick rebuttal stating that his work contained no falsehood, and that it did no harm to the truth of the scriptures, provides a glimpse of the anxiety involved in translating religious texts. In addition to this, the complexities of translating verse, or translating "into verse" places several linguistic and metrical constraints on the translator, and in the process reveals the complexities, or the "fault lines", inherent in in the act of translation (Cronin et al. 2007, 254). The translation of "figurative language" and metaphors exposes all the complexities that are present in cultural translation (Cronin et al. 2007, 254). When the problems of scriptural translation and poetry come together in a text such as *Kristapurāṇa*, these questions become even more conspicuous. The translator in such a case teeters on the verge of "accuracy" and "heresy", and the translated work becomes a site where these tensions are constantly at play. When a poetic genre from local Hindu repertoire is chosen by Stephens to translate the biblical narrative into Marathi, cultural nuances associated with the genre enter the biblical stories. In addition to the reshaping that needs to occur to fit the Bible into the metrical framework of the *ovi*, sacred concepts which were deeply ingrained in the poetic purāṇic tradition begin to collide and merge with biblical concepts, revealing the "fault lines" in the translatorial enterprise.

The "fault lines" in the domain of translation practice begin to widen as these complexities merge with cultural differences and colonial power. Translation, now, is being perceived not just as "simple linguistic transpositions or literary creations" but as "records of cultural contestations and ideological struggles" (Tymoczko 2015, 443). In the twentieth century, translation crosses the boundary from being within a "philological enclosure" where it is studied in relation to language and literature to being "a central category of cultural theory and the politics of culture" (Wolf 2008, online). The significance of cultural nuances in the act of translation, and the centrality of translated works in shaping cultures, are two significant aspects of this shift.

The moment "culture"[10] is invoked in the context of translation, the anxiety associated with dislocation and uprooting is brought to mind: "Precisely by becoming cultural, translation opens up the problem of its intrinsic political meaning" (Buden et al. 2009, 196). The foregrounding of the "cultural" in translation is associated with the opening up of the discipline for a discussion on the political repercussions of the translatorial enterprise. The use of translation as a colonial tool for subjugation (Niranjana 1992, 3) or as a mechanism for creating an empire based on colonizers' cultural aspirations becomes an important part of the discourse when "culture" becomes a focal point in Translation Studies.

Further, in invoking culture in the study of translation, the focus shifts from the text as an isolated product to the cultural setting of the translation and to the translator who functions within the framework of this cultural setting. The translator, who was hitherto invisible, is now brought to the fore and situated in the socio-cultural setting of translation practices. According to Bassnett and Lefevere:

> Translations are not made in a vacuum. Translators function in a given culture at a given time. The way they understand themselves and their culture is one of the factors that may influence the way in which they translate.
>
> *(Bassnett and Lefevere 1990, 31)*

The translator's experience of the culture and their interpretation of a certain cultural context determine their approach towards translation. It becomes necessary, therefore, to dwell on the translator figure in order to make sense of the way in which they translate. In the words of Michael Cronin, in "Double Take: Figuring the Other and the Politics of Translation" (2007), "translations were no longer to be seen as free-floating aesthetic artefacts generated by ahistorical figures in a timeless synchronicity of language but as works produced by historical figures in diachronic time" (254). The cultural turn is significant as it highlighted the idea that translation takes place in a time-space continuum and is a network of complex transactions. It is a departure from the concept of translations as isolated instances of linear transfer at sporadic intervals in the "synchronicity of language". The cultural turn also shifts the position of the translator to an "all-powerful reader" and "a free agent as a writer" (Bassnett and Trivedi 1999, 5).[11] Translators no longer remain "ahistorical figures" who borrow and create secondary copies of texts, but are instrumental figures in shaping literary and cultural traditions. This book marks a conscious attempt to treat Stephens as a historical translator-figure in diachronic time, in order to address the cultural complexities of his acts of translation.

Lawrence Venuti addresses the issue of invisibility of the translator in *The Translator's Invisibility: A History of Translation* (1995). Venuti argues that the invisibility of the translator had to do with the "transparency" expected of a translated work: "The more fluent the translation, the more invisible the translator, and presumably, the more visible the writer or meaning of the foreign text" (Venuti 1995, 1). Any indication that the work was a translation was considered an indication of a flaw in the translation. Venuti makes a distinction between the "foreignization" and the "domestication" of translations, based on the two methods put forward by Schleiermacher in the nineteenth century (Venuti 1995, 15).[12] For Venuti, it is the preference for domestication of translated works which leads to the translator's invisibility. In a domesticating translation, the text is brought home to the target culture, in a form that is familiar to the readership. Venuti argues for "foreignizing" translations where the differences of the foreign text are highlighted, in order to "stage an alien reading experience" (16). In other words, Venuti argues for translations where readers from the target culture are taken towards the culture of the source text. The shape and function of the translated work is influenced by the culture which is privileged in the act of translation.

The focus on specific cultural contexts also served to expand the understanding of the term "translation" itself. Translation could now be visualized as a form of rewriting which is shaped by factors such as power, ideology, institution, and manipulation:

> Rewritings can introduce new concepts, new genres, and new devices, and the history of translation is the history also of literary innovation, of the shaping power of one culture upon another. But rewriting can also repress innovation, distort and contain, and in an age of ever increasing manipulation of all kinds, the study of the manipulative processes of literature as exemplified by translation can help us towards a greater awareness of the world in which we live.
>
> *(Bassnett and Lefevere 1990, 31)*

Lefevere and Bassnett argue that as "rewritings", translations have the potential to reshape cultures and manipulate literary landscapes. In this process, "new concepts", "new genres", and "new devices" are introduced into cultures. One instance of such rewriting and reshaping is analysed by Chandrani Chatterjee in her work *Translation Reconsidered: Culture, Genre and the "Colonial Encounter" in Nineteenth Century Bengal* (2010), where she studies the introduction of the genre of novel into nineteenth-century Bengal. Chatterjee argues that translations were primarily responsible for the introduction of the novel into the Bengali literary tradition (Chatterjee 2010, 47). The "cultural turn" foregrounds the translatorial enterprise and firmly locates it as a practice rooted in specific political and cultural contexts.[13] The complexities of cultural differences and conflicting worldviews within the process of translation were fully acknowledged during the cultural turn.

The focus on culture(s) in the study of translation also demonstrates that it is not merely an "intercultural" activity, a give and take between two distinct cultures

(Tymoczko 2015, 445). It also has "intracultural" implications, on the ways in which a single culture or its language builds its identity through translation. An example of such "intracultural" translation may be given from the Tamil language: G.J.V. Prasad, in "Caste in and Recasting Language" (2009), argues that in the case of Tamil, the translation was more internal or within Tamil, in an attempt to standardize the language and resist the hegemonic influence of Sanskrit. This "internal translation", according to Prasad, was far more "consequential to the evolution of the language" (Prasad 2009, 17) than any interlinguistic translation that took place.

This period of the twentieth century within Translation Studies denotes a shift in ways of studying the translation itself with a focus on issues of ideology and power structures. Postcolonial Studies was one of the areas that contributed towards this turn towards "culture" in translation. Translations were no longer to be sanitized of any "odorous" cultural references that jarred European sensibilities (Bassnett and Trivedi 1999, 7). The act of translation was to be placed squarely within the framework of culture(s), in order to bring to the fore critical questions on power politics and translation.

I.3 Colonization, Cultures, and Postcolonial Translations

Translation has been one of the "hegemonic apparatuses" that were used by colonizing societies to serve the interests of their imperial missions. In *Siting Translation: History Post-Structuralism and the Colonial Context* (1992), Tejaswini Niranjana states, "translation reinforces hegemonic versions of the colonized, helping them acquire the status … of objects without history" (3). She argues that translation shapes and is shaped by "asymmetrical relations of power that operate under colonialism" (2). Niranjana uses the Derridean framework of translation to problematize the superior position of the original and proposes an idea of translation that does not subscribe to the use of translation as a hegemonic apparatus. According to her, "The most profound insight Derrida's work has afforded to post-colonials is the notion that origin is always already heterogenous, that it is not some pure, unified source of meaning or history" (Niranjana 1992, 39). The translation (whether a text is translated or not) is inherent in the spaces in the original, it is the "afterlife" of the original.

Translations of English literature were often used as a means to portray a superior image of the British in India (Viswanathan 1988, 86). This also illustrates Niranjana's argument that translation was used as a hegemonic apparatus to promote British rule in India. The unequal power politics between languages, in this case, between English and Indian languages, are also brought to light by an examination of translation in colonial settings, making translation an important ground where cultural complexities are highlighted.[14] Tymoczko and Gentzler, in *Translation and Power*, describe the cultural turn as the "power turn" in Translation studies, as it highlights key issues of the power politics involved in translation histories and strategies (Tymoczko and Gentzler 2002, xvi).

The largely one-sided translations of the colonial period, from colonial languages to European ones, consolidated an image of a culturally superior empire and the inferior status of the colonized. Gayatri Spivak, in "The Politics of Translation" (1993), stresses the role of translation in colonization and in conveying an image of the colonies to the rest of the world. A postcolonial reading of these translations attempts to correct these cultural wrongs that are highlighted in the act of translation. Spivak argues for a "commitment to correct cultural politics" and states that "the history of the language, the history of the author's moment, the history of the language-in-and-as-translation, must figure in the weaving as well" (Spivak 1993, 403). The cultural turn in Translation Studies endeavours to "re-look" these hegemonic translation practices and redefine them in terms of the diversity and challenges that exist within languages and their cultures. An attempt has been made to figure the "history of the author's moment", and the history of the languages of *Kristapurāṇa* in the weaving of this book.

The preceding discussion has given some idea of the way in which postcolonialism informs the foundation of the cultural turn in translation studies. The dynamics of power politics between languages in cultural translation comes from postcolonial investigations into the translations that began in the colonial period. In the Indian context, language and translation were used to depict the quintessential Englishman as superior, and to paint Indian society and culture in an inferior light and justify British rule in India (Metcalf 1994, xi, 66). Educational initiatives in British India were aimed at creating a colony that reflected the glory of its ruling culture. Inequalities in the treatment of texts in translation reflect the inequalities between cultures. The colony itself was seen as a translation or "copy" of the "original" colonizing culture.[15] Translation becomes a major trope in understanding these unequal, problematic relationships that were created by colonial enterprises.[16]

The orientalist view of undeniable superiority of Europe and the unfitness of the "orient" to understand or interpret itself is reflected in early orientalist discourse about India. The "morally superior" British had to take on themselves the "imperial responsibility" (Metcalf 1994, 53) to educate the "uncivilized" natives. Translation was used as a means for European colonizers to propagate essentialist views of colonized cultures and to bring a superior picture of the "West" to the locals in their colonies. In South Asia, classical Sanskrit texts were translated by the colonizers to familiarize themselves with indigenous knowledge systems while ignoring the variety of literature that was available in the regional languages of the subcontinent. These translations were done in such a way as to make the works palatable to a European readership. The translation by Sir William Jones (1746–1796) of Kalidasa's *Abhijnanashakuntalam* as *Sacontala*, is a significant example of colonial translations (Bassnett and Trivedi 1999, 7). The sanitization of cultural references to make translations of South Asian texts appealing to a European readership was one of the translation practices followed during the colonial period.

The significant volume of Orientalist works which were produced in the colonial period is significant in this context. Translations of classical South Asian texts by Indologists such as William Jones (1746–1794), Horace Hayman Wilson (1786–1860), and Max Mueller (1823–1900), among others, contributed to this volume of colonial translations. The discourse on Orientalism concerns itself with the imagination and "construction" of the "Orient" by the West. Early travel writers such as Marco Polo (c.1254–c.1324) wrote about the exotic lands of the Orient in their travelogues. These texts portray the Orient from a Eurocentric perspective and are often studied as skewed portrayals of Eastern realities, influenced by European political interests. Orientalist imaginations about India and other Asian regions have received much attention through years of scholarship, especially so after the publication of Edward Said's *Orientalism* (1978).

A large volume of Orientalist works were produced in the era before the period of "High Orientalism" discussed by Said. Ângela Barreto Xavier and Ines Županov, in their work *Catholic Orientalism: Portuguese Empire, Indian Knowledge* (2015), add to the discourse on Orientalism by arguing that "Catholic Orientalism" has been consistently sidelined in the study of Orientalism.[17] The book attempts to bring Catholic knowledge practices into the discussion on Orientalism and emphasize its role in the formation of all later "Orientalisms." These practices under the Portuguese regime, of constructing India for the European imagination, "fed into" all future practices of Orientalism, including British efforts to produce knowledge about India (289).

Portuguese attempts to create their own imperial identity and establish their position in the hierarchy of empires take place simultaneously with their ventures into the Indian Ocean. The creation of "mental maps" about India in the imagination of Europeans was shaped by the literature and arts emerging out of imperial ventures in India. The earliest Portuguese orientalists like Joao de Barros (1496–1570) and Garcia de Orta (1501–1578) created an archive of knowledge about the subcontinent, with a view to translate it for a European readership. Barros' *Asia* (1552–1615) is introduced as "the first truly orientalist work" (20). These orientalist works by Catholic agents of the Portuguese regime were dismissed as overly religious or unscientific while at the same time their work was being used to build other "scientific" interpretations of the region.[18]

A postcolonial reading of translations highlights the significance of these translatorial enterprises in establishing and maintaining empires. Both translation and postcolonial literature bring literary forms of one culture into another, thus playing a part in culture formation. Confident assertions of literary and cultural "difference" by postcolonial writers, unlike the colonial impulse to homogenize everything to conform to European standards, influences the cultural turn in Translation Studies to re-think hegemonic relationships as they are reflected in the problems of translation.

Postcolonialism also brings to notice the phenomenon of "transculturation". Transculturation is a phenomenon of the "contact zone", a space where "disparate cultures meet, clash and grapple with each other, often in highly asymmetrical relation of dominance and subjugation" (Ashcroft, Griffiths and Tiffin 2000, 233).[19] Transculturation signifies the reciprocal effects of representation and cultural practices, where not only does the "metropole" define the margins, but the margins, in turn, determine the "metropole". Vicente Rafael, in his book *Contracting Colonialism: Translation and Christian Conversion in Tagalog Society under Early Spanish Rule* (1988), juxtaposes the ideas of translation, conversion, and conquest and how they all involve a "transaction of radically distinct languages, bodies, and material objects among colonizers and colonized" (Rafael xvii, xiii). Translation becomes a means for the colonizer to negotiate the language, and, consequently, the culture of the colonies. In this process, the language and its people are codified into forms that are familiar to the colonizing culture.[20] In Rafael's work, the native Tagalog community begin "translating back" in their attempts to come to terms with the culture of the colonizer in a bid to brace themselves against the shock of threatening conquest. In the postcolonial age, when the colonies start writing back, newer and unexplored aspects of the process of translation come to light.

In the colonial setup, the cultural history associated with the language and inherent in the landscape of the colony had to be negotiated by the conquerors in order to facilitate colonization and further translation. In "Translation as Culture" (2007), Spivak argues that translation is an act of "reparation" towards the mother tongue:

> ... translation in the narrow sense, as it were, is also a peculiar act of reparation – towards the language of the inside, a language in which we are responsible, the guilt of seeing it as one language among many.
>
> *(265)*

In the postcolonial context, this idea of "reparation" could be taken to mean a focus on culture(s) in the process of translation in order to make amends for the inequalities of colonial translations. Postcolonial readings of translation are significant in acknowledging the role of translation in building and sustaining empires. Postcolonial readings of the act of translation contribute towards foregrounding the cultural politics inherent in translation.

1.4 Aspects of Cultural Translation

In this journey of translation through culture(s), the term "cultural translation" has become associated with a range of meanings – from the ethnographic to the literary (Sturge 2009, 67).[21] It may refer to the task of an anthropologist, wherein he/she has to interpret a "field" or a new culture to readers in a different culture. It may also refer to the translation of a literary text while keeping in mind the cultural subtleties of the text and the target audiences. In either of these cases, the translator's interpretation of a text or of culture(s) shapes the way in which the text is formed and the role played by the translated text in the target culture.

Trivedi, in his essay "Translating culture vs Cultural translation" (2007), points out that the "cultural" began to enter the discourse on translation when it began to be noticed that literature is created by language and that language is extremely culture-specific:

> ... in a paradigmatic departure, the translation of a literary text became a transaction not between two languages, or a somewhat mechanical sounding act of linguistic "substitution" ..., but rather a more complex negotiation

between two cultures. The unit of translation was no longer a word or a sentence or a paragraph or a page or even a text, but indeed the whole language and culture in which that text was constituted.

(Trivedi 2007, 280)

According to Trivedi, culture becomes a complex negotiating space in the act of translation. The entirety of languages and cultures are recognized as units of translation. This is what Trivedi describes as the 'cultural turn' in Translation Studies – the place where Culture Studies meets Translation Studies and redefines it.[22]

The term "cultural translation", as it is used today, is a completely different concept, according to Trivedi. If it implies sensitivity to culture while translating a text, then that is already a part of the cultural turn in translation. To decode Trivedi's anxiety with the term "cultural translation", it is necessary to understand its use by Homi Bhabha in *The Location of Culture* (1994). In a chapter titled "How Newness Enters the World: Postmodern Space, Postcolonial Times and the Trials of Cultural Translation", Bhabha approaches the idea of cultural translation through the condition of the migrant.[23] He applies Benjamin's idea of "untranslatability" and Derrida's interpretation of it as "sur-vival" to the unassimilability of a migrant individual in an alien culture. The migrant has the choice either to stay unchanged, "unassimilated", or to integrate into the culture. Bhabha describes cultural translation in metaphoric senses as "the borderline condition" (Bhabha 1994, 11) and as "hybrid sites of meaning" (Bhabha 1994, 234). The translation that Bhabha refers to is not textual. It is rather an attempt to understand the in-between spaces, the "third space" where these questions of the migrant condition are enacted.

Pym, in *Exploring Translation Theories* (2010), points out that though Bhabha formulates his ideas on translation as metaphors, his contribution is significant as it focuses on the "(figurative) translator" who inhabits the in-between spaces of languages and cultures (Pym 2010, 142). By locating "a translatory discourse that enacts hybridity", Bhabha highlights the idea that translation opens up cultures to one another (Pym 2010, 142).

Trivedi comments on Bhabha's idea of cultural translation in an attempt to unravel its significance:

What is nevertheless clear and indisputable in Bhabha's formulations of what he calls cultural translation is, firstly, that he does not at all by this term mean literary translation involving two texts from two different languages and cultures, and secondly, that what he means by translation instead is the process and condition of human migrancy.

(Trivedi 2007, 283)

In this context, cultural translation also becomes the need of the Western world to translate the migrants in their world in an attempt to understand them. Cultural translation, thus, comes to signify the shift or the process of transformation that is on-going when an individual comes in contact with a new culture.

Trivedi makes a distinction between the cultural turn in Translation Studies and "cultural translation". He expresses the anxiety that the extreme generality with which the terms "cultural translation" and "translation" are used currently may erase the essentially multilingual nature of the discipline.

> … one may suggest that there is an urgent need perhaps to protect and preserve some little space in this postcolonial-postmodernist world, where newness constantly enters through cultural translation, for some old and old-fashioned literary translation. For, if such bilingual bicultural ground is eroded away, we shall sooner than later end up with a wholly translated, monolingual, monocultural, monolithic world.
>
> *(Trivedi 2007, 286)*

For Trivedi, cultural translation is the stream through which "newness constantly enters" the field and, as such, he fears that it may end in a wholly translated and monolithic field. It may be argued, however, that this stream of "newness" that cultural translation infuses into the field could also uncover newer complexities and multiplicities of translation practices rather than erasing the ones that already exist.

There are scholars who, similar to Trivedi's position, are anxious about the extreme metaphoricity with which the term cultural translation is used. Antoine Berman uses the term "vagabondage conceptuel", where, according to him, cultural translation is used as an excuse for intellectual wandering (Pym 154). Sherry Simon questions the necessity of such a term by arguing that "… the very notion of "cultural translation" becomes tautological (is there any sense in which translation is not somehow cultural?" (Simon, in Buden et al. 2009, 209).

The term, however, is significant as it highlights the material movement of people between cultures as a condition for translation (Pym 2010, 142). The significance of spaces where cultures meet and overlap, as spaces of translation, is opened up in this context. It also brings to mind the idea of transculturation, and "the agency of translators and mediators" (Tymoczko 2015, 255; Cortés, in Pratt et al. 2010, 102). The idea that cultures speak to each other in the process of translation is emphasized by cultural translation. According to Pym, "The social and cultural spaces that once set up equivalence theory are no longer there. Cultural translation might thus offer ways of thinking about the many situations in which translation now operates in the world" (Pym 2010, 156). Chatterjee elucidates this idea further when she states:

> Cultural translation enables us to rethink the ways in which cultures relate to one another, recognizing their internal differences and also questioning the poles from which and to which cultural products travel, thus emphasizing the dimension of negotiation and exchange in any cultural interaction.
>
> *(Chatterjee 2010, 166)*

Cultural translation, here, becomes a mode of understanding the negotiations and exchanges that take place when cultures encounter one another. Cultural translation enables one to read into these spaces of exchange, note the similarities and differences between cultures, while acknowledging the complex routes by which texts travel between cultures.

The "cultural" aspect leads one to think of translation not just in terms of what is traditionally called Translation Studies and comes from the European tradition of translation, but also at the various different practices and conceptions of translation that may exist in other geographical and cultural locations. It helps to bring into focus the ways in which "other" cultures translate, and the understanding that their processes of translation or the very meaning of what they call translation, may differ from the Western framework. Cultural Translation, in its attempt to privilege a comparative study of cultures through the medium of translation, brings to light various "non-Western" conceptions of the idea of translation. Regions such as South Asia, being multilingual, have a long and rich history of translated works. However, whether India and other South Asian countries have a "theory" of translation is something that has been the subject of recent study and debate among scholars who are keen to explore the non-Western perspective on Translation Studies.

Judy Wakabayashi and Rita Kothari, in their edited volume *Decentering Translation Studies* (2009), discuss the possibility of a "de-Westernization" of Translation Studies. In this anthology of essays on translation, Wakabayashi and Kothari attempt to historicize and inquire if a "non-Western" theory of translation exists in reality. In the "Introduction" to the volume, they point out the fallacy of applying the Western concept of translation or translation theory as an umbrella term for all kinds of translation all over the world. One point that comes through clearly in this "Introduction" is the wonderment of the editors at "the relative lack of polemics around translation in a country like India" (Wakabayashi and Kothari 2009, 13) where the practice of translation has been taking place for over a millennium now. One of the explanations provided for this is that multilingualism in South Asia was a much more natural and "everyday" phenomenon than it was in European countries. This pervasive multilingualism may have led to an effortless movement between languages without a conscious acknowledgement of the process of translation:

> Perhaps one reason for the relative dearth of theorization was that languages were seen along a continuum, and the movement between languages was so effortless that it was no movement at all.
>
> *(Wakabayashi and Kothari 2009, 13)*

Wakabayashi and Kothari argue that even though there was a considerable volume of translations taking place in India for over a millennium, there was no theorizing on the act of translation. This lack of theorizing could have been because multilingualism and crossing over from one language to another was a natural part of everyday life for translators from these regions. In the South Asian milieu, translators worked with "much looser notions of text" (Simon and St-Pierre 2015, 10), leading to a creative and continuously evolving corpus of translated works. This approach to translation may be seen in the early translations from Sanskrit into the regional vernaculars of South Asia. Ramanujan has suggested that cultural traditions in India "are organized through at least two principles, (a) context sensitivity and (b) reflexivity of various sorts, both of which constantly generate new forms out of the old ones" (Dharwadker 1999, 137). The early translations that took place from Sanskrit into the regional languages of South Asia were context-specific and reflexive, and gave rise to new literary genres out of "old" Sanskrit material. In most cases, these translations inaugurated the literary traditions of these vernaculars (Devy 1999, 183).

E.V. Ramakrishnan, in "Translation as Resistance: The Role of Translation in the Making of a Malayalam Literary Tradition" (2009), asserts that the Malayalam literary tradition was inaugurated by translations from Sanskrit and Tamil. According to Ramakrishnan,

> One of the functions of translation is to articulate that which is latent in a culture but for which no vocabulary, discourse, image or metaphor is available. In this sense, translation creates a script for that which is hitherto unexpressed and invisible.
>
> *(Ramakrishnan 2009, 30)*

Ramakrishnan argues that the literary milieu of Kerala is shaped in major ways by translation. He discusses the fifteenth-century Malayalam classic *Krishnagatha*, believed to be written by Cherusseri. This is a translation of the tenth canto of the *Bhagavatha Purāṇa*, based on the legend of Krishna. The most striking feature of the text, according to Ramakrishnan, is the "symbiosis of Dravidian vocabulary and Sanskritic figures of speech" achieving "a stylistic breakthrough" (31). Cherusseri has "localized" the text by including metaphors and images familiar to the regional audiences while telling the *Bhagavatha Purāṇa*'s story of Krishna.

Ramakrishnan notes that the source text became a "mere pretext" for creating a new text in the vernacular.

> The Sanskrit original becomes a pre-text or a mere pretext, as it is pluralized to accommodate divergent elements of a living culture. Translation here can be seen as a means of assimilating the alien into the literary matrix of the local society.
>
> *(Ramakrishnan 2009, 32)*

This vernacularization contributed to the linguistic development and the standardization of Malayalam as a language. For Ramakrishnan, "Translation is a multi-layered process that demands interpretation of an entire tradition from a local and contemporary perspective" (Ramakrishnan 2009, 39). An understanding of what the practice of translation involves and its implications on culture should be derived from the specific cultural contexts of works of translation. "Cultural Translation" opens up the field to these inclusive ideas of the term "translation" itself.

In the Western perspective, translation was viewed against the backdrop of the myth of the Tower of Babel. Multilinguality was seen as a punishment to the aspiring builders of the tower, and translation as a means to "reconcile" or make up for what was lost or confounded at Babel. In the South Asian context, however, this was not the case. Multilingualism was accepted as a more natural part of everyday life. Cronin, in *Across the Lines: Travel, Language, Translation* (2000), recounts the Hassidic myth of Babel. In the Hassidic version, multilingualism is not a punishment for aspiring towards heaven, but rather a boon from God to alleviate the boredom and repetitive nature of monolingualism (Cronin et al. 2000, 57, 58). The South Asian attitude towards multilingualism is similarly positive, as opposed to the punitive overtones suggested by the biblical Babel. Sheldon Pollock, in "India in the Vernacular Millennium" (1998), notes that in the case of South Asia, "Diversity was not a punishment, multilinguality was not a sin that needed to be expiated…" (62). Translation, then, no longer remains an aspiration towards the "pure language" that was lost at Babel, but a negotiation of the intercultural differences inherent in a multilingual context.

This "everydayness" of multilingualism and translations practices may be one of the reasons why there is no widely accepted term equivalent to "translation" in India:

> We borrowed *anuvad* from Sanskrit (where it means 'speaking after') and *tarjuma* from Arabic (where it is nearer to 'explicate' or 'paraphrase'). More recent borrowings are *rupantar* (in Bangla) or *vivartanam* (in Malayalam) or *bhashantar* (in Hindi).
>
> *(Mukherjee 1997, 160)*

Translation, here, is a "speaking after", what is spoken after the "original" has been spoken. According to Mukherjee, translation in the South Asian context meant "to speak or write or read to each other."

In this sense, a translation did not have to be "equivalent" to the original. There was also no idea of a "primary" original and a "secondary" translation. According to Mukherjee, "[W]hen we admired a literary text in one language, we used it as a take-off point and composed a similar text in another language" (Mukherjee 1997, 160). In spite of this, "enough of the original remained in the new texts for listeners – later, readers – to be able to relate it, if they wanted, to the old texts" (Mukherjee 1997, 160). Mukherjee advocates the use of the term "transcreation" for this South Asian phenomenon of translation.[24] Within this conception of translation, a translator could make considerable changes to the form and matter of the text to suit the needs of their audience or readers. A sizable proportion of the regional literatures created during the period of vernacularization in medieval India consisted of Sanskrit texts translated into the vernacular.

The idea of translation that emerges from this discussion is different from the "translation proper" that constituted early discussions in translation theory. There is a whole different worldview towards the act of translation, different from that of a "superior" original and a "secondary" translation trying to live up to the standards of the original. The idea of translation that emerges from the vernacular millennium in South Asia is one of a dynamic give and take between Sanskrit and the vernacular languages. Though the translations were mostly from Sanskrit to the vernacular, they were hardly literal copies. They were new creations with a life of their own, "localized" texts infused with the colour of the region in which they were being "transcreated". A study of these translated texts shows that a translated text was a free text that used the original as a point of departure, rather than as a text to be faithfully carried over into another language. It creates a complex inter-mingling of the original with the translation rather than a linear relationship with the two (Bassnett and Trivedi 1999, 10). In this sense, "cultural translation" may be used to imply the cultural multiplicity of the term "translation" itself and the various connotations of the term in different cultural contexts.

By using the term "cultural translation", translation is taken out of the framework of the "philological enclosure" of linguistics and literature within which it was studied. "Cultural Translation" implies a focus on the act of translation itself, and an attempt to bring it into the forefront as a key process which is constantly at play in the (re)formation of cultures. This act of situating translation as a central category in cultural systems brings into focus the aspects of politics of power, inclusion, and exclusion that are constantly at play in the process of translation. Cultural Translation also connotes the idea that translation practices are deeply rooted in their geographical and cultural contexts and that any study attempting to understand the practice of translation must take these complexities into account. However, while approaching "cultural translation" in the context of Translation Studies, one has to be cautious about the still-emerging grammar and methods associated with cultural translation as a theoretical paradigm.

I.5 Outline of the Book

The possibility of studying *Kristapurāṇa* as a milestone in the history of translated works is underscored by this book. The uniqueness of the present study emerges from an attempt to situate *Kristapurāṇa* and Stephens in the rich tradition of translated texts and cultures of South Asia. The chapters of the book make an earnest attempt to open layers of new perspectives into an old, yet remarkable lineage of missionary scholarship. This book reads *Kristapurāṇa* as a translation of the biblical narrative. Translation is studied here as the process through which Stephens mediated the spaces between Hinduism and Christianity. A reading of the cultural translation undertaken by Stephens provides a glimpse into the travel of texts during the early missionary period in South Asia. In this process, certain key questions on cross-cultural transactions, as reflected in acts of literary translation, are discussed. One of the contributions of this work is that it consolidates the Marathi and English scholarship available on *Kristapurāṇa* today.

One of the aspects of cultures in Translation Studies is the critical relationship between travel and texts. Chapter 1, "Texts, Travels, and Christianities in South

Asia", is a survey of the routes by which Christian writings travelled in South Asia. The earliest works of scriptural translation and the "ports of entry" through which these texts entered are discussed. The purpose of this chapter in the larger study of *Kristapurāṇa* is to understand the diverse translation practices adopted by different groups of missionaries and translators who arrived in the subcontinent. The methods adopted by Catholic missionaries and Protestant missionaries provide interesting insight into translation and cultural practices that existed in colonial settings in South Asia. After this, the specific context of the Jesuits, of whom Stephens was one, is analysed from existing scholarship. The region of Salsette, where Stephens lived and worked for forty years, is also briefly introduced. This chapter primarily intends to locate Stephens and his monumental text in the larger context of Christian writings that existed prior to and after Stephens' time. The chapter begins with a discussion of the concept of "inculturation" within the church with specific reference to its relationship with cultural translation. This chapter offers a perspective for the rest of the study.

Chapter 2, "Into the Languages of This Land", introduces the primary text, *Kristapurāṇa*, and its composer Stephens. Details of Stephens life and the motivation for this research have been discussed in this chapter. The transformation of Stephens into a poet-priest and his role as a "creative" translator is highlighted. This chapter reads deeper into the transformation of the priest into a participant in the saint-poet tradition in the Marathi language. Stephens awareness of the literary nuances of the language, and his location within the edicts of the church, led him to practise a "creative Christianity" which is evident the translation strategies adopted by him. His epistolary correspondence is analysed to get a sense of the times and circumstances within which he was working. This chapter also introduces the textual aspects of *Kristapurāṇa* – its parts, division of cantos (Avaswaru), and the language and metre used in the text. Debates surrounding the language and original versions of *Kristapurāṇa* are also discussed.

Chapter 3, "Genre, Novelization, and Translatability in *Kristapurāṇa*", addresses the generic complexities of *Kristapurāṇa*. Genre is one of the sites through which cultural translation is approached in this work. The purāṇic tradition within which Stephens placed his work is studied in this chapter. The features of Purāṇas, specifically their translatability and their potential for "novelization", is analysed in order to understand the manner in which they travelled to the regional languages from Sanskrit. A close reading of the purāṇic term "Vaicunttha" is undertaken as one instance of the manner in which Stephens conveyed the Christian narrative in a genre sacred to the Hindus of the region.

Chapter 4, entitled "(Re)Painting Landscapes, (Re)Inventing Tradition", presents the abundance of vivid landscape writing in *Kristapurāṇa*. Landscape is one of the tropes in which Stephens's poetic genius and cultural translation is evident. This chapter also addresses the recent "spatial turn" in Translation Studies. The use of landscapes as symbol and images in the narrative is a significant thread in *Kristapurāṇa*. The landscapes that Stephens painted also provide glimpses into the everydayness of life in seventeenth-century Goa. The terrains in the text are a mix of the Palestinian imagery of the Bible, and the geography of the Konkan region in which the text was composed. Landscape is read in this chapter as intimately connected with the memory of people inhabiting it. It is argued in the chapter that a repainting of these lands, ruptured by colonial ventures, is a way of (re)inventing the memories and traditions that were connected to the landscape.

Chapter 5, "Speaking After", is a reflective chapter on the implications of this research. The unexplored parts of *Kristapurāṇa* are highlighted, and there is also a discussion of the avenues that it opens up for research in translation and allied fields. The discussions ends with a reaffirmation of the centrality of cultural translation and highlights the relevance of the complexities opened up by this book in contemporary times.

Notes

1 Friedrich Nietzsche, "Translation as Conquest", *Western Translation Theory: From Herodotus to Nietzsche*. 2nd ed. Edited by Douglas Robinson, p. 262.
2 The story of the Tower of Babel is described in the Book of Genesis (Chapter 1, verses 1–9) of the Bible. This scene is revisited and quoted in Chapter 4 of this book as part of a critical discussion on landscape.
3 The practice of translation existed centuries before the emergence of Translation Studies as a discipline. Translation Studies as an academic discipline was inaugurated in the late twentieth century.
4 The need for studying translation as intimately related to the cultural contexts that are involved in its practice, and not merely as sanitized instances of linguistic transfer, has been acknowledged in Translation Studies, specifically through moves such as the "Cultural Turn" within the field. However, scholars of Translation Studies have expressed discomfort and anxiety about the use of the word "translation" in the sense of its etymological meanings. The fear is that the basic meaning of translation as "textual transfer" from one language to another, or rewriting of a text into a language different from the one in which it was first written, is being eroded by this indiscriminate use of translation as a metaphor. This anxiety has been discussed in some detail in the following sections of this "Introduction".
5 In the linguistic approach to translation, translation was understood as a transfer from one linguistic code to another. For Roman Jakobson, a translator is someone who decodes the language of source text and "recodes" it into the language of the target text (Jakobson 1959, 233).
6 "Différance", or "deferment-difference", was a term coined by Jacques Derrida. He wrote about it in an essay titled "la Différance" (1963). The idea is further developed in *Of Grammatology* (1967). "What we note as *différance* will thus be the movement of play that 'produces' (and not by something that is simply an activity) these differences, these effects of difference. This does not mean that the *différance* which produces differences is before them in a simple and in itself unmodified and indifferent present. *Différance* is the nonfull, nonsimple "origin; it is the structured and differing origin of differences" (Derrida *Différance* 286–287).
7 Tejaswini Niranjana drew upon this deconstructionist understanding of translation in her work *Siting Translation* (1992), to question the status of the original in the hierarchy of translation (Niranjana 39).
8 According to Bastin, this adaptation may be either "local" or "global". Local adaptation entails the use of terms from the target culture in order to make up for inadequacies in the source text, in terms of equivalence. Global adaptation refers to change of genre or other strategies that are deliberately applied to the text as a whole (Bastin 2009, 5).

9 Bassnett and Trivedi argue, in their "Introduction" to *Post-colonial Translation: Theory and Practice* (1999), that the idea of the original as superior gained currency only with the advent of printing and widespread literacy (6). Until medieval times, translators were not burdened with a reverence to a superior "original". However, it is important to note that theories of translation which emerged primarily from Europe used the "original as superior" model in early discourses on translation, which in turn influenced the way the discipline of Translation Studies has evolved.

10 Culture has been studied in various ways in different academic disciplines. David Katan, in *Translating Cultures: An Introduction for Translators, Interpreters and Mediators* (2014), begins his discussion on culture by noting that it has been a "notoriously" difficult concept to define. He differentiates between the external manifestations of culture, "High Culture" and Low Culture", and "culture" that is "internal", "collective", and "acquired rather than learned" (26). In the context of translation, Katan suggests a possible definition of "culture as a shared system for interpreting reality and organizing experience" (26). Discussions on "culture" in the field of Translation Studies stemmed primarily from the cultural problems which had to be addressed during literary translation. "Culture", in this sense, is the collective set of practices and symbols which correspond to a language, either of the source text or of the target text. As the study of cultures through translation and the study of translation through cultures progressed, "culture" in translation has also come to imply the politics and power relations inherent in intercultural transactions (Brems et al. 2014, 8). Currently, culture is studied by Translation Studies scholars in relation to material artefacts, "power", "space", and neurological mechanisms involved in translation, among other aspects.

11 It is significant to note that this idea of translator as a "free agent" and all-powerful reader, who wielded authority over the source text, was already present in the South Asian context since medieval times. In Jnaneswar's *Bhavarthadeepika*, a commentary of the *Bhagavad Gita* into the Marathi language composed in the thirteenth century, the translator, far from being invisible, enters the narrative as one of the characters elucidating the meaning of the text. Jnaneswar's *Bhavarthadeepika*, also known as the *Jnaneswari*, is studied as one of the earliest translations into the Marathi language (Choudhuri 2010, 119). Ketkar argues, in "Lighting a Lamp with a Lamp: The *Bhavarth Deepika* as Translation" (2018), that Jnaneswar entered the text from time to time as one of the characters and contributed to the narrative.

12 Schleiermacher's envisioned two methods for translation: "Either the translator leaves the author in peace, as much as possible and moves the reader toward him; or he leaves the reader in peace, as much as possible and moves the author toward him" (Schleiermacher 49). For Schleiermacher, these were the two choices available to a translator while translating a text.

13 The "cultural turn", though not inaugurated by Lefevere and Bassnett, was heralded by their seminal works on translation in which they emphasized the role of translation in shaping cultures. The chapter, "The Cultural Turn in Translation Studies", jointly written by Bassnett and Lefevere in their book *Translation, History and Culture* (1990), is considered as an important moment signifying the turn towards culture.

14 Susan Bassnett and Harish Trivedi, in their book *Post-colonial Translation: Theory and Practice* (1999), emphasize on the colonial encounter and on the manner in which translation has been used "to establish and perpetuate the superiority of some cultures over others" (17).

15 Bassnett and Trivedi, in their "Introduction" to *Post-colonial Translation: Theory and Practice*, note that Europe, the colonial master, was the great "original", while its colonies are copies or translations of it (4).

16 The inherent violence of translation and the violence of translation in the exercise of colonial power are emphasized by Anuradha Dingwaney in her "Introduction" to *Between Languages and Cultures: Translation and Cross-cultural Texts* (Dingwaney and Maier 1996, 3, 4).

17 Xavier and Županov's *Catholic Orientalism* is a historical study of the "Orientalist" works produced by Catholic agents of the Portuguese empire. In order to bring out the influence of knowledge production by the "Catholic" empire, Xavier and Županov attempt to retrace the trajectory of Catholic knowledge as it came into contact with the colonies and developed into a massive volume of literary and cultural records. These documents are spread across various archives like the Biblioteca Nacional and the Biblioteca Publica in Lisbon, the Archivio della Congregazione di Propaganda Fide in Rome, and the Historical Archives of Goa in Panjim, among others in various European and Indian cities. The historical period addressed by the book primarily extends from the fifteenth century to the nineteenth century. The "knowledge practices" examined by the authors throughout the volume are illustrated through works on natural history and medical texts (pp. 77–115), administrative documents such as land records, inventories of temple lands and fortresses, and collections such as the *Livros das Communidades* (pp. 46–77), missionary texts, and translations of mythologies (pp. 115–158, 202–245).

18 Barros was a grammarian, historian and moralist and an important official in the House of India (Xavier and Županov 2015, 18), which was the institution that controlled maritime commerce. His *Asia* was a "narrative of Portuguese overseas experiences" (21), written on the basis of manuscripts Barros accessed in the House of India. Xavier and Županov's major contention in this work is that Protestant missionaries who began arriving in India in the eighteenth century and British orientalist scholars appropriated the knowledge produced by Catholic agents without acknowledging them. They utilized the works that were of use to them in their enterprises and neglected the rest. The material amassed by Catholic orientalists can be found in the archives of these later "Orientalisms," albeit unacknowledged. According to Xavier and Županov, the Jesuit missionary Memnius Rene Gargam wrote about "samcroutam" as a "mother language" in 1728 (317), long before the British scholar William Jones' celebrated "discovery" of Sanskrit and the Indo-European languages. Apart from this, English scholars like Francis Whyte Ellis used the Jesuit Beschi's writings for the Tamil literary renaissance of the nineteenth century without giving credit to Beschi's works (320, 321). Several other instances of appropriations by the agents of "High Orientalism" are discussed by the authors in this book. The anticlimactic end of the ambitious project of the Catholic empire is partially attributed to such "theft" by later scholars (317, 319).

19 The term "contact zone" was first coined by Mary Louise Pratt in her 1991 essay "Arts of the Contact Zone".

20 This is evident in the numerous grammars written by early Catholic (and non-Catholic) missionaries. After learning the language, the next step was to formalize it in a grammar. One familiar example is *Arte de Lingoa Canarim* by Stephens written in sixteenth-century Goa.

21 The term cultural translation has been, and continues to be, the subject of much debate in translation studies (Sturge 2009; Maitland 2017; Conway 2020).

22 Jeremy Munday writes about the interaction between Culture Studies and Translation Studies: "Cultural studies brings to translation an understanding of the complexities of gender and culture. It allows us to situate linguistic transfer within the multiple 'post' realities of today: poststructuralism, postcolonialism and postmodernism" (Munday 2001, 131).

23 Bhabha reads the works of Salman Rushdie to explain his concepts of hybridity and cultural translation. Salman Rushdie, in *Imaginary Homelands*, states that "we are translated men" (Rushdie 1991, 17). This understanding draws upon the etymological meaning of the word "translation": a human being who has been carried across from one land to another. It could also denote the process of transformation which brings a person to a moment where she or he can translate a culture through literature.

24 Transcreation is defined by the *Oxford Advanced Learners Dictionary* as "creative translation seen as producing a new version of the original work" (Mukherjee 1997, 158). Prasad also uses the term "transcreations" in his article on Tamil translation (Wakabayashi

and Kothari 2009, 17). Bassnett and Trivedi note that Mukherjee used the word "transcreation" to describe acts of translation in the South Asian context, probably without realizing that "transcreation" was being used in the South American context as a strong anti-imperial movement (Bassnett and Trivedi 1999, 17). According to Else Vieira in "Liberating Calibans" (1999), Haroldo de Campos used the term "transcreation" in the 1960s in the Latin American context. For Campos, "transcreation" involved an appropriation of the "translator's contemporaries' best poetry, to use the existing local tradition" (Vieira 1999, 110).

1

TEXTS, TRAVELS, AND CHRISTIANITIES IN SOUTH ASIA

> What should we do but sing his praise
> That led us through the wat'ry maze
> Unto an isle so long unknown,
> And yet far kinder than our own?
>   (Andrew Marvell, *Bermudas*)[1]

1.1 Times, Places, and People

Textual traditions, sacredness, and translation are the major threads of this work. One of the primary ways of grappling with the sacred through the ages has been through religious texts.[2] The central texts of the religions of the world have been read as some of the finest literary works known to humankind. In addition to their literary value, religious groups consider them sacred, setting them apart from other works of literature. One aspect of the sacredness accorded to religious texts was the divine authorship attributed to them. The "received" or "revealed" nature of these texts – non-human (*apauruseya*) authorship of the *Vedas*, the creative power of the "Word" of the Judeo-Christian Bible, or "divine revelation" of the *Quran*, among numerous other sacred texts – remain a challenge for critical study.[3] The primary reason for the challenging nature of such studies is the attribution of faith, reverence, and emotional value to these texts by the "practitioners" of these belief systems. The words contained in these texts had power, so much so that merely hearing them read out, or wearing amulets with these "words" written in them were seen as channels of divine power. Though these texts have often been dismissed as not subscribing to scientific rationality or to social "realities", they are significant records of the human quest for truth and search for roots (Dandekar 1937, 233). These sacred texts have direct implications on the way in which communities

DOI: 10.4324/9781003146544-2

perceive the world around them, order their social structures, and they delve into the inmost workings of the human soul.

In addition to the "internal" function of these texts in reflecting the human quest for meaning, these texts also played vital roles in the larger arena of the shaping of public institutions. Religious texts have often been used to establish empires, validate and sustain monarchies, and justify colonial ventures (Finer 1997, 50, 52; Riches 2000, 84). The symbiotic relationship between religions and power structures has drawn heavily on the reverence given to sacred texts. Divinely ordained monarchs and religious nation states held these texts as central to the continuation of their dynasties. For precisely these reasons, the "ownership" of these texts became a question which was deeply entangled in the power politics of cultures.

The possession of these religious texts had historically been a privilege of the elite. For instance, the Sanskrit-reading higher castes of the Indian Subcontinent had sole access to the Sanskrit texts which governed religious practices and the laws of society. The Latin of the Catholic Church was inaccessible to the large number of vernaculars of Europe where the Church flourished. The need to preserve the "sanctity" of these texts ensured that they remained untranslated. Any attempt to disseminate the knowledge of these texts had to be mediated by the existent powers who claimed ownership of them. Early attempts at translating these texts were, thus, branded as heresy and punishable by death (Zogbo 2009, 22). When these translations were into cultures where "other" religions were practised, the "cultural translation" that religious texts underwent came under further scrutiny. Ancient sacred traditions are renewed in processes of cultural translation. When cultures clash and overlap in sites of conquest, new soul is breathed into "what is old" leading to a discovery of the "selves" of individuals and coommunities involved in these encounters (Nietzsche 2002, 67). Cultural translation becomes one of the processes through which texts and traditions are conquered and made new. A study of cultural translations of religious texts, thus, provides significant insight into the complexities of the translation process as well as the cultural politics inherent in the act of translation.

The Christian Bible has been one of the most prolifically translated sacred books of the world (Zogbo 2009, 21). With the onset of European colonial ventures backed by missionary cadres from the Church, it became necessary to translate sacred texts to facilitate exchange of knowledge and religious conversion. Sites of colonial encounters are important locations where these questions of sacredness, power, and translation intersect in fundamental ways. When colonial agents justify their invasions through civilizing missions and religious conversions, the question of the sacred becomes interlinked with the power politics of the region (Metcalf 1994, 53). The complexities of textual translation are intensified in sites of cultural encounters, such as in regions of colonial establishments. A layer of complexity is added in these acts of translation when the texts being translated are sacred texts. A third complex strand is the use of regional literary traditions to adapt narratives for a local readership. A study of sacred texts from this period also provides insight into the ways in which translation was used as one of the tools to strengthen and sustain colonial ventures. All these complexities find a space in *Kristapurāṇa* (1616), making this South Asian text an ideal site for reading the problems of cultural translation of sacred texts.

Kristapurāṇa, a Marathi poetic retelling of the Bible composed by Father Thomas Stephens (1549–1619), is a site where there is interplay of multiple texts and traditions.[4] The arguments in this volume reflect the three major strands of cultural translation, sacredness, and transformations that occur at the intersections of these texts and traditions. *Kristapurāṇa* is one of the earliest texts from South Asia which provides spaces for reading the complexities of translation and the role of translation in the cultural practices of the region. Given that it is a missionary text from the Catholic period of Goa, a former Potuguese colony on the Western coast of India, the sacred texts which are studied in this work are the Christian compositions of the period, along with the local Hindu literary traditions that existed in Goa in the seventeenth century.

Cross-cultural encounters between Christianity and indigenous religious practices in South Asia have been dated back to the first century AD (Frykenberg 2008b, 92; Koepping 2011, 14). These encounters have led to innovative expressions of cultural exchange, especially in the form of literature in South Asian languages composed by missionaries. Christian texts were written with the primary intention of supporting evangelization. Some of these Christian texts entered the corpus of South Asian literatures and were woven into the varied linguistic fabric of the subcontinent.

Scholarship on Bible translation in the Indian Subcontinent take the eighteenth century as their starting point, with a cursory glance at the ages that have gone before (See Hooper 1938; Israel 2011). The eighteenth century is notable for the first "translation proper" of the Bible into a South Asian language – the Tamil New Testament, published in the year 1715 (Neill 1985, 477). This was followed by a surge in Bible translation activity by missionaries in the eighteenth and nineteenth centuries. However, the period of early missionary work by the Catholics under the Portuguese regime produced some critical works which are significant in understanding the development of sacred-text translation in the subcontinent. A large volume of orientalist works by Catholic agents of the Portuguese empire were created, beginning in the sixteenth century (see Xavier and Županov 2015). Catholic missionaries, specifically Jesuits, composed several works in the languages of the regions which were their mission fields. Translation of the Bible, however, was not one of the priorities of these early missionaries (Hooper 1938, 8). Their works were largely Catechisms, lives of saints and other poetic pieces and commentaries to familiarize converts with Church culture. *Kristapurāṇa* is a rare sighting, in this period, of an attempt to translate the biblical story into a South Asian language.

Kristapurāṇa stands out in the corpus of South Asian Christian writings because, (a) it was composed in the seventeenth century and may be claimed as the earliest retelling of the Bible in a South Asian language, (b) it uses local Marathi narrative traditions to tell biblical stories, and (c) it provides insight into the period of "Catholic orientalism", as texts from this period have largely remained unexplored in the study of translated works. The seventeenth century, in which *Kristapurāṇa* was published, becomes a significant component of discursive reflections in this book, providing a route to follow the trajectories of Portuguese missionary texts and their travels. The acknowledgment and location of the large volume of texts and translations from the Portuguese era in the literary canvas of the subcontinent is critical in reading the cultural history of the region with clarity. *Kristapurāṇa* is a work of scripture translation from this age of Portuguese rule. A reading of this text provides hitherto unexplored insight into the act of translation as it was approached by early missionaries like Stephens.

As a Jesuit, Stephens was expected to study regional languages and compose Catholic literature in them. However, Stephens, unlike other Jesuits of his time, chose to tell the entire story of the Bible in the seventeenth century. *Kristapurāṇa* is a text that is located at the critical intersection of scripture translation, cross-cultural encounters, and distinct literary and religious traditions. In *Kristapurāṇa*, the listeners, the new Christians of Goa, ask the *Padre-guru*, the narrator, to bring the "blessed" story of the Bible "into the languages of this land" (*Kristapurāṇa* 1.1.161). Stephens's attempt to bring the biblical narrative into the languages of South Asia is a critical moment in the literary history of the region.

Kristapurāṇa was originally published under the title *Discurso Sobre a Vinda de Jesu Christo Nosso Salvador ao Mundo* in Rachol, Goa in the year 1616. According to A.K. Priolkar (1895–1973), Stephens's "claim to a place among the immortals of the Marathi literature" is because of this "classical presentation of the Biblical story in Marathi verse" (Priolkar 1971, 41). *Kristapurāṇa* is a grand poetic telling of the biblical story from the creation of the world up until the resurrection and ascension of Christ. Stephens described his composition as a "Purāṇa". Purāṇas were originally Sanskrit texts, held in reverence by various sects of Hindus in the Indian Subcontinent. In the period between 1000 AD and 1500 AD, these Sanskrit texts began to travel to the vernacular languages of the subcontinent through translations, including Marathi (Das 2005, 191–193). *Kristapurāṇa* participates in this tradition of Marathi Purāṇas.

Kristapurāṇa is written in verse in the purāṇic style. It has a total of 10,962 strophes *(Ovi)*. There are thirty-six cantos (*Avaswaru*) in the *Paillem Puranna* and fifty-nine cantos in the *Dussarem Puranna*. The *Paillem Puranna* roughly corresponds to the passages of the Old Testament and the *Dussarem Puranna* to the New Testament of the Bible. Throughout the first and second Purannas, Christ is the undisputed, glorified hero of the narrative (see Figure 1.1).

As a retelling of biblical episodes from the Latin Vulgate of the Catholic Church into the Marathi language composed in the Portuguese colony of Goa, *Kristapurāṇa* provides spaces for reading it as a cultural translation of the biblical narrative. It is composed in a contact zone of cultural encounters. It has multiple "source texts", orality, and traditions to draw from, and as such it is not possible to draw a linear relationship between the source materials and target text. It provides significant insight into the way in which intercultural differences are negotiated in mission fields. It reveals the ways in which local Goan communities displaced by colonial ventures came to terms with cultural shifts in the everydayness of life, making it a critical text for reading cultural translation. One of the ways in which missionaries negotiated the cultural complexities of mission fields was through cultural translation as a channel for inculturation in the Church.

FIGURE 1.1   Title page of the handwritten manuscript of the 1654 edition of *Kristapurāṇa* at the Krishnadas Shama Goa State Central Library (MS–57).

Photograph mine (Courtesy: Krishnadas Shama Goa State Central Library).

1.2 Inculturation and Cultural Translation

In an event narrated in the New Testament, the disciples of Jesus were gathered together in a room, in the first century AD, and the Holy Spirit came upon them for the first time. The passage can be found in the book, Acts of the Apostles, Chapter 2, Verses 1–12, of the Bible. The following quote is from the New International Version:

> When the day of Pentecost came, they were all together in one place. Suddenly a sound like the blowing of a violent wind came from heaven and filled the whole house where they were sitting. They saw what seemed to be tongues of fire that separated and came to rest on each of them. All of them were filled with the Holy Spirit and began to speak in other tongues as the Spirit enabled them.

Now there were staying in Jerusalem God-fearing Jews from every nation under heaven. When they heard this sound, a crowd came together in bewilderment, because each one heard their own language being spoken.

Utterly amazed, they asked: "Aren't all these who are speaking Galileans? Then how is it that each of us hears them in our native language? Parthians, Medes and Elamites; residents of Mesopotamia, Judea and Cappadocia, Pontus and Asia, Phrygia and Pamphylia, Egypt and the parts of Libya near Cyrene; visitors from Rome (both Jews and converts to Judaism); Cretans and Arabs – we hear them declaring the wonders of God in our own tongues!" Amazed and perplexed, they asked one another, "What does this mean?"

Some, however, made fun of them and said, "They have had too much wine".

The passage describing this event in the Bible is considered as one of the foundational passages of Christianity. It was after this episode that the disciples went out to different parts of the world in order to evangelize. It can be argued, therefore, that it is inherent in the Christian tradition, from its earliest days, to take the gospel to people in their own language (Phan 2003, 4). In practice, however, the process is not as simple as this symbolic passage seems to portray. Christian encounters with new cultures, especially those that originated from European colonizing missions, have been rife with violence and intercultural struggles for supremacy. In this context, it is important to understand the concept of "inculturation", the concept as (a) envisioned by the Church, (b) as seen in actual practice in Christian missions, and (c) in its relationship with cultural translation.

Peter Phan, in his work *In Our Own Tongues: Perspectives from Asia on Mission and Inculturation* (2003), defines inculturation as "a double process comprising of (a) insertion of the gospel into a particular culture, and (b) introduction of the culture into the gospel" (6). The Second Vatican Council (1962–1965) of the Roman Catholic Church devoted important discussions to the subject of inculturation in mission fields (Phan 2003, 3). Though the term itself is a recent one, the process of inculturation has been taking place for several centuries, in both Catholic and Protestant evangelical missions. Over the centuries, different terms, such as "translation, accommodation, adaptation, localization, indigenization, contextualization, incarnation, acculturation, inculturation, interculturation" (Phan 2003, 4), have been used to describe the transformative, transmissive processes that take place during evangelization.[5]

The process of inculturation includes not only Christian literature, but also Church rites and liturgy being (re)shaped and accommodated into local culture. Church culture, here, is appropriated by the local culture, while local culture is being appropriated to disseminate the Christian message. Christianity begins to be 'translated' as soon as it comes into contact with a new culture, irrespective of whether its texts are linguistically translated or not.[6] It is a process where the new religious culture seeps into local culture, using local, "pre-Christian" forms as a means to convey the Christian message, or finding ways of incorporating local culture into the Church. This leads to a transformation in the Church itself, giving it a new colour and shape, and not just in the converted masses. Phan notes that inculturation leads to

> ... both the transformation of the culture from within by the gospel and the enrichment of the gospel by the culture with its new ways of understanding and living it. Hence, the end result of inculturation is something new, a *tertium quid*, going beyond the current culture and the previous ways of understanding and living the gospel.
>
> *(Phan 2003, 6)*

Inculturation involves the translation – of written works, practices and rituals connected with Christian living – into cultures that came into contact with Christianity. Vengco divides this process into three stages. The first stage is the initial encounter, when the Church is "translated" for the local culture, but in terms of the missionary's culture, as a "foreign" religion. This step introduces Christianity into the field of the new culture. Vengco describes this stage as a 'cultural translation' or acculturation, where elements of both cultures begin to cross over and inter-mingle. The second stage is an "assimilation" of the Church into local life while the third is a process of "transformation", where the Church begins to reshape local culture to spread its message (Vengco 1984, 193). It is also a continuous process, an on-going dialogue between the Church and local culture.

Inculturation is a process initiated by the Roman Catholic Church to effectively evangelize peoples of various cultures. However, we can argue that rather than a "method" which has been recommended and used by the church, inculturation is a process of cultural translation that takes place at "contact zones" where missionary meets native. We can argue that it is not accurate to study inculturation as a technical method devised by the Church for effective Christianization of world cultures. The moment a missionary reaches a "new" culture, a process of negotiating begins between two cultures, which can be studied as a "cultural translation", and, in this case, a part of the process of inculturation. Robert Frykenberg, in his review of *Christian Inculturation in India* (2007) by Paul M. Collins, states that Christianity is not bound by forms that originated in Europe. Since its beginnings, as it moved out of its Jewish birthplace, it has transcended and negotiated cultural barriers (Phan 2003, 3; Frykenberg 2008a, 1118).

> Christian cultures of India, with their norms or rituals, are not mere instances of "legitimization", or "recognition", by alien Christians from the West. Rather, each reflects an instance of the "indigenous discovery of Christianity" by one among manifold Indian peoples, for themselves.
>
> *(Frykenberg 2007, 1118)*

A study of inculturation in any region of South Asia, or any other Christian community in the world, should not be from the point of view of the Church which imposes its methods and successfully Christianizes a society. Rather, it needs to be studied as a process of cultural translation that happens when the culture comes into contact with Christianity, and discovers, for themselves, their own form of "indigenous Christianity". According to Frykenberg, "Inculturation coming out of decisions and discussions of the World Council of Churches, Vatican II, and Lambeth Conferences seems little more than another futile importation, if not a neo-colonial imposition" (1118). Frykenberg asserts the importance of recognizing the local roots of inculturation rather than studying it solely as a conscious approach by the Church.

Francis X. Clooney argues that Roberto de Nobili (1577–1656) used inculturation centuries before the church adopted it officially as a term (Clooney 2020, 7, 32). De Nobili's easy assimilation into the local culture in the Madurai mission and his adaptation of classical concepts from Hindu texts to translate Christian doctrine became a precursor for future methods of inculturation in India and the subject of many controversies within the Church.

Stephens's *Kristapurāṇa*, though written in an age before the use of the term "inculturation" came to be used for "cultural translation" in Christian missions, is an example of the "tertium quid", the third, new thing that emerges out of a transaction between two cultures. *Kristapurāṇa* can be studied as a specimen of inculturation and to understand how cultural translation functions to create the transformative forces that lead to inculturation.[7]

A close reading of *Kristapurāṇa* as a cultural translation brings into perspective the manner in which the Bible was appropriated by the community of new converts in Goa. In this process of cultural translation, both the narrative and the local culture are transformed. The term "cultural translation", in this study, is taken to mean the appropriations and transformative processes that occur in the text as it crosses the boundary from one culture to another. A reading of *Kristapurāṇa* enables one to rethink the idea of translation itself, to include an understanding of translation as it was practiced in the literary milieux of South Asia in the seventeenth century.

It may be argued that texts like *Kristapurāṇa* were not meant to replace the Latin Vulgate in the Catholic Church neither were they meant to be used for liturgy in churches. They functioned more as "para-text" to the Bible. It is argued in this book that the local Hindu audience, however, ascribed sacredness to poetic, purāṇic works. A translated text may have meaning(s) unintended or not necessarily desired by the translator. *Kristapurāṇa* was composed in a genre in which the sacred texts of the locals had been composed for centuries. The local audience considered purāṇic works as scriptures and ascribed historicity and sacredness to them. As Stephens appropriated indigenous sacred forms to translate the Christian message, his readers responded by actively "interpreting" it through their own worldview. It is likely that the converts of Goa, who had no Bible to read in their own language, attributed the position of scriptures to this Christian text. Stephens was fully aware of the sacred reverence his work was likely to receive, as he states boldly in his prose "Introduction" to the Purāṇa that his work would convince the locals of the truth of Christianity. It is necessary, therefore, to treat Stephens's work, not just as biblical poetry,[8] but as one of the earliest retellings of the biblical narrative in a South Asian language.

Stephens practised cultural translation in the sense that he made his poetic epic available to readers in a form that was accessible to them. It was his intention not only to take the Christian "truth" to his readers but also to "thrill" (2.2.115) his readers with his poetic composition. In this process, biblical places had to be painted in Konkani colours, old landscapes were transformed and new landscapes created. Stephens's cultural translation is, thus, both a transformative process as well as a creative one. This reading of *Kristapurāṇa* as a cultural translation underlines how traditions are transformed and new traditions are created by Stephens's poetic text.

In the following sections, a clear understanding of the travel of Christian writings in South Asia is developed. The purpose of the next sections in this chapter is to temporally and spatially locate *Kristapurāṇa* within the context of early missionary translation practices.

1.3 South Asia and Its "Christianities"

The next few sections of this chapter contemplate a panorama of Christian textual practices and translations in South Asia, before focusing on Salsette in Goa, where Stephens lived and worked. The purpose of this discussion is to foreground the critical routes by which power, knowledge, and textual cultures travelled in the subcontinent.

It seeks to locate *Kristapurāṇa* in the framework of Christianity in South Asia, with specific focus on the journey of scriptural translations. While reading *Kristapurāṇa* as a cultural translation of the biblical narrative, it is crucial to situate it within the context of the practices associated with scripture translation in the region. Locating the text within the context of translations in South Asia enables an understanding of the cultural factors that may have influenced the translator and his narrative. In this process of situating the text in a spatio-temporal framework, the variety and complexity that is brought to mind by the term "Christianity in South Asia" is revealed. The focus of these sections is to follow the routes by which biblical narratives first began to appear in South Asian languages. The lens through which this history is viewed in the present work is that of the earliest scriptural translations that were composed in South Asian languages.[9] While this chapter may appear to be a digression from the reading of *Kristapurāṇa*, these discussions have been consciously placed in this work in order to locate *Kristapurāṇa* as a critical text in the network of South Asian Christian writings.

Phan, in *Christianities in Asia* (2011), prefers to use the plural term "Christianities" to describe Asian Christianity. Phan points out that the church in South Asia is marked by cultural, theological, and liturgical diversity and by multiple Christian denominations present in the region (Phan 2011, 3). The sheer multiplicity of forms taken by Christianity in the South Asian region makes it important to study it with special focus on the regions in which it flourished. In order to facilitate an understanding of Christianity as a possible cultural, religious alternative, Christian narratives and writings were designed specifically to make them accessible to the common masses. The texts that were chosen to be translated into the vernacular, the language to be used, the form of the translated work, are all subject to the peculiarities of the missionaries' "field". A study of Christianity in South Asia cannot be a monolithic, linear study. It is a study of each of these micro-Christianities that flourished in different regions of South Asia. A close reading of *Kristapurāṇa* provides insight into one such "microcosm" of Christianity. It brings to light the way in which translation of religious literature took place in specific microcosmic settings, providing insight into the routes by which texts travelled, and the role that translation played in shaping these cultural ecosystems. The purpose of this analysis is also to underline the varied translation practices that were adopted by different missionaries who arrived in the region and the relevance of these practices in understanding how the Christian Bible was culturally adapted to the South Asian context.

In the chapter titled "India, Pakistan, Bangladesh, Burma/Myanmar" in Phan's edited volume *Christianities in Asia*, Elizabeth Koepping lists the factors that have to be taken into account while studying Christianity in this region:

> Caste, class, and ethnicity, local and foreign missions, contested contextualization, inter and intra-religious pluralism, colonialism, politics, poverty, nationalism: this sample list gives some indication of the complexity of Christianity in South Asia.
>
> *(Koepping 2011, 10)*

The abovementioned intricacies are knit into the complex fabric that is South Asian Christianity. When factors like those enumerated by Koepping, which are inherent in South Asian societies, are brought in contact with a religion like Christianity, it brings about changes in both the foreign religion and indigenous cultural practices. This leads to accommodation as well as conflict in both the host culture and the new religion. When a person is "converted" to Christianity, she or he does not suddenly transform into a completely Christian person. The new convert carries the traces of memories and traditions of an indigenous culture, while being expected to embrace the culture of the new religion. This encounter between disparate cultures involves a process of cultural translation, wherein the convert moves towards a transformation into a Christian. Such transformations are rarely complete. They lie somewhere in between the spectrum of the old culture and the new.[10] These interactions bring about "new manifestations" of Christianity which are peculiar to the region (Bayly 1989, 1).

Christianity had its beginnings in South-West Asia, in Palestine. However, after its spread and growth in Europe, it "re-entered" Asia as a Western religion, specifically as the religion of Asia's "colonizers" (Phan 2011, 2). An understanding of Christianity in South Asia, rather than being linear and chronological, could be a study of the three major "waves" (Jones 2012, 93) of Christianity that entered South Asia, beginning in the first century AD. These waves interacted and clashed with each other, leading to unique Christian practices and denominations. South Asia, as a society, is marked by religious and political pluralism in addition to its massive geographical and linguistic diversity. On its arrival in South Asia over several periods, Christianity evolved into multiple shapes based on the cultures that it came into contact with. These interactions were manifested in church culture, architecture, and in the literary landscapes of these regions (Koepping 2011, 18, 19).

The first "wave" of Christianity to arrive in South Asia came from West Asia (Koepping 2011, 14; Jones 2012, 93). Oral traditions and songs of the Thomas Christians of South India are based on the belief that the Apostle Thomas came to India in the first century and founded Christianity in the region. This group of Christians was assimilated into the socio-cultural milieu of South India and over two millennia have emerged as a distinctly South Asian expression of Christianity (Visvanathan 1993, 20). Early churches were also found in Sri Lanka, as has been recorded in the travelogue of Cosmas Indicopleustus (c. 547) (Wilfred 2014, 31).[11]

The second wave was the arrival of the Roman Catholics at the end of the fifteenth century. The Catholics were unable to make large inroads in terms of territorial expansion and were converged around power centres like Goa and Sri Lanka (Jones 2012, 94). Early Catholic churches may also be found in Lahore (1579), Agra (1611), and Dhaka (1677), among other places (Koepping 2011, 19). However, agents of the Catholic-Portuguese empire – missionaries, traders, adventurers, and administrators – created a vast corpus of Orientalist literature which shaped the portrayal of South Asia to Europe (Xavier and Županov 2015, 60). These meticulous records and translations of religious texts which were created for the benefit of the Portuguese empire and the Roman Church became storehouses of knowledge that would be used by the future orientalists, the British.

The third wave of Christianity in South Asia came with the Protestant missionaries. The first Protestant group to arrive was that of the Dutch missionaries. A significant influence of Dutch Protestantism may be seen in Sri Lanka, where the Dutch took over power from the Portuguese in 1658 (Rasiah 2011, 47). With the arrival of the British, the position of the Protestants in South Asia was consolidated, and the imperial aspirations of the Catholic Portuguese Empire drew to an end.[12] Catholicism, however, continued to flourish in, and beyond, the parishes which had been established in the centuries in which the Portuguese had been in power. These three waves overlapped and interacted both in terms of time and geographical territory, thereby contributing to the manner in which Christianity in South Asia shaped up. Koepping notes that one of the significant features of Christianity in the region is its long and continuing history, beginning in the first century AD. She characterizes South Asian Christianity as a "faith in the making", a cultural phenomenon which is continuously shifting shape and being reformed by the socio-political forces at work in the region (Koepping 2011, 35).

The following sections consider two of these these three waves of Christianity in South Asia in an attempt to understand how Christian texts travelled in the region. In this process, the role of translation practices in shaping the Christian communities of South Asia is highlighted. These sites of Christianity became the "contact zones" where cultural translation was a means for both the missionary "translator" and the "translated" convert to read each other. The literary translations that emerged out of South Asia in this period signified a two-way process of inter-cultural transfer. Texts from South Asian vernaculars were translated into European languages, while at the same time texts from the languages of Europe were trans-lated into the vernaculars. *Kristapurāṇa* is located as an early text in this network of South Asian literature, where cultural translation took place in the spaces created by imperial encounters. A journey along the routes that these texts travelled is also a journey that reveals the intimate relationship between cultural translation, religious practices, and colonial itineraries.

The first extant translation of the Bible into an Asian language was the protes-tant missionary Albert Cornelius Ruyl's translation of the Gospel of Matthew into the Malay language, in 1629. This was the "first printed portion of the Bible in a non-European tongue to be used as a tool for evangelization" (Bullard 1990, 896).[13] The movement towards composition of literature and translation of Christian works into the languages of South Asia was to begin in earnest with the second wave of Christianity which was ushered in by the Roman Catholics, which also coincided with the establishment of Portuguese colonial rule in the region.

1.4 The Catholic Wave

The earliest foreign Christians in India were profoundly Portuguese. The arrival of the Portuguese traveler Vasco da Gama and his company in Calicut on the Western coast of South India in the year 1498 inaugurated the discovery of a sea route to India.[14] Da Gama's meeting with the Zamorin of Calicut opened up trade relations for the Portuguese with the rulers of Kerala and the Thomas Christians (Disney 2009, 150). Regular expeditions by different companies of Portuguese followed, leading to the establishment of the *Estado da India*, or the Portuguese State of India, by the first Governor Albuquerque.[15] The aim of the Portuguese was to get a share in the trade route from India, which was monopolized by the Arabs for centuries (Disney 2009, 149). In 1502, the King of Portugal was conferred with the title "Lord of the Conquest of Navigation and commerce of India, Ethiopia, Arabia and Persia". Owing to the battles between the kingdom of Vijayanagara and the Muslim leaders of South India, Goa, which was under the rule of the Adilshah of Bijapur, was won by the Portuguese with the help of local Hindu rulers (D'Souza 2012, 277). Thereby, Goa became the power centre of the Portuguese in South Asia.

The influence that the Portuguese had can be better understood if it is remem-bered that they were armed with the *Padroado Real*: "The *Padroado Real*, granted by the Church of Rome to the Portuguese Crown, gave it exclusive authority to fill clerical positions within its Portuguese domains" (Frykenberg et al. 2008b, 127). This meant that any Catholic mission to be conducted in the colonies, since the fif-teenth century, had to come via the Portuguese crown and be subject to Portuguese authority. Frykenberg argues that "The earliest Pfarangi Christians in India were not just Catholic, nor just 'Roman' Catholic. They were profoundly 'Portuguese'" (Frykenberg et al. 2008b, 127). *Pfarangi* was a name given to Europeans in India, and was used as a derogatory term in some instances (Frykenberg et al. 2008b,

19). Portuguese settlements began to grow as Christian centres. Goa was the focal point of the Portuguese power in India and the heart of missionary activity of the Catholics. The number of converts in Goa began to rise steadily and the Goan landscape began to be dotted with elaborate churches which would become symbols of power and the focal point of Portuguese/Jesuit presence in the region. A.R. Disney, in *A History of Portugal and the Portuguese Empire* (2009), states that visitors were struck by the number and splendor of churches in places like Goa (Disney 2009, 148), pointing to the Portuguese influence on the rapidly changing landscape of the region. The Portuguese armed with their monopoly on both navigation and religious mission, became a formidable force in South Asia in the sixteenth century.

The *Estado da India* justified its rule partly through the argument of religious superiority and conversion. For missionaries, the need to understand indigenous knowledge and interpret it for a European audience was necessary to fulfil their religious calling. Translation of indigenous religious texts was necessary to understand indigenous religions and refute their tenets so that Christianity could be firmly established. These missionary endeavours led to systematic studies of Indian languages and religions. The result of this was a massive corpus of grammars, dictionaries, translated texts, and original compositions in native languages along with administrative documentation of Church activities. Missionaries such as Roberto de Nobili conducted "experiments" in creative forms of Christianity in order to engage with the intellectual tradition of the Brahmins, who were the missionaries' preferred group for conversion during the period. Rather than preach Christianity as it was practiced in Europe, de Nobili attempted to insert Christianity into the framework of Indian religious thought.

The translation of the Christian message into local poetic forms was one of the ways in which missionaries attempted to reinvent Christianity. In the process, the missionaries themselves were culturally translated, as is illustrated by the life of Roberto de Nobili. He was well known for his physical transformation into an Indian monk. He dressed like the locals and ate the food eaten by high-caste Brahmins of the region, transforming himself in the process of translating Christianity for the locals. De Nobili wore the sacred thread of the twice-born Brahmins and stressed that he was not a "*Parangi* [Portuguese], but a *sannyasi* from Rome, born to a Rajah's family" (Koepping 2011, 17). In a work titled *Disputed Missions: Jesuit Experiments and Brahmanical Knowledge in Seventeenth-Century India* (1999), Županov analyses the life and epistolary correspondence of de Nobili as a significant voice located on the borders between the "Orient" and the "Occident." De Nobili separated Indian "civility" from "religion" and grafted Christian meaning onto indigenous semiotic forms (Mosse 2012, 32; Clooney 2020, 19).[16]

Xavier and Županov argue that the systematic foundation of religious and linguistic works laid by the Catholic missionary enterprise led to the development of the comparative study of religions and linguistics under the British in later years. British scholars accessed Jesuit writings through intermediaries like Abbé Dubois and A. Muttusami Pillai[17] and referred to these writings while composing their own scholarly works about India (Xavier and Županov 2015, 320, 321).

The Catholics translated large volumes of texts from South Asian languages to European languages. They wrote grammars and translated catechisms and prayers into the vernaculars of the region to aid conversion. The Catholics, however, never translated the Bible into any of these vernaculars. Bible translation as a systematic activity was inaugurated with the arrival of the Protestants in the eighteenth century. Protestant scholars like J.S.M. Hooper and Claudius Buchanan note that the Catholic Church never took the "good and perfect gift" (which for Buchanan was the Bible) to the people to whom they were preaching (Buchanan 1812, 10). Hooper points out that the Church did not provide the Bible "un-interpreted" to the people, without the Church's mediation (Hooper 1938, 8). Such debates can be attributed to the fact that Catholic missionaries were largely involved in translating Church culture, whereas Protestant missionaries who arrived in India took up Bible translation projects soon after their arrival. This difference of perspective towards holy-text translation could primarily be attributed to the difference between Catholic and Protestant theologies.

After the conquest of Goa by the Portuguese, Dominican priests were the first to arrive in the region, followed by the Augustinians. However, the Jesuits, who arrived in 1542 and started missionary work in earnest, soon became the most influential religious group in the region (Moffet 2005, 16). The Jesuits in South Asia are discussed in this section in order to locate Stephens and his work in the temporal and spatial framework of missionary culture in India.

There were priests from several Catholic orders working in South Asia in the sixteenth and seventeenth centuries – Augustinians, Franciscans, Dominicans, and Jesuits, among others. Of these, the Jesuits[18] attained major influence and success as missionaries. In terms of the magnitude of missionary work, the work of Jesuits in South Asia is much more influential than of any other order (Frykenberg et al. 2008b, 129). The Jesuits spread all over the Indian Subcontinent and continued their work, influencing the religious, linguistic, and political landscape of the region. There are records of Jesuit priests in Akbar's court which demonstrates the routes which the Jesuits traversed in order to disseminate the message of the Catholic Church (Rezavi 2008, 204).[19] They became well known for their achievements in areas of evangelization, arts, and sciences as much as for their controversies (O'Malley 2014, 27, 68). The focus on Jesuits in this work is relevant in the context of their role in developing a religious vocabulary for Christianity in South Asia and for their role in shaping the landscape of Portuguese Goa in which *Kristapurāṇa* was written and published. In addition, it is important to understand the Jesuit order as the author of *Kristapurāṇa* was himself a Jesuit who was situated within the framework of his missionary calling while composing his magnum opus.

The founding mission of the Jesuits is critical in understanding the textual traditions that emerged in their mission fields in subsequent centuries. The Society of Jesus officially came into existence on 27 September 1540, when Pope Paul III signed the papal bull, *Regimini militantis ecclesiae* (O'Malley 2014, 3). The *Formula Vivendi*, "plan for life", which was the founding document of the Jesuit order is significant as it reveals the basic tenets on which the Order continued to function in the subsequent centuries.

"Travel" was one of the central themes in this document. The first Jesuits vowed that they would be prepared to travel "among the Turks, or to the New World, or to the Lutherans, or to any others whether infidels or faithful" (O'Malley 2014, 4). This idea was so central to the mission of the Jesuits that it was called the "Fourth Vow", in addition to the three customary vows of poverty, chastity, and obedience. Travel did become a significant part of the way in which the Jesuits functioned and shaped their identity as a missionary order. The mission of this society was to go out into the world and spread the Catholic faith, while maintaining allegiance to the Pope.

In keeping with this vow of travel, Francis Xavier (1506–1552), one of the founding members of the society, set out for India and arrived in Goa in the year 1542. Xavier was the Jesuit who inaugurated the work of the Society of Jesus in South Asia. He began working in the Malabar region and in Tamil Nadu with the help of local translators from Goa (Fernando and Gispert-Sauch 2004, 90). Xavier appointed people to translate small instruction books into Tamil (Fernando and Gispert-Sauch 2004, 90; Malshe 1961, 22). He committed a Tamil sermon to memory and preached in villages. In addition to his work in India, he travelled to Malaysia, Japan, and China. He died in 1552 on an island near China. Xavier's significance in Goa and in the spread of Catholicism in Asia goes far beyond his actual missionary work in these regions. He became a symbol of the devout Catholic missionary travelling across borders and braving all odds to spread the gospel. The veneration accorded to Xavier's mortal remains which have been preserved at the Basilica of Bom Jesu in Goa is symbolic of the way he is embodied in the narrative of missionary work in South Asia. Xavier's work soon became renowned all over Europe through missionary networks and his life became an inspiration for later generations of Jesuits to travel to South Asian regions for missionary work.

The *padroado* provided a great deal of autonomy to these missionaries enabling them to interpret local culture and Christianity in new and ingenious ways. One instance of this interpretation is when, on encountering the institution of caste in India, the missionaries devised indigenous forms of worship that gave a distinct Indian flavor to local Catholic worship. These Jesuit interventions and their interaction with Indian society and culture have been studied by scholars like Županov and David Mosse. Mosse, in *The Saint in the Banyan Tree: Christianity and Caste Society in India* (2012), discusses the manner in which Jesuits such as de Nobili negotiated the system of caste in the Madurai mission. The literary compositions by Jesuits in local languages were ways in which both the locals and the Jesuits "reprocessed" their knowledge of each other (Županov 2012, 415).

Xavier is also remembered in the context of the Inquisition of Goa. The Inquisition was established in Goa in 1560 to punish apostate new Christians – Hindus, Jews and Muslims who converted to Catholicism, as well as their descendants – who were now suspected of practicing their ancestral religion in secret. It also targeted non-Catholic Christians like the Syrian Christians of Kerala. The guilty were tried for heresy and punished. In his study of the Inquisition of Goa, Priolkar presents an extract from a letter written by Francis Xavier to the King, D. Joao III, on 16 May, 1545, requesting that the Inquisition be brought to the region: "Another need in

India to protect Christian life of those who have been baptized into the Christian faith is that your highness should order the establishment of the Holy Inquisition" (Priolkar 2008, 21, 22). This request by Xavier, however, did not bring about any result. The Inquisition was established in Goa much later, in the year 1560, during the reign of D. Sebastiao. Priolkar terms the Inquisition as a "terrible tribunal for the East" as it struck fear into the heart of the locals. The palace of the Inquisition in Goa was a site where culture(s) came face to face in a fundamental way, and had fatal implications for those who did not "translate" well into the Catholic faith.

Apart from the Inquisition, there were numerous instances of violent conquests, forced conversions, and desecration of Hindu temples (Malshe 1961, 19, 22, 24; Disney 2009, 165). In order to repair this damage to the Church's reputation, Provincial Councils were set up in 1575 and 1585 to revisit the Jesuits' approach towards conversion. More "accommodative" methods were devised and it was decided to create a "compendium of Catechism in the Portuguese language" and then translate it into the vernacular (Malshe 1961, 24). According to S.G. Malshe, Stephens's *Doutrina Christa*, *Kristapurāṇa*, and similar works by Jesuits all over the country were in accordance with these councils. These councils also urged Jesuits to learn the local languages of the regions in which they resided. They were given special schooling in local languages and in the indigenous literature of the region (Malshe 1961, 26; Županov 2012, 424). Indigenous texts were translated into Portuguese to facilitate the Jesuits' study of them. The whole corpus of texts in the regional languages of South Asia that were brought out by the Jesuits was a result of such training.

Henrique Henriques (1520–1600), de Nobili (1577–1656), John de Britto (1647–1693), and Constanzo Giuseppe Beschi (1680–1747) are some of the well-known Jesuits who followed Xavier to India. They composed important works in Tamil. Henriques, who served as the Superior of the mission from 1549 to 1576, translated Christian doctrines into Tamil and arranged for their printing (Somaratna 2012, 299). Županov, in her article "I am a Great Sinner: Jesuit Missionary Dialogues in Southern India (Sixteenth Century)" (2012), discusses a confession manual in Tamil, the *Confessionairo*, published by the Henriques in 1580. Županov underlines the role of such texts in creating "self-conscious Catholics" after the initial conversions, which were largely "communal events" (Županov 2012, 417).

De Nobili is famous for his work in the Madurai mission and for his interpretation of Catholic theology in order to fit Christianity into local Tamil culture (Mosse 2012, 10, 32, 33). He studied Sanskrit and Tamil texts and came up with his own methods for "accommodation" in the mission field. Accommodation is a missionary principle which encouraged the adaptation of Christianity to local culture of mission fields. De Nobili's accommodation included both a physical transformation into the appearance of a Tamil ascetic as well as the study and use of Indian religious texts in shaping Catholic doctrines for converts (Amaladass 2012, 497). His willingness to adapt to local customs gave rise to controversy within the Church leading him to explain his rationale in three Latin works: *The Apology* (1610), *The Narration*, and *Report on Certain Customs of the Indian Nation* (1615). His Tamil works, such as *Tushana Tikkaram* (Refutation of Calumnies) (1941), were based on his careful study of local texts and cultural nuances.[20]

Tembavani is a Tamil poem written by Beschi (also known as *Veeramamunivar*) about Joseph, the earthly father of Jesus. It is considered as a fine example of Tamil poetry and contains 3,615 stanzas. Beschi, considered one of the finest poets among missionaries in the Madurai mission, expressed disgust at the first Tamil Bible which was translated by Protestant missionary Ziegenbalg in the Tranquebar region (1715). In *Ved Vilakkam* I (1728), he compared Ziegenbalg's Bible to a "gem thrown in the mud, like poison mixed with ambrosia, and like black ink spilt on a beautifully drawn picture" (Frykenberg 2012, 79).

The Jesuits, then, could be considered some of the earliest *dubashis*, bilinguals, who served as intermediaries between the Catholic religion and the people whom they converted to Christianity, in order to bring them closer to Christian thought and ideals. Though there is not a single available instance of a Bible translated by the Jesuits, they did bring out translations of prayer books and other pieces of literature used in church services and worship. These *dubashi* Jesuits were in fact using indigenous semiotic forms and investing them with Christian meanings to draw the locals into Christian worship. Christian worship was made to fit into indigenous cultural spaces, while this process re-organized the identity of the new converts. The cultural translation undertaken by these missionaries involved a two-way process of being transformed in order to have been able to translate Christianity for the locals. Among early Catholic literary compositions, Stephens's *Kristapurāṇa* is the only available example, of an attempt to convey the entire biblical story in a regional language.

1.5 Bible Translation in Protestant Missions

Two major sites of translation from the non-Catholic missions are discussed in this section: The Tranquebar Mission and the Serampore Mission. Both these missions were remarkable for their Bible translation activity. These two missions are discussed in this section in order to locate their translation practices within the cultural-linguistic framework of South Asian languages. Though the first of translated Bibles from these missions, Ziegenbalg's New Testament, appeared almost a hundred years after Stephens's completion of *Kristapurāṇa*, it is significant to note the translation practices adopted by these missionaries whose focus was the translation and dissemination of Bibles, above all other aspects of missionary work. Protestant translations have been studied as some of the earliest Bible translation practices in South Asia, making them a critical point of connection while analyzing sacred text translation in the region. This critical survey will also set the stage for the study of genre in Chapter 3 of this book.

1.5.1 The Tranquebar Mission

The Tranquebar group is remarkable for being the first missionary centre to attempt a "translation proper" of the Bible into a South Asian language. On 9 July, 1706 two German missionaries, Barthelomaus Ziegenbalg (1682–1719) and

Heinrich Plutschau, arrived in Tranquebar on the eastern coast of India (Neill 195; Frykenberg 146). Plutschau began working among the Portuguese in the region while Ziegenbalg focused on the local Tamils. The rigour with which Ziegenbalg set to learning Tamil is the stuff of missionary legend. He sat with schoolchildren, learning and memorizing Tamil sounds and verses. Within one year of his arrival, Ziegenbalg wrote a tract and delivered his first sermon in Tamil. In 1708, he came out with two dictionaries and a grammar in Tamil (Frykenberg 2008b, 147). By 1714, Ziegenbalg had acquired 645 Tamil books; each carefully catalogued, described, and wrapped (Frykenberg 2008b, 148). These contained several palm leaf manuscripts in Tamil. Manuscripts that could not be purchased were painstakingly copied down and preserved. Frykenberg writes:

> Long before newspapers or other forms of public media could convey such information across the world, reports from Tranquebar told Europeans about significant local events – virtually everything that lived or moved in South India, both animate and inanimate, whether small and great, was described and then subjected to analysis concerning its importance. Reports sent to Europe pertained to historical events, social structures, elements of natural philosophy or natural theology and much more.
>
> *(Frykenberg et al. 2008b, 148)*

A copy of each of these books was sent to Europe, along with volumes containing Ziegenbalg's everyday observations.[21] This thorough, scientific method of study adopted by Ziegenbalg led him to an exceptional understanding and respect for indigenous scriptures and local culture:

> His Tamil sermons, hymns, ethical writings, and translations demonstrated a profound appreciation for Tamil culture, both classical and contemporary, and a remarkable sensitivity to the feelings and dignity of those with whom he dealt – especially the lowly.
>
> *(Frykenberg et al. 2008b, 150)*

According to Stephen Neill, in *A History of Christianity in India 1707–1858* (1985), all this was in preparation for what Ziegenbalg considered his most important mission: translating the Bible into a language the people could read (Neill 1985, 33). Ziegenbalg began his efforts to translate the New Testament into Tamil around the year 1708 (Neill 1985, 477). This translation of the New Testament was completed in 1714 and it was printed in Tranquebar in 1715. He died in 1719, before he could complete translating the Old Testament.[22] The translation of the Old Testament that was left unfinished by Ziegenbalg was taken up by Benjamin Schultze (1689–1760). The Tamil Bible that was published in 1719 is symbolic as it was the first complete Bible to be translated into an Indian language.

Ziegenbalg was one of the long stream of *dubashi*, Protestant missionaries who were to arrive in India. He was followed by Benjamin Schultze, Johann Philip

Fabricus (1711–1791) and Christian Friedrich Shwartz (1726–1798), among others. Schultze gained mastery over Telugu and did work comparable to that which was done by Ziegenbalg in Tamil. Fabricus, revised and perfected earlier translations of the Bible by Ziegenbalg. It is considered one of the best translations of the Bible into Tamil (Neill 1985, 44, 45). Schwartz is written about by scholars of Christianity as "one of the most successful missionaries since the Apostles" (Frykenberg et al. 2008b, 158), for the influence he had in the mission. A special feature of the mission in Tranquebar was the training of local Tamils to be *dubashis* and ministers in the churches that were established in the region (Neill 1985, 36; Frykenberg and Low 2003, 25).[23] These *dubashis*, both foreign and local, were the conduits that bridged the gap between disparate cultures and negotiated the process of translation that was taking place in these cross cultural encounters.

1.5.2 The Serampore Mission

The Serampore Mission and their translations of the Bible are significant landmarks in the study of Christianity and the Bible in South Asia. Historically, Augustinian and Jesuit missionaries were present in Bengal since the late seventeenth century (Neill 1985, 98). Nevertheless, it was the arrival of William Carey (1761–1834) in Bengal that actually brought Serampore and Bengali Christianity to the limelight.[24] Carey and his contemporaries in the Fort St. William College and the Serampore press were pioneers of Bible translations into at least thirty South Asian languages.[25]

The Bengali New Testament was brought out in 1801. The Old Testament was completed in 1809. The Sanskrit New Testament came out in 1808, followed by the Old Testament in 1818. The Hindi New Testament was completed in 1811 and the Old Testament in 1818. These were followed by the Marathi Bible in 1811, followed by translations into Punjabi in 1815, Telugu in 1818, Kannada in 1822 and Malayalam in 1840. Carey supervised the translation of the Bible (or parts of it) into a minimum of thirty other languages, including Bikaneri, Braj-bhasha, Sindhi, Kashmiri, Odia, Magadhi, Assamese, Khasi, Manipuri, Kanauji, Udaipuri, Jaipuri, Bhugeli, Marwari, Haraoti, Ujjaini, Bhatti, Palpa, Kumaoni, Garhwali, Nepali, Gujarati, Konkani, Multani, Dogri, Pushtoo, Baloochi, before the year 1825 (Hooper 1938, 20, 21).

Apart from translations into Indian languages, Serampore also became the epicentre of translation into languages of neighbouring Asian countries. Carey supervised translations into Persian, Burmese, Chinese (with Dr. Marshman), Javanese, Sinhalese, Maldivian, and Arabic. In his work Buchanan gives details about the people involved in these translations. Mirza Fitrut, who worked on the Persian, Meer Bahadur Ulee, who translated the "Hindostanee", and Ananda Rayer, who translated into Telugu, are some of the names he mentions (Buchanan 1812, 7, 84, 250, 251).

This first version of the Bengali Bible by Carey was not very successful and had to be revised soon. In 1799, William Ward and Joshua Marshman, along with some of their missionaries, joined Carey. Carey, Ward, and Marshman would later come to be known as the famous "Serampore trio" (Neill 1985, 98; Frykenberg et al. 2008b, 145, 153).

Based on his six years of training before they shifted to Serampore in 1800, Carey and his associates worked on the following principles. Neill describes these principles in his book, *A History of Christianity in India 1707–1858* (1985):

  i.   Non-Christians should be approached in their own language. The missionary should have a working knowledge of these languages.
 ii.   The missionary should read the religious literature of the locals and observe and understand customs and traditions
iii.   The primary duty of the missionary is to spread the Gospel. In case the people are illiterate, he should devise ways of doing this orally.
 iv.   The firm belief that the "Word of God" is the greatest instrument in converting people, and that every effort must be made to make it available and accessible.
  v.   Education must be made available to the locals and primary schools set up for this purpose.

(Neill 191–195)

Each of these principles was a step towards cultural translation of the biblical message for local audiences. The missionaries were expected to find ways of making the biblical message "accessible" to people in their own languages. They were also to find "oral" ways of spreading the gospel to illiterate audiences. The message was to be translated in such a way that it was accessible and in forms with which the receiving audiences were familiar. This approach of the *dubashi* missionaries of Serampore, as well as the Tranquebar Mission, inaugurated a new chapter in the discipline of translation in India. Their work signifies a shift to "linguistic" translation in South Asia. Hephzibah Israel argues that the indigenous notion of translation "creatively reused subject matter, style and genre" and were "rewritings" (Israel 2011, 52). The idea of faithfulness in translation was introduced only with early Bible translation pursuits (Israel 2011, 5). Biblical translation signified the shift to more formalized efforts of translation, and, in order to achieve this, the mastery of regional languages by missionaries. The centrality of the Bible in the process of Protestant evangelization and missionary attempts to translate it provided a new lease of linguistic and cultural exchange into these Indian missions. The Jesuits and missionaries from other Catholic orders had been translating for at least two centuries before Ziegenbalg's translation of the Bible, but their primary focus was on translating church culture and liturgy, rather than the Bible.

Buchanan, in *Christian Researches in Asia*, gives a close account of the work done by the Serampore group. Buchanan was the first Vice-Provost of the college at Fort St. William and had observed closely the work done by the translators at Serampore. Buchanan also secured for Carey, a position as professor of Bengali at the College (Buchanan 1812, 3). The college had a department devoted to the translation and printing of the Scriptures. Buchanan's *Christian Researches* is full of rich details from the translation efforts of the missionaries in Bengal.

Carey and his associates, like Buchanan, and the German missionaries in Tranquebar, believed that the best way of evangelizing any region is to give the "word of God" in the language that the people spoke (Buchanan 1812, 10; Neill 1985, 195).[26] The Serampore translators did pioneering work in documenting the languages of India, creating grammars, and in preserving the scripts of many languages which are no longer in use. These are valuable archival materials in understanding the linguistic-cultural history of South Asia. George Grierson, who compiled the first Linguistic Survey of India (1898–1928), credited these early missionaries for being the first to systematically map the country out into linguistic fields (See Grierson, *Linguistic Survey of India*).[27]

While transforming themselves into *dubashi* foreigners in a new culture, these missionaries were fulfilling their mission of Christianizing the masses and, at the same time, documenting the literary and linguistic scene in India. The mapping out of the region into linguistic fields by missionaries may have helped later colonial linguists like Grierson and William Jones in their study of Indian languages. The last section of this chapter revisits the Catholic period in Goa with the purpose of focussing on Stephens's mission field and the cultural environment within which he functioned.

1.6 Cultural Palimpsest and the *Estado da India*

The Roman Catholic Church in South Asia, with the patronage of the Portuguese Crown, may be read as a site of "the intimate connection between production, power and ritual" (Robinson 1997, 338). The "knowledge" that was produced by imperial agents in the colonies was "recycled" and brought back as imperial knowledge. The production of knowledge and the routes by which such knowledge travelled was intimately linked to the power of the empire (Xavier and Županov 2015, 57, 58). "Raw" information was gathered at the village level, in order to be repurposed as "useful knowledge" for the empire. This information, which included land records, lists of temples and their assets, and details of traditional village administration in Portuguese territories like Goa, travelled from the colony (periphery) to the seat of power (center) and was processed and sent back to the colony as Portuguese "knowledge."

The transactions that took place among the natives and Portuguese agents in these processes are important in the study of the contribution of local Indians to the production of "Portuguese" knowledge. These agents included administrative officials, missionaries, individual travellers, and adventurers. Xavier and Županov bring to light the relationship between the natives and these agents in descriptions of village life as reflected in Portuguese records. The Portuguese created "registers" on village administration and recorded minutes of meetings and conversations between villagers, enabling readers to get a glimpse of village life during Portuguese rule. According to Xavier and Županov, there are up to a hundred registers for a single village between the sixteenth and eighteenth centuries, affording a rare insight into the development of the relationship between the villagers and their colonizers. Cultural translation is used as one of the important channels of knowledge production in these colonial endeavours. The culture of the colony was closely studied and documented, and translated into Portuguese texts in an attempt to feed the colonial machinery and ensure its smooth functioning.

The *Estado da India* arrived in Goa in the early sixteenth century with aspirations of building a transnational empire (Xavier and Županov 2015, 202). Along with the massive force of its conquering naval power came the *Padroado Real*, whereby the King of Portugal became the legitimate guardian of Christian missionary work in the colonies. Portuguese, the language of the expanding empire, became the language that would help the colonizers negotiate the newly conquered realms. The period of early conquest was also a period when the Portuguese language was consolidating its position in the European linguistic framework. There were attempts to position Portuguese in relation to Latin, the classical language and the language of the Church. Rafael, in his volume *Contracting Colonialism*, points out that in Philippines, Castilian, the language of the Spanish conquerors, was the intermediary between native Tagalog language and Latin, the language of the Church (Rafael, 10). Similarly, Portuguese was the intermediary between native languages and Latin in Portuguese colonies (Xavier and Županov 2015, 209). These "vernacular" European languages aspired to gain prestige by highlighting their familial relationship with Latin.[28] The native language of the colonies, by this same argument, was inferior because it was unrelated to Latin.

The critical relationship between linguistic mastery, translation, and religious conversion shaped the manner in which textual traditions evolved in the region. The Portuguese empire had aspirations to establish the Portuguese language in the colonies along with Christianity. For this, it was necessary to establish the superiority of Portuguese as a language in relation to native languages. However, missionaries recognized the absolute necessity of learning the local idiom for proselytizing. The Portuguese language, therefore, never really replaced regional languages completely in the colonies, although the administration undertook stringent measures to establish Portuguese as the language of the region. Despite the 1684 ban on regional languages, translation and religious conversion were inextricably linked as the translation of religious texts into local languages was directly related to the conversion of locals to Christianity.

Catholic missions in Portuguese colonies were under the patronage of the King of Portugal. The missionaries themselves, however, were from different European nationalities and classes of society. These monks brought with them their own linguistic and literary traditions and sensibilities. Portuguese, being the language of the colonizing rulers, naturally acquired a position of power. Županov, in her study of the Jesuit mission in Madurai, discusses the dispute between de Nobili, an Italian, and his co-worker and fellow Jesuit, Gonzalo Fernandes, a Portuguese individual, about their style of evangelization (Županov 1999, 35). She argues that the tensions between Jesuits within the Company were European in origin:

> ... the European origins of the conflict, that is the explosive cultural baggage that the Jesuits brought with them to Madurai. The social distance prevailing among them due to ethnic, or to put it in their own words, "national", class and educational differences, created in the colonial context a heteroglossia of European voices. Some of these voices were, for the first time, given space and incentive to talk about themselves and to articulate "their own" perspective. These belong to the Jesuit missionaries recruited from popular *milieux*, generally Portuguese, a fair number of whom were recruited in India from among disabled soldiers, impoverished merchants, etc. ... Jesuit European "ethnic" and, in particular, class issues were decisive prisms for an early ethnographic condensation and an epistolary vision of India.
>
> *(Županov 1999, 34)*

Jesuit priests hailed from several European nationalities. The Portuguese being the administrative overlords, their language had official prestige and power. The chaotic linguistic scene in Jesuit centres, and the contesting "nationalisms" among Jesuits, led to several complex strands of translation in these Jesuit centres. In addition to the translatorial movements required to engage with the locals, learn their languages, and facilitate conversion to Christianity, these Jesuits were grappling with the tensions created by their European "ethnicities". Cultural translation was, thus, taking place both within the company of Jesuits and in terms of their relationship with the locals of the mission fields.

The Jesuit mission in Goa, where Stephens lived and worked, was no different from the Madurai mission described by Županov. The period in which Stephens wrote *Kristapurāṇa* was characterized by a polyphony of languages such as Portuguese, Konkani, Marathi, and Latin, among others, in the region. A work like *Kristapurāṇa* emerges from the "contact zones" between these languages. The tension where these languages and, consequently, the corresponding cultures intersect, the spaces between them, contain the seeds of such cultural translations as illustrated in *Kristapurāṇa*. The European settlers, therefore, had to simultaneously negotiate the interaction and power politics between the European languages, while at the same time reaching out to the natives in an attempt to understand local culture. Translation, here, functions at various levels as a complex, multi-layered process. *Kristapurāṇa*, being a product of such an intricate, multicultural setting, becomes an ideal space to locate and decipher the various cultural complexities at play in a work of translation.

It must also be remembered that Stephens was the only English Jesuit in the mission at the time (Wicki 1970, 800).[29] For Stephens, translating Christianity for the locals was a multi-layered process, requiring encoding and decoding these messages through several linguistic and administrative filters. The licences printed at the beginning of the 1658 edition of *Kristapurāṇa* give an indication of the multiple languages that Stephens had to negotiate. The licence for the first edition of 1616 reads:

> By order of the very Revv. the Inquisitors, I have examined this book enti-
> tled 'Treatise on the coming of the Redeemer into the World', written in the
> Brahmin-Mahratta language and collating it with another written in Portuguese
> – which accompanies it – I find that it agrees with the latter, as far as the lan-
> guage permits. Goa, this day the 3rd April, 1614. – Paulo Mascarenhas.
>
> *(Drago 1996, 891)*

It is evident from the above statement that *Kristapurāṇa* was compared to a
Portuguese version before it was sanctioned to be printed and circulated. The
image that a reader of these licenses forms is that of an Englishman, writing in
Marathi, while also producing a Portuguese version for it to be compared with.
His work was also influenced by the Latin source texts from which he may have
translated biblical episodes. This interplay between the several languages present in
the region is reflected in the narrative of *Kristapurāṇa*, where Marathi is interspersed
with Konkani, Portuguese, and Latin words.[30]

The struggle of the Portuguese language for ascendancy during Portugal's
endeavour to expand its empire continued during the regime in Goa. A significant
step in this direction was the banning of Konkani and all other regional languages
in 1684 (Xavier and Županov 2015, 211). It was mandatory for locals to learn
Portuguese and it was legally prohibited to use any regional language. However, as
early as the year 1548, systematic attempts were made to discourage literature in
regional languages:

> It will be seen that destruction of all vernacular literature as "proved or sus-
> pected of containing the precepts and doctrine of idolatry" formed a prom-
> inent feature of this campaign against Hindu religion. Among the official
> records at the Torre do Tombo in Lisbon is preserved a letter from D. Fr.
> Joao de Albuquerque, the first Bishop of Goa, written from Goa on the
> 28th November, 1548. In this the writer gives an interesting account of his
> conscientious efforts to collect Hindu literature with the object of destroying
> it and describes how he refused to honour a message from the Governor of
> Goa himself, asking him to return some books to their owners. It is clear,
> therefore, that the attitude of the early Portuguese to Indian languages and
> literature during this early phase of their missionary activities was one of
> undisguised antagonism.
>
> *(Priolkar 1971, 38)*

Clearly, the Portuguese were anxious about the polyphony of tongues in the region
and its effect on their own effort to consolidate their empire. Added to this was
the belief in the superiority of one language over another. Important Christian
terms remained in Portuguese or Latin and were not translated into the target language.[31] The strict vigilance on translation, one example of which can be seen in
the language of the licences given to *Kristapurāṇa*, is evidence of the suspicion and
fear that the colonizers had of the act of translation. If sacred terms were translated

into native languages, there was the danger of them slipping back into the meaning and significance that the people attached to them during their pre-Christian life. Stephens, in his letter to a superior in 1601, noted with satisfaction that the local people were slowly but surely forgetting the idols of their Hindu past (Drago 1996, 898). We understand from this that it was one of the aims of the missionaries that the memories of the old religion should be wiped out from the minds of the natives and that Christianity should be firmly rooted in them. For this reason, translation of key religious terms was approached with caution.

For Catholic missionaries, words were empty icons that could be filled with the meaning of their choice by translation. Under the Spanish rule in the Philippines,

> the writers of *artes* and *vocabularios* were charged with the task of retaining the syntax and sound of Tagalog while creating a space behind the words within which to lodge referents and meanings other than those that had previously existed.
>
> *(Rafael 2012, 29)*

The indigenous meaning of the sign was erased and overwritten with Christian meaning, in these spaces that were consciously created "behind" the words. Ines Županov writes of a similar method "emptying" and filling with Christian meaning in the Madurai mission by de Nobili (Županov 1999, 78). In his writings about de Nobili's work on the Madurai mission, Clooney writes that the translation of Christian ideas into Indian languages was "unproblematic" and another version of the clothing problem: "just as one replaces trousers with a *dhoti*, a black cassock with a *samnyasin's* robe, the word 'Bible' gives way to the 'Veda', 'Messiah' to *divya guru*, and salvation to 'reaching the farther shore' and so on" (Clooney 2020, 46). The effect of such practices of cultural translation is that of a "palimpsest", of multiple layers of meaning lying just under the top layer that has been inscribed by the missionaries. This palimpsest, the overwriting of multiple threads of narrative, can be seen not just in language, but also in other narratives like architecture. One example is the unearthing of Hindu idols and artefacts found below churches and other Christian buildings.[32] Erasing indigenous meanings of forms and superimposing Christian ones was a method used by Catholic missionaries all over India. In Goa, where the Portuguese had a glorious rule and the presence of missionaries was exceptionally strong (Disney 2009, 148, 165), this palimpsest effect is much more visible in its structures than in other regions.

The region of Salsette[33] in South Goa, where Stephens lived and worked, was a microcosm of all the complexities associated with a contact zone. Traditionally, it was a group of sixty-six villages, hence the name "Salsette", from the local name "Sasashti" (meaning the number sixty-six). Although the conquest of Goa began in 1510, Salsette and northern Bardez were conquered only in 1543 (Robinson 1997, 334). The Jesuits came to Salsette in the same year and began earnest efforts to convert the residents. Salsette was a "difficult mission field" and there was not much progress as far as conversion was concerned for the first twenty years. In an official report, the Jesuit Valignani wrote that the sixty-six villages of Salsette were "obstinate and rigid" in their idolatry. They are said to have resisted conversion for a long time (Wicki 1979). In the 1560s, missionaries began entering the villages and preaching "bravely" (Robinson 1997, 334). The locals retaliated by attacking the priests with lances. To avenge this "indignity" to the priests the Portuguese ordered destruction of the temples in Salsette. The clashes between locals and missionaries continued and reached its climax in the village of Cuncolim. Cuncolim was described by the Catholics as the "worst of all the villages in Salcete" (Robinson 1997, 334).

The Cuncolim Revolt is also referred to as the "Cuncolim Martyrdom" based on whether the event is narrated from the Catholic perspective or the local Hindu perspective. The village of Cuncolim was inhabited by Kshatriyas who rose up in arms against the destruction of their temples by the Portuguese army. On 25 July 1583, five Jesuits and fifteen Christians were killed by the *gauncars*[34] of Cuncolim (Robinson 1997, 340). The priests killed in Cuncolim were beatified by Pope Leo XIII in the year 1893 (Stephens and Saldanha XXXII, *footnote*). According to Rowena Robinson, in "Cuncolim: Weaving a Tale of Resistance" (1997), "Cuncolim's revered are its gauncars, who were treacherously killed by the Portuguese for the 'crime' of defending their temples, houses and lands from their destroyers" (340). The event at Cuncolim is significant in understanding the way Christianity, conversion methods, and local traditions interacted and clashed in colonial settings such as Goa It also highlights the role of missionaries like Stephens who seemed to be negotiating a "middle path" in these sites of physical and metaphorical violence.

This struggle for translating the Bible while maintaining a middle path is reflected in the verses of *Kristapurāṇa*. The text can be read as a cultural translation as every biblical episode that was being translated had to be located and justified against the background of local culture and religious practices. The physical violence that occurred in episodes such as the Cuncolim Revolt is mirrored in the metaphorical violence of negotiating the biblical narrative. Local practices had to be refuted, Christian practices had to be established, and the newly converted locals had to be convinced to accept them as "truth". Stephens's cultural translation symbolizes the step that came after "conversion" to Catholicism, that of creating "self-conscious Catholics" who were rooted in the doctrines of their new faith. Stephens's intended readership were already members of the Catholic Church. It was an attempt to convert the heart of the locals, to justify to them the truth of the Christian message that Stephens preached. In Avaswaru 8 of the First Puranna, readers get a glimpse of the struggles that the new converts of the region underwent to defend their newly-accepted faith (1.8.78, 105). This cultural translation of the Bible was meant to equip them with the doctrinal foundation and the knowledge to justify themselves to those locals who had not converted to Catholicism. In order to do this, the Padre-guru attempted to explain in the light of each biblical episode he translated why idol worship was wrong (1.8.44–60), why the interpretation of dreams and witchcraft was to be condemned, and why belief in rebirth ("yerzari") and reincarnation was not sound faith (1.5.156), among numerous other practices.

Kristapurāṇa also reveals the socio-political condition of the region which necessitated the formulation of "creative Christianities", where missionaries and translators had to come up with novel ways of overcoming local challenges and approaches towards Christianity. These challenges were multi-layered and complex. It is mentioned in the text itself that the converts often resorted back to Hindu religious practices after accepting Christianity (1.19.53), forcing the missionaries to give serious thought to the "spiritual" and "civil" aspects of life in cross-cultural missions. Often, these disparate and clashing cultures had to be reinterpreted within the framework of Catholicism in seventeenth-century Salsette. The secret Hindu practices of the newly converted locals are significant because the text reveals the ways in which the translator used biblical passages to address these issues. Cultural translation, in Stephens's work, is a two-way process: (a) the translated work "speaks to" the local culture in an attempt to Christianize it, while (b) the culture speaks to the translation and moulds it into a form unique to the region. In his translation of the biblical story of the Golden Calf, for instance, Stephens used the opportunity to underline the destructive effects of worshipping idols. The golden calf made by the people of Israel for worshipping led to their eventual destruction. After describing the episode from the Bible, the Padre-guru exhorts his listeners not to worship idols like the biblical Israelites did (1.19.83).

The text also reveals that the newly converted Christians feared their compatriots who remained Hindus. The Padre-guru urges them not be afraid of them as the Christians were under divine protection and no one would be able to harm a "hair of their heads" (1.8. 111, 112). The converts were branded as "batlele", or polluted by other locals of the region (Henn 2014, 174). Another detail which emerges from the text is that many locals accepted Christianity with the hope of getting material benefits (2.32.49). In these passages, the Padre-guru exhorts his listeners that without real devotion (bhakti), no one could aspire to receive salvation (2.32.33). These insecurities of the converts and regional nuances entered into the text in the process of cultural translation. The Church was portrayed as the ark which would protect them from the uncertainties of life and transport them safely to the kingdom of God (1.7.128). The cultural translation of the Christian narrative in Goa led to the creation of a new way of expressing and practising Christianity which was specific to the region. *Kristapurāṇa* is a reflection of these translatorial dilemmas which were manifested in colonial locations such as Goa.

It was in such an atmosphere of linguistic variety, socio-political tension, and multiple contact zones as seen in the region of Salsette that a "tertium quid" (a new way of disseminating Christianity in the local culture) was practised by Stephens. In the encounters between empires, religions, and languages, the spaces were created in which cultural translation of the biblical narrative could take place, into a form that was distinctly South Asian. Until the publication of the Tamil New Testament in 1715, *Kristapurāṇa* was the closest text available to the complete Bible story in an Indian language in a period when other Jesuits were writing catechisms and prayer books to be used in churches. Stephens's work mediates the space between the interpretative role of the Catholic Church and the non-Catholic missionaries' zeal to take the text directly to the people. By his cultural translation of the biblical narrative, Stephens's work transcended the boundaries of evangelization and entered the stream of what is called South Asian literature today.

Notes

1 Andrew Marvell, "Bermudas", *The Poems of Andrew Marvell*. (Edited by Nigel Smith, pp. 56–57.

2 The term "sacred" as used in this book refers to the reverence given to religious texts, institutions, and practices. The feeling of "awe" and "majesty" associated with the "holy" is one of the senses in which this term has been used throughout this book (Otto and Harvey 1926, 5, 13, 22).

3 V.S. Apte's *The Practical Sanskrit-English Dictionary* (1957–1959) defines "apauruseya" as "superhuman, not of the authorship of man, of divine origin".

4 The term "tradition" has been used here in two senses: (a) literary traditions such as the biblical and the purāṇic, which are reflected in *Kristapurāṇa*, (b) a specific set of beliefs and practices which are associated with particular groups or religions, for instance, Hindu customs, or Church practices. "Tradition", in literature is "an inherited past which is available for the writer to study and learn from" (Cuddon 1998, 730). T.S. Eliot, in "Tradition and the Individual Talent" (1919), argues that artistic creation does not take place in a vacuum, but is a continuation of the traditions that have gone before. This surrender to the "dead poets" is not a repetition of poetic ancestors but a "historical sense" which makes "a writer acutely conscious of his place in time" (Eliot 1998, 28). According to Eliot, by surrendering to a particular tradition of poetry, a poet does not give up his/her individuality; novelty in literature is possible only by acknowledging a work as part of a continuing tradition.

5 Sabino Vengco, in his paper "Another Look at Inculturation" (1984), delineates the differences between the terms "inculturation" and "enculturation". Enculturation is a term used in cultural anthropology. According to Vengco,

> By enculturation is meant the learning process, by which an individual becomes inserted into his own culture, is initiated and grows into it. By inculturation we mean, on the other hand, the process by which the Church becomes part of the culture of a people.
>
> *(188)*

Vengco also attempts to differentiate between the ways in which the three terms "accommodation", "acculturation", and "inculturation" are used:

> The first is simply adapting to the special needs of a particular group; the second means that cultural elements are incorporated into the Roman Liturgy as complements; and for the last, an indigenous pre-Christian rite is taken and given a new meaning.
>
> *(Vengco 1984, 187, footnote)*

6 Vicente Rafael, in *Contracting Colonialism: Translation and Christian Conversion in Tagalog Society under Early Spanish Rule* (1988), gives an account of how the local Tagalog people translated Christianity, appropriating it into their own systems of meaning, while the Church was in the process of translating Christianity for them. Rafael's study of Spanish Catholic translations in Tagalog society have been revisited in the following chapters of this book.

7 The Bible has been "transmitted, received, appropriated and even subverted" by different cultures (Sugirtharajah 2001, 1). Translation is one of the processes by which this transmission and appropriation takes place.

8 It is significant, at this point, to compare Stephens's text to work like Milton's *Paradise Lost* (1667–1674). *Paradise Lost* was published in a cultural context where Bibles already existed in the English language. It is likely that Milton's readership composed of individuals who had access to the Authorized King James Version of 1611. Milton was composing poetry on the Bible. In Stephens's case, his poetry *was* the only Bible available to the new Christians of Goa in their own language.

9 Taking into account the cultural and religious diversity in South Asia, Christianity has been studied through various angles: studies based on geographical spread of Christianity, theological nuances, caste-based studies, and worship and Church practices, are some of the lenses which existing studies on Christianity in South Asia have used. The present study takes account of all these available works and attempts to reconstruct a trajectory of early scriptural translations in South Asia.

10 Susan Bayly, in *Saints, Goddesses and Kings: Muslims and Christians in Indian Society, 1700–1900* (1989), begins her work by raising questions such as "What kinds of meetings and interactions occurred when practitioners of the so-called world religions encountered the values and cultural norms which already prevailed in South India?" and later, "The result of these interactions was a rich array of cults, sects and confessional attachments, a process of mixing and borrowing which created remarkably sophisticated and cohesive new manifestations of Christianity and Islam" (Bayly 1). These new manifestations carried the marks of the cultural contexts within which they were placed leading to varied expressions of South Asian "Christianities".

11 The interim period between the rise of the Syrian Christians and the arrival of the Portuguese is largely a period of darkness as far as information about Christianity in South Asia is concerned. Frykenberg is of the view that the Syrian Christians self-insulated themselves from all external invasions for their own survival and this led to a kind of spiritual hibernation (Frykenberg et al. 2008b, 245). There were occasional Christian and other European visitors to South Asia in the period before 1498, such as Sighelmus and Aethelstan who are said have visited South India in the ninth century (Malshe 1961, 38; Frykenberg et al. 2008b, 117), John of Monte Corvino, a papal emissary (Wilfred 2014, 32) who visited the subcontinent in the thirteenth century, and Jordanus Catalini, who came to Thane in Maharashtra at the beginning of the fourteenth century (Frykenberg et al. 2008b, 118). These travel accounts seem to be the limited sources available to understand early Christian traditions in South Asia. However, in all these travelogues, no mention has been made of Christian writings or Bibles in the local languages of South Asia.

12 Xavier and Županov, in their work *Catholic Orientalism: Portuguese Empire, Indian Knowledge* (2015), trace the manner in which the Portuguese empire that began with high hopes of a grand empire ended in "tragedy" (p. 329) with the arrival of the British: In the "Epilogue" to the volume, the authors draw a parallel between the tragedies staged by the Viceroy Marquis de Tavora and his wife in their palaces in Goa and later in Lisbon. Tavora was the Viceroy of Goa between 1750 and 1754 and his court was a symbol of the splendour of the Portuguese empire. The viceroy and his wife were eventually executed in 1759 for conspiring against the King (pp. 331–340). Similar to the tragic fate of the Tavoras, the splendor of Catholic orientalism began to decline" (George and Rath 2016, 5).

13 See Daud Soesilo, 2007. "The Bible Translation in Asia-Pacific and Americas". *A History of Bible Translation*. Edited by Philip C. Noss. Roma: Edizioni di Storia e Letteratura, pp. 163–181.

14 John F. Richards writes that "Europe's discovery and exploitation of reliable sea passages throughout the globe was its single most important advantage over other early modern societies" (1997, 199). It was the "commercial, military, and diplomatic edge" that access to these global routes provided that aided the rise of Portuguese colonialism in the Indian subcontinent and other parts of the world.

15 The Portuguese territory in India stretched from Cochin in the South to Diu in western India and up to Hugli on the eastern coast. The Estado da India began to take root and flourish, even as the Mughals were consolidating their power in North India.

16 In his essay, "Roberto de Nobili, Adaptations, and Reasonable Interpretation", Clooney writes that de Nobili lived in a time before Europe had discovered the vocabulary of "religions" and "cultures" (2020, 39). During this period, it fell upon the missionaries to find ways of adapting the message of the Church for the diverse cultures of the mission field, in the absence clear edicts from the Church on adapting the gospel for culturally distant missions.

17 Abbé Dubois was a missionary who belonged to the Société des Missions-Étrangères and worked in Mysore. He wrote a manuscript in French in 1808, titled *Moeurs, institutions et cérémonies des peoples de l'Inde* and sold it to the British. It was later found out that large portions of his text were borrowed from a manuscript by a Jesuit, Laurent-Gaston Coeurdoux (Xavier and Županov 2015, 321). A. Muttusami Pillai was employed by the college of Fort St. George as a *munshi* or a teacher who taught Tamil to the Tamil teachers who trained the civil servants of the East India Company (Xavier and Županov 2015, 238, 320). Tamil "literati" like Pillai were *pundits* trained by the Jesuits and other Catholic agents and were important figures in British knowledge production.

18 A consideration of the Jesuits as a priestly order and their influence in South Asia is especially significant now, with the current Pope being the first Jesuit to hold the papal throne in the history of the Roman Catholic Church. Pope Francis (Jorge Mario Bergoglio) was elected to the papacy in the year 2013 (See O'Malley 2014).

19 Rezavi, in "Religious Disputations and Imperial Ideology: The Purpose and Location of Akbar's Ibadatkhana" (2008), writes of the Jesuits depicted in an illustration in the *Akbarnama*:

> The miniature depicts the emperor seated before a chamber fronted with a pillared veranda. Four arches above which a white dome is visible are placed in the background. Facing the emperor on the carpet-covered platform are seated a number of scholars, including the two Jesuit priests.
>
> *(Rezavi 2008, 204)*

Rezavi discusses this while describing the secular nature of Akbar's theological and philosophical discussions in the hall called the *Ibadatkhana*. H. Beveridge (1837–1929), in the "Introduction" to his translation of Akbarnama discusses in detail the relationship between Akbar and the Jesuits, Monserrate and Acquaviva, who are believed to be the two Jesuits in the painting of the Ibadatkhana (*Akbarnama*, Trans. H. Beveridge, Vol. 3).

20 It is interesting to note that de Nobili and Stephens were contemporaries. De Nobili's biographer Vincent Cronin wrote that it was customary to invite new missionaries to visit Salsette, where Stephens worked, as Salsette was "then the showpiece of Christianity in India" (Cronin 1959, 174). Cronin is of the opinion that de Nobili and Stephens may have met soon after de Nobili arrived in India in the year 1605. He further states that though they may never have met, de Nobili had heard of Stephens's name and works and was influenced by Stephens's literary work (Cronin 1959, 176).

21 Ziegenbalg's correspondence with Europe is preserved in the "Halle Reports" and the collection known as the "Malabarische Korrespondenz". Two of his major works are *Malabarisches Heidenthum* (Malabar heathenism) in 1711 and *Genealogie der malabarischen Gotter* (Genealogy of the South Indian Deities) in 1713.

22 Ziegenbalg is described by historians as having died of a broken heart. His superiors in Copenhagen did not understand the undue focus and sympathy for local culture that Ziegenbalg displayed. Christopher Wendt wrote to Ziegenbalg accusing him of neglecting apostolic work. Neill wrote that Ziegenbalg was heart-broken by this incident (Neill 1985, 38). Though the Catholic de Nobili and Protestant Ziegenbalg belonged to radically different groups, doctrinally and in approach to holy-text translation, the suspicion that their establishments displayed towards their adaptation of local idiom in missionary work is comparable.

23 Daniel Jeyaraj, in his essay "Indian Participation in Enabling, Sustaining, and Promoting Christian Mission in India", discusses the primary role played by Indian Christians, many of them *dubashis*, in the establishment and growth of the Tranquebar Mission (Jeyaraj 2009, 26–42).

24 Carey arrived in Calcutta from London on 11 November, 1793. His early years as a missionary in Bengal were full of challenges. Frykenberg writes that the conditions that Carey encountered on his arrival in Bengal were not favourable to missionary activity and he soon found that the East India Company wanted to have as little to do with evangelism as possible. One of his sons died and his wife gradually slipped into insanity. A well-wisher gave him a job at an indigo factory at a small village called Madnabati. It was during this time that he and his sons became proficient in Bengali (Frykenberg et al. 2008b, 145). His formative years in the village of Madnabati played an important role in shaping his linguistic and cultural sensibilities. Here he also met a common friend, Ram Basu, a scholar of Bengali, who agreed to work as his *munshi*. By the time Carey left his job at the factory, he had already completed his translation of the New Testament into Bengali, and started translating the Old Testament.

25 Having received no support or encouragement from the East India Company, these missionaries shifted base to Serampore (Srirampur), a region under Danish settlement. The Danish governor welcomed them and extended them the protection they required.

26 The work done by these missionaries eventually got associated with the British and Foreign Bible Society which was established in the year 1807, with the aim of providing affordable Bibles to people in Britain and other countries. The Bible Society began to print and publish Bibles for Carey and his contemporary translators. The Archives of the Bible Society of India contains the Annual Reports of the Bible Society from the year of its establishment to the present date. The early reports show correspondence between the Society in London, and Carey and his contemporaries in Bengal. Their work was noticed and supported by the Society.

27 In his *The Bible in India* (1938), J.S.M. Hooper reproduces a map created by early missionaries dividing the Indian Subcontinent into linguistic regions.

28 Joao de Barros, one of the first grammarians of the "Portuguese Vernacular", stated how learning Portuguese helped him learn Latin, thus highlighting the relationship between the two languages (Xavier and Županov 2015, 208, 209).

29 Wicki, in his *Documenta Indica, Vol. I–XVIII* (1948–1988), compiles the history of eastern Jesuit missions. The volumes are a compilation documents related to the Indian mission from the Jesuit Archives. A search of these volumes does not show any record of other English Jesuits in the region during Stephens's times.

30 Early modern India had a linguistic and cultural diversity that was markedly different from the neat divisions of "classical Hindu", "medieval Muslim", and "modern British" classification that is used to characterize the subcontinent (O'Hanlon 2013, 769). Western India in the early modern period was overwhelmingly multilingual. The combined cultural and political influences of Brahminical religion, influences of the Bahamani kingdom, regional rulers, the advent of Portuguese colonialism and Catholicism, and trade routes which had flourished for centuries led to an atmosphere of multilingualism and cultural diversity (Richards 1997, 205; Washbrook 2009, 139). This multilingualism was the crucible in which texts such as *Kristapurāṇa* were moulded.

31 The aspect of "untranslatability" of certain terms related to Church culture has been discussed in some detail in Chapter 3 of this book.

32 The Pilar Seminary museum has several such Hindu and Christian artefacts on display. The museum also houses an ancient Nestorian cross excavated from the banks of the Zuari river in Goa, similar to crosses found in Kerala and Sri Lanka. The stone cross is on display at the museum.

33 "Salsette" is also spelt as "Salcete", and "Salcette". In this book, the spelling followed by Saldanha in his 1907 edition of *Kristapurāṇa*, "Salsette", is followed. In case of quotes, the spelling used by the original author is retained.

34 According to the *gauncari* system followed in Goa, the village land was commonly owned by clans of *gauncars*, who were the male descendants, of the original clearers of the land. They claimed hereditary rights in the land, maintained roads and irrigation facilities, and demarcated places for common use and wards for artisans. Gauncars paid the taxes and administered the villages. They were also the founders of the main village temple, maintaining its servants and paying for its upkeep. It is among the gauncars that one would find the leaders or village "elites" (Robinson 1997, 334).

2

INTO THE LANGUAGES OF THIS LAND

... with foreign lips and strange tongues
He will speak to this people ...[1]
(The Book of Isaiah)

2.1 Travelogue

This section discusses the life and travels of Stephens in some detail. The journeys of Stephens's famous predecessor, Francis Xavier S.J., became legendary, especially in the annals of Catholicism (O'Malley 2014, 3). His "heroic" ventures into India and China and subsequent martyrdom for the cause of the gospel gave rise to an army of Jesuits who were ardent to follow in his footsteps.

Stephens was one such young priest who reached the shores of Goa in the year 1579, and would live and die in the land of Goa. It is crucial that Stephens's life be discussed in a study of *Kristapurāṇa*, specifically a study that focuses on "cultural translation" in sacred encounters. The material movement of individuals between places and their negotiation of nuances of the region is one of the aspects of cultural translation. Stephens's development into a saint-poet of Marathi reveals one of the many complex layers in the process of cultural translation, one where the individual is transformed in the process of composing a work of literary magnitude such as *Kristapurāṇa*.

Stephens was born in Bushton in the diocese of Salisbury in Wiltshire, England in the year 1549. His father, Thomas Stephens (spelt Stevens in some sources), was a well-to-do merchant in London. His mother's name was Jane and he had a brother, Richard, who was to teach Theology at the Douay Seminary in France. Limited information is available on Stephens's boyhood and education. Many scholars writing about him claim that he was a student of New College, Oxford, but college registers do not show any records of him having been at Oxford.

DOI: 10.4324/9781003146544-3

Monier Monier-Williams (1819–1899), for instance, was of the view that it was unlikely that Stephens studied at Oxford. Malshe discusses this debate in some detail and comes to the conclusion that Stephens most likely did not study at Oxford, because of insufficient evidence to support the claim (Malshe 1961, 32, 33). James Southwood, in his essay "Thomas Stephens, S. J., the First Englishman in India" (1924), writes that the records show that a "Thomas Stevens" was "elected on the Foundation of Winchester College in 1564 when he was thirteen years of age" (Southwood 1924, 231). In the application Stephens submitted for admission to the Society of Jesus, it was mentioned that he had studied the "humanities" (Malshe 1961, 34).

According to one of Stephens's biographers, Georg Schurhammer, soon after completing his scholastic career, he met and befriended Thomas Pounde, who was attached to the court of Queen Elizabeth and was greatly favoured by her. However, the persecution of Catholics at the hands of the Protestants forced Pounde and Stephens into hiding for almost two years. Being devout Catholics, they made a plan to go to Rome and study to attain priesthood and from there sail to India to do mission work. Pounde was imprisoned before departing for Rome, leaving Stephens to undertake the journey on his own. After reaching Rome, he applied for admission to the Society of Jesus, for himself and for Pounde,[2] *in absentia*. Stephens gained admission immediately.

Joseph Wicki S.J., in his *Documenta Indica* (1970), notes from official Jesuit records that a twenty-six-year-old Stephens commenced studies in the Society of Jesus on 20 October, 1575 (Malshe 1961, 33; Wicki 1970, 27) in the Seminary of Sant' Andrea in Rome (Stephens and Saldanha 1907, XXV). Wicki writes that Stephens knew the celebrated Catholic martyr Edmund Campion while he lived in England (Wicki 1970, 818). In addition to this, Stephens had heard of the work of Francis Xavier in India. It was probably because of his fascination with these glorified examples of Catholic piety and martyrdom that he expressed a desire to travel to India for mission work. Accordingly, his superiors gave him orders to leave for India before his studies in theology and philosophy could be completed.

On 4 April, 1579 Stephens boarded a ship called the *S. Lorenzo* and set sail for India (Wicki 1970, 571). Wicki lists six Jesuits who arrived on the ship to India.[3] Stephens was the only Englishman among them.

The entry in the *Documenta Indica* reads: "Father Thomas Stephanus–anglus–sarisburgensis dioecesis–29–3–Romanae–romani–phisicus" (Wicki 1970, 571). In a footnote to this entry Wicki has written that this was the same Englishman, Thomas Stephens, who would become the celebrated author of a *Purāṇa*.[4] Further information of this six-month-long journey may be derived from a letter that Stephens wrote to his father, dated 10 November, 1579. He wrote in the letter that the journey was perilous. People on the ship fell into "sundry diseases" (Stephens and Saldanha 1907, XXIX) such as swellings and fevers. It may be understood from Stephens's letter that close to a hundred and fifty people on the *S. Lorenzo* were affected by these diseases. However, he reports with gratitude to God that only twenty-seven of them died during the journey. The ship reached Goa on 24 October, 1579.

In Goa, Stephens was known by various names given by the Portuguese and used by the locals. His *Kristapurāṇa* is published under the Portuguese version of his name, Thomas Estevao. The other names listed by Malshe and Wicki are Thomas Busten, Etienne, and Thomas Stephanus (Malshe 1961, 31; Wicki 1970, 571). Malshe gives an extract of a chronological table of Stephens's service from the Roman archives. He mentions in the footnotes that this was procured for him by Father Georg Schurhammer S.J.[5] Malshe procured this table from the records of the Roman Church through his personal correspondence with Georg Schurhammer. Later editors of *Kristapurāṇa* and researchers have used this table from Malshe's work (see Figure 2.1: Timeline of Stephens's career as Jesuit, from Roman records). From this table it is clear that apart from a short period between the years 1611–1612 which he spent in Bassein,[6] Stephens spent the rest of his life in Goa doing missionary work. Schurhammer also wrote a biography of Stephens in German, *Der Marathidichter Stephens* (1957), which gives a modern Jesuit's perspective of Stephens's life and works.

The chronology provided by Malshe reveals that Stephens knew the local languages well in enough by 1594 to preach and hear confessions "in lingua canarin", or Konkani (Malshe 1961, 40). In an entry from November 1581 reproduced by Wicki in *Documenta Indica*, it is mentioned that "P. Thomasso Stefano" of "Salsete" heard confessions in the language of the land, "Lingua aryana Konkani", and that his use of the language was excellent (Wicki 1972, 437). It is evident from this entry in Church records that Stephens had begun to learn the language and use it in Church affairs soon after his arrival in Goa.

Stephens assumed responsibility as the Rector of the Seminary in Rachol in the year 1609. In a letter to his Superior written in the year 1608, Stephens mentioned that construction work of seminary buildings had to be stopped because of lack of funds. It may be understood from this that Stephens was actively involved in mission work in the region before he was appointed Rector of the College. The original buildings of the Rachol seminary, built during Stephens's times, stand even today.[7] Stephens's magnum opus was printed in the printing press housed in this college, marking a symbolic moment in the history of the printing press in India and the literary history of the subcontinent (Priolkar 1958, 8). However, the only traces of Stephens that remain in this seminary are a picture of him (a modern artist's imagination) on the wall of the library, and copies of modern editions of *Kristapurāṇa*. No original printed copy of *Kristapurāṇa* is known to be extant today.

Stephens died in 1619 in Goa, three years after the publication of his magnum opus, *Kristapurāṇa*. He breathed his last in the Professed House adjoining the Basilica of Bom Jesu in Old Goa. Saldanha writes that he was "probably" buried at the Seminary of Rachol. In spite of the scarcity of information about the life of Stephens in England and in Goa, his legacy lives on in the land he called his mission field. The "Thomas Stephens Konknni Kendr" is an institution run by Jesuits and is dedicated to the study of Konkani language and culture. It is named after Stephens in honour of his *Arte*, which is considered the first grammar of the Konkani language and for his services to Konkani.

<u>Goa 24</u>   1579

Folio 123   arrived in India in the ship S.Lourenço : Fr.
             Stephens, Scholastic.

      139V   Salsette college : Fr. Thomas Stephens 1584.

      160   1587 Mormugão cum socio ex-convalescentibus.

      176   1588 Mormugão.

      220V   1594 Margão, rector.

      229V   1594 ib. preaches and hears confessions " in
             lingua canarin ".

      267V   1596 Mormugão, Vicar

      273   1597 ib.

      312   1599 Benaulim, Vicar.

      288   1589 Vows as coadjutor Spiritualis.

      316   1601 Vicar of Benaulim (perhaps resident in Margão).

      366   1605 25 years in Salsette, knows the language.

      390V   1606 Loutlim, Vicar.

      407   1608 knows the language well.

      414   1608 Loutlim, Vicar.

<u>Goa 27</u>

Folio 11   1610 Salsette,rector of the college.

      17V   Bassein college," Mestre da Lingoa". The college
             has 11 Fathers, 13 Scholastics and lay-brothers.
             1611 December.

      20   1612 Salsette,Vicar (Goa Salsette)

      24V   1613 ib.

      30   1614 ib.

      33   1616 ib.

      37V   1618 Navelim, Vicar.

FIGURE 2.1   Timeline of Stephens's career as Jesuit, from Roman records. Table taken
from Malshe's unpublished doctoral thesis (Malshe 1961, 40, 41).

J. Courtenay Locke, in his work *The First Englishmen in India: Letters and Narratives
of Sundry Elizabethans Written by Themselves* (1930), reprinted a letter by Ralph
Fitch from Hakluyt's *Voyages* exemplifying Stephens's charitable nature. Fitch and
John Newberie were English adventurers who were arrested by the Portuguese in
Ormuz and taken to Goa. Fitch, in writing to Leonard Poore in 1583, wrote grate-
fully of the help rendered them by Father Stephens in releasing them from imprison-
ment and spoke highly of his preaching (Southwood 1924, 240; Locke 1930, 86, 87).

This humane side of Stephens is described in another letter by Thomas Pounde S.J., his friend from England:

> My first imprisonment was in the town of Ludlow, and the shortest of all other, but for one forenoon's space; but much the sweeter for my fellow and partner in that imprisonment, Father Thomas Stevens, these thirty-nine years since a famous preacher of the Society at Goa, where their colony of St. Paul's is, at the East Indies, of whose great favours, there showed to many of our English Protestants there sometimes arriving, they have in the history of their navigation given good testimony.
>
> *(Foley 1883, 595)*

These are a few of the "fleeting glimpses" (Southwood 1924, 240), that exist today, of Stephens's life in Goa.

Another debate on Stephens's life is centred on the issue of him being the first Englishman to set foot in India. Saldanha asserts that Stephens was the first Englishman to land in India. He quotes an *Encyclopaedia Britannica* entry:

> The first Englishman who actually visited India was Thomas Stephens, in 1579, unless there be any foundation in fact for the statement of William of Malmesbury, that in the year 883 Sighelmus of Sherborne, being sent by King Alfred to Rome with presents to the Pope, proceeded from thence to the East Indies to visit the tomb of St. Thomas at Mylapore … and brought back with him a quantity of jewels and spices.
>
> *(Stephens and Saldanha 1907, XXIII)*

Malshe argues that it is possible that Sighelmus did visit India in 883 AD. Apart from that, Malshe also had access to the work of Schurhammer (1882–1971) who, in his 1955 article "Thomas Stephens 1549–1619", mentions that there are records of two Englishmen who were wounded in the siege of Diu in 1546, "Lancarote Barbudo, Englishman … Esteram Lopez, Englishman often wounded and therefore in bad condition" (Malshe 1961, 39). Malshe, therefore, prefers to agree with the statement that Stephens was the first "English Jesuit" to come to India. In any case, it is clear that he was the only English Catholic missionary among the many Portuguese and other nationalities in Western India at the time.

The multiple geographical borders crossed by Stephens in his lifetime are symbolic of the multiple cultural borders traversed in the process of cultural translation. He travelled from England to Rome, and from there to Portugal, before he reached his mission field, Goa. Just as Stephens crossed the boundaries over from one land to another to reach his mission field, Goa, the biblical narrative negotiated through several linguistic and cultural borders before it came to be embodied in Goa as *Kristapurāṇa*.

As a translator, Stephens entered the polyphony of the Goan linguistic scene and extracted this new landscape for his readers.[8] Seventeenth-century Goa had a multiplicity of languages. Marathi was the literary language used during this period. Konkani[9] was spoken by the locals, while Portuguese was the administrative language. Added to this was the Latin of liturgy and Stephens's first language, English. His role as a translator lay in navigating the spaces between these languages and retrieving a "Christian" landscape for the new Christians of the region. For this task, his personal transformation into a participant in the saint-poet tradition of Western India was an important step of cultural translation.

2.2 Epistolary Networks

At present, five letters written by Stephens are known to be extant. Stephens's letters are discussed here in order to develop an understanding of the times in which he lived and worked. They provide insight into the process of Stephens's personal transformation as well as the socio-cultural background of the composition of *Kristapurāṇa*. Missionaries of the Jesuit order were bound together by a code of conduct and lifestyle that they were expected to follow, especially while on distant mission fields. One such guideline followed by Jesuits was to write annual letters or reports concerning the work done in their respective missions. Each Jesuit was required to write a minimum of one letter a year. Županov writes, in *Disputed Missions* (1999), that there were clearly laid out guidelines on letter writing within Jesuit ranks (Županov 1999, 9, 11, 33). The "public" and "private" sections of letters had to be written separately. Disputes among individual Jesuits, for example, had to be included in the "private" portion of the letter. Each annual letter was to be written in triplicate and sent via three routes to ensure that the letters reached their destination. Stephens spent forty years in the Jesuit mission in India. Considering that he wrote one letter a year as per the regulations, a minimum of forty letters by Stephens should have been found in Portuguese and Roman records. However, these letters, if they ever existed, seem to be lost to the vagaries of time for now.

Of the five known letters written by Stephens, three are addressed to his Superior in Rome. Apart from these, there is one letter to his father and one to his brother.[10] The two letters included by Saldanha in his biographical introduction give an idea of Stephens's first impressions of Goa, his outlook towards the missionary activity for which he had come, his work in Goa, and life in Goa during Stephens's times.

Stephens began his letter to his father by justifying his decision to travel to Goa. He wrote that the reason for his journey to India was "obedience":

> I wrote unto you taking my journey from Italy to Portugal, which letters I think are come to your hands, so that presuming thereupon, I think I have the less need at this time to tell you the cause of my departing, which nevertheless in one word I may conclude, if I do but name obedience.
>
> *(Stephens and Saldanha 1907, XXVI)*

One gets a sense from these lines that Stephens may have expressed his desire to depart for India in his previous letters. After this clarification, Stephens quickly moved into a meticulous description of his voyage. There are descriptions of the lands that the ship passed, and the animals, birds, and plants that Stephens encountered on his journey. A good part of the letter is a description of the landscape as viewed from aboard the *S. Lorenzo*. He wrote that all the wine drunk in Goa was brought from Portugal and that the local drink was "good water" (Stephens and Saldanha 1907, XXX). The letter ends with a promise that he would write again, though there is no way of knowing if he wrote to his father again.

The letter written by Stephens to his brother, Richard Stephens, who was also in priestly orders in France, is written in Latin.[11] After expressing relief that their father was spared from the persecution of Catholics in England, Stephens goes on to give advice to his brother on how to conduct himself in the difficult times in which they were living. He gives exact geographical descriptions of the land of Salsette. It may be gathered from this letter that there were eight churches in the region when Stephens began his work there and three more churches were added since then. In the letters written by Stephens to family and to his superiors, the creation of architectural edifices of the Church such as churches, colleges, and chapels seems to be a parameter for measuring the success of mission work. This architectural development contributed to the changing landscape of the region of Goa in the sixteenth and seventeenth centuries. The idea of landscape as reflected in *Kristapurāṇa* is critically analysed in "Chapter 4" of this work.

Stephens wrote to his brother of the progress of his missionary work and the challenges that missionaries faced while working among locals. The reader can sense from this letter that Stephens's work in Goa was not without challenges. There was a shortage of staff, financial problems, and intense opposition from local Hindus towards conversion to Christianity (Stephens and Saldanha 1907, XXXI). He recounts to his brother the story of a Brahmin convert who was abducted and taken back to his family, and how he escaped from them and returned to the mission. The intense hostility between the Brahmins and the Jesuits is evident here (Stephens and Saldanha 1907, XXXIII). This letter is significant as it provides insight into the life of newly Christianized locals in Goa during Stephens's time. It is clear that the converts tended to go back to Hindu rituals and faced violent opposition from those who were not converted to Christianity. This letter also seems to describe the incident of the Cuncolim Revolt (discussed in the previous chapter). Stephens recounts the horror of the massacre to his brother (Stephens and Saldanha 1907, XXXII).

Father Rudolph Acquaviva, who was well known for his meeting with the Mughal emperor Akbar, and was killed in the Cuncolim Revolt, is mentioned by Stephens. Stephens wrote:

> It is unnecessary to say who Fr. Rudolph Acquaviva was, as he is very well known in Rome and is illustrious for the nobility of his birth and the lustre of his virtues. Rudolph, whom the most powerful moghul king had not the courage to face and who was safe among so many thousands of hostile

Mahomedans, a year or two after he had returned to Goa, fell in the same week and on the same day, and was put to death near Goa by a few barbarians who were subjects of the Catholic king.

(Stephens and Saldanha 1907, XXXI)

Through these lines and at other places in the letter, Stephens attempts to acquaint his brother with the hostility faced by missionaries while working in Goa and other regions of the subcontinent. For a modern reader, these letters provide a window in to certain key events in Portuguese Goa and Jesuit responses to these encounters with locals.

The remaining two letters were written on 6 December, 1601 and 5 December, 1608 to his Superior in Rome, Father Claudius Acquaviva, Superior General of the Society of Jesus. The first letter, written in the year 1601 from Margao, spoke of a dearth of missionaries in the region leading to difficulties in mission work. Stephens emphasized the fact that many parishes were "lost" because there were no resident priests in them. It is also clear from this letter that locals were appointed as priests but the Christians paid them "little regard" (Drago 1996, 897). Stephens appealed for additional missionaries to be sent to Goa so that these parishes could be saved. He also noted with satisfaction that the children of the region had learnt to sing and recite the catechism in the "vernacular".

In the second letter, written in 1608, Stephens wrote with satisfaction that the "spiritual" matters in Salsette were progressing well. The priests, wrote Stephens, "have sufficient knowledge of the language" (Drago 1996, 900). He went on to describe the construction of the college at Rachol and the financial difficulties because of which the construction of the college buildings had to be stopped (Drago 1996, 901).[12] He also expressed a desire to have books printed in the language and script of the region to aid missionary work. The superiors, apparently, were against this idea of printing books in the language of the region (Falcao 2003, 2). Stephens attempted to convince Acquaviva of the benefits of printing such books:

> … I wish to bring to the notice of your Paternity the fact that for many years I have ardently desired to see in this province some books printed in the language and in the script of the place as was done in Malabar, with great profit for the Church in those regions.
>
> *(Drago 1996, 901)*

The letter reveals that Stephens had given significant thought to the problem of printing in local script. He suggested solutions for the problems of creating typefaces for local language characters. In addition, he appealed to Acquaviva to write to the Father Provincial so that he could be granted the desired licenses for printing in local languages. In spite of these appeals, *Kristapurāṇa* was not printed in local script. This may be due to the lack of permissions, or the practical difficulties of printing in local characters.

Stephens's letter to his father has provoked its share of debates. It is argued that it was this letter that sparked off an interest among merchants in London to explore India for trade and that it led to the eventual establishment of the East India Company. The argument was that since Stephens's father was a well-placed merchant in London, news from the letter may have circulated and led to such an interest. It is clear from Stephens's letter, however, that its value is mostly as a travelogue and does not contain any indication as to the suitability of the region for trade. Malshe discusses this debate:

> Stephens's letter, from its beginning to the end, is a travelogue. Even that was rare during those days. However, there is not a single sentence in the letter from which it can be said that a Roman Catholic missionary like Stephens took an interest in trade. There is no attempt in the letter to indicate that England would benefit from building trade relations with India.[13]
>
> *(Malshe 1961, 38)*

Saldanha seems to be in agreement with Malshe on the discussion on Stephens's relationship to the arrival of the East India Company (Stephens and Saldanha 1907, XXVI). Stephens's biography has evoked much interest and historical debates such as these, probably because of his unique location as a lone Englishman in sixteenth- and seventeenth-century Goa.

Stephens spent his early years in India learning the language and reading Indian literature. Malshe gives a comprehensive list of the Marathi writers who influenced Stephens and his works. He devotes an entire chapter to the discussion of Marathi writers' influence on Stephens's work (Malshe 1961, 424–480). Stephens was transforming into a *dubashi*, a bilingual, like many of his predecessors, preparing to be an intermediary to bring the biblical story into a distinctly local form. His translation from an English Jesuit to a Marathi- and Konkani-speaking Jesuit, learned in indigenous forms of literature, is visible from his letters and the trajectory of his career as a Jesuit. He comes across as a fine linguist who understood the nuances of the languages he studied. In his letter to his brother he wrote:

> Many are the languages of these places. Their pronunciation is not disagreeable, and their structure is allied to Greek and Latin. The phrases and constructions are of a wonderful kind. The letters in the syllables have their value, and are varied as many times as the consonants can be combined with the vowels and the mutes with the liquids.
>
> *(Stephens and Saldanha 1907, XXXIV)*

Stephens had noticed the similarities between Latin and Sanskrit and had made a note of them in his letter to his brother in the year 1583 (Zwartjes 2011, 46). This was two hundred years before William Jones made the connection between Latin and Sanskrit, coming up with his formulations on Indo-European languages and laying the foundations of comparative philology (Singh 1995, 150).[14] Brijraj Singh, in his biographical essay on Stephens, writes that his success as a missionary lay in his command over the languages of the region: "If he achieved greater success in winning converts than Acquaviva and Monserrate did with Akbar, part of the credit must go to his gifts as a linguist" (Singh 1995, 148). *Kristapurāṇa* is the finest example of this linguistic accomplishment. His letters show an early promise of this mastery.

2.3 Kristapurāṇa

The printing press was envisaged as an aid to the proselytization of locals in India. The story of the press in which *Kristapurāṇa* was printed is itself noteworthy in understanding the relationship between power, print technology, and the routes by which knowledge was produced and disseminated. Priolkar, in his work *The Printing Press in India: Its Beginnings and Early Development* (1958), delineates the advent and development of print technology in India. He writes that on 20 November, 1545, Father Johannes de Beira, a Jesuit who worked at the Casa de Santa Fé, a school for recent converts in Goa, wrote in a letter that if books were printed in India, the students would receive much profit from it (Priolkar 1958, 3). However, Beira's request bore little fruit. The printing press that eventually arrived in Goa on 6 September, 1556 was the result of "a happy accident" (Priolkar 1958, 2). A printing press which was meant to be sent to Ethiopia happened to land in Goa.[15] As a result of this, when Stephens arrived in Goa in the year 1579, a fully functional printing press existed in the region.

One of the first books to be printed in this press was Francis Xavier's *Doutrina Christa*, in the year 1557. Stephens *Kristapurāṇa* was one of the earliest works to be printed in this press. In addition to the letters of Stephens, there are three existing works attributed to him. All three of them were printed in this press, according to Priolkar:

1 *Arte da Lingua Canarim* – A Grammar of the Konkani language (Malshe prefers to call it the Gomantaki dialect of Marathi (Malshe 1961, 48) written in Portuguese. According to Saldanha, at present its only value is bibliographical (Stephens and Saldanha 1907, XXXVII). Nevertheless, it is accepted to be the first grammar of the language ever written. It is believed to have first circulated in the hand-written form, and was probably used by missionaries attempting to learn Konkani. Priolkar notes that the grammar was written and used before *Kristapurāṇa* even though it came into print only later. In 1640, Father Diogo Ribeiro S.J. edited it and got it printed at Rachol (Priolkar 1958, 18). Priolkar writes that a copy of the first edition can be found in the National Library of Lisbon. In his grammar, Stephens discusses the orthography, phonology, morphology and syntax of Konkani (Zwartjes 2011, 45–58).

2 *Doutrina Christa em Lingua Bramana Canarim* – This was a translation of the Portuguese Catechism written by Padre Marcos Jorge (Saldanha XXXVII). It was published after Stephens's death, in 1622. Priolkar notes that this catechism, too, was written and used before *Kristapurāṇa*, but came into print only in 1622 (Priolkar 1958, 17, 18). Copies of this catechism may be found in Lisbon and Rome.

3   *Kristapurāṇa*: The original title of *Kristapurāṇa* is *Discurso Sobre a Vinda de Jesu Christo Nosso Salvador ao Mundo*. Being translated this means, "Treatise on the coming of Jesus Christ the Redeemer into the World". It was printed in Rachol in the year 1616. Among all of Stephens's works this is considered the magnum opus.

The first two works of Stephens were in keeping with the Jesuit tradition of translating church culture into regional languages. *Kristapurāṇa* sets Stephens apart from his predecessors and contemporaries by its literary beauty and magnitude.

   The narrator of *Kristapurāṇa*, the Padre-guru, states in the text that the Puranna was narrated over the course of fifty-two Sundays to the new converts and Brahmins of Salsette in Goa. It can be understood from the text itself that the composition of *Kristapurāṇa* was completed in the year 1614 AD:

Jesu suamy bh*a*ctancha c*a*iuary	Lord Jesus, Saviour of the faithful,
Zadĩ z*a*nmu ghet*a*la s*a*unssarĩ	Took birth in this world
V*a*russẽ solla setẽ chout*a*rd*a*ssa veri	Sixteen hundred and fourteen years
T*a*ĩ lagoni zahali	Have passed since then
To s*a*nqhu chal*a*te varussĩ	In that year,
V*a*ss*a*nta callĩ v*a*issaqh*a* massĩ	In the spring of the month Vaisakha,
Deu*a*gr*a*nthu M*a*ratthiyessi	This holy book has been dedicated
Abh*a*ngu quela	To Marathi
(2.59.119, 120)	

It is significant to note the contemporaneity of the text vis-à-vis the Authorized King James Version (KJV), an English translation of the Bible, which was published in England in the year 1611. The distinct religious needs and cultural nuances of England and Portuguese Goa in the seventeenth century gave rise to two distinct approaches to Bible translation. The importance of translation in disseminating the "sacred" is evident in both these instances. The difference in translation strategies of these two texts also foregrounds the manner in which the cultures of the source text(s) and the target text, along with the politics prevalent in the period, interact to create unique texts in the process of translation.

   The title page of *Kristapurāṇa* was inscribed with

> Discurso Sobre a vinda Jesu Christo Nosso Salvador ao mundo, dividido em dous Tratados, pelo Padre Thomaz Estevão, Inglez, da Companhia de Jesu. Impresso em Rachol com licencia da Santa Inquisicão, e Ordinario no Collegio de Todos od Santos da Companhia de Jesu Anno 1616.[16]
>
> *(Stephens and Saldanha 1907, XXXIX)*

A second edition of Stephens's work, brought out by Father Gaspar de S. Miguel along with other priests, replaced this title with "Puránna" (Stephens and Saldanha 1907, XXXIX). This may probably have been the beginning for the work to be popularly known and disseminated as the "Kristapurāṇa". However, this is certainly not the only reason why Stephens's work came to be known as *Kristapurāṇa*. Stephens stated clearly in his prose "Introduction" to the work that he was writing a Purāṇa. The tradition of purāṇic literature within which Stephens placed his composition has been discussed in critical detail in "Chapter 3" of this work.

Commentaries on Bible translation into Marathi mention Stephens and his *Kristapurāṇa*. Scholars rarely comment on Christian writings in Marathi and Bible translations in the region, without mentioning Stephens's epic work. *Kristapurāṇa* was published a hundred years before the Protestant translation of the Tamil Bible, and considering the attention given to other Jesuit works, *Kristapurāṇa* has remained fairly unknown until recent times. J.S.M. Hooper, in *The Bible in India* (1938), mentions Stephens with great reverence, as a predecessor of the Bible in Konkani, which he considers a dialect of Marathi. Hooper, who was the General Secretary of the Bible Society of India in the early twentieth century, writes:

> But under the Roman Catholics a new literature came into being, the first writer being an Englishman, Thomas Stephens, [...] among other works, he wrote a Konkani paraphrase of the New Testament in metrical form which was reprinted several times and is said to be a favourite book among Christians to this day.
>
> *(83)*

Hooper defines *Kristapurāṇa* erroneously as a "paraphrase of the New Testament". Stephens's work encompasses both the Old and New Testaments. *Kristapurāṇa* is a grand narrative which traces a "Christianized history of the world up to the Resurrection" (Singh 1995, 154). The stories included are biblical with some extra-biblical episodes from the Catholic tradition. Episodes such as the description of the early life of the Virgin Mary (*Dussarem Puranna*, Avaswaru 2) and the story of the Sybils (1.36.10), which are not present in the Bible but is prevalent in Catholic literature, have been included in Stephens's narrative.

Kristapurāṇa seems to have been well-received by locals of the region, and appreciated by fellow-churchmen. In the 1648 edition of *Kristapurāṇa*, Father Gaspar de S. Miguel (c.1595–1649) wrote a tribute to Stephens. This poetic tribute may be found in the handwritten manuscript preserved at the State Central Library in Panjim, Goa.[17] The poem, written after Stephens's death, praises the priest's saintly nature and poetic skill:

Sadhu chaturagu Padre	A saint and a wise man,
Hea Purāṇaca adhikary	Is the priest, author of this Purāṇa
Tomas estevam kavitva sringhari	Thomas Stephens composed a poem,
Miravala cangu	Adorned beautifully[18]

Miguel was a priest who worked in Goa and has a grammar (*Arte*) of the Konkani language and several other Konkani compositions to his credit (Zwartjes 2011, 47).

It is clear from this tribute and from the reprints of the text that it was well-received among fellow priests in the region. As a poet himself, Miguel was competent to recognize the literary and practical value of the text in strengthening the new Christian community of Goa. In an annual letter from Goa dated 1619 found in *Lettere Annue Del Giappone, China, Goa Et Ethiopia* (1621), the author mentions Stephens's epic composition with much praise and mentions that not only the Christians of the region, but also the Hindus speak of it with much pride (Vitelleschi and delle Pozze 1621, 112, 113). Until the Portuguese ban on using regional languages and texts in the year 1684, Stephens's text seems to have enjoyed the appreciation of his fellow priests of the Catholic fold.

Saldanha, in the "Introduction" to his 1907 edition of *Kristapurāṇa*, writes that it was "held in great esteem especially by the middle and the lower classes of the Roman Catholics in the Konkan" (Stephens and Saldanha 1907, XLIII). It was probably read out on Sundays and during other devotions. Saldanha also notes that it was also read during a ceremony called *soti* (*shasti-pujan*), a ceremony conducted six days after a child's birth (Stephens and Saldanha 1907, XLIII). He records that *Kristapurāṇa* was found among the Christians of Mangalore. When sixty thousand Catholics were imprisoned by Tipu Sultan at Seringapatam (1784–1799), they seem to have sung verses of *Kristapurāṇa* for solace and strength (Stephens and Saldanha 1907, XLIII).

Achyut Narayan Deshpande, in his *Pracheen Marathi Vangmayacha Itihas – Bhag Choutha* (1977), lists Stephens along with the great saint-poets of the period: "Eknath, Tryambak, Dasopant, Vishnudasnama, Father Stephens…" (Deshpande 1977, 510). Deshpande discusses the background of the Portuguese rule under which Stephens's work was composed. The violence with which the Portuguese and the missionaries conducted their rule in Goa, especially the horrific violence of the Inquisition, is remembered as a background of Stephens's work. A study of Stephens's translation inevitably brings to mind the conflict and violence accompanying the cultural translation of scriptures in the early missionary period. Nevertheless, Deshpande writes that as a literary work, Stephens's text is a remarkable contribution to Marathi literary history and marks the beginning of a tradition of Christian Purāṇas. Malshe describes Stephens as a "Catholic devotee of the Marathi language" (Malshe 1961, 480). He is of the opinion that Stephens thoroughly studied the old Marathi literature available to him so that he could produce a satisfactory work for the converts who were keen to read in their own language. The fact that Deshpande places Stephens in the same line as Eknath, Tryambak, Dasopant, and Vishnudasnama, who were revered saint-poets of the Marathi language, is a tribute to Stephens and gives an idea of how his work was received in the centuries following its publication.

In the four centuries following its publication, *Kristapurāṇa* has been read as a part of both Marathi and Konkani literary-historical traditions. The nineteenth-century scholar J.H. da Cunha Rivara, in his essay "An Historical Essay on the Konkani Language" (1856), lists it as a work of Konkani literature. Other historians of Konkani have followed suit, including more recent examples such as Manoharārāya

Saradesāya's *A History of Konkani Literature: From 1500 to 1992* (2000). Marathi literary histories stake equal claim to *Kristapurāṇa*. S.G. Tulpule and Malshe count Stephens among the "Marathi purankaars" of medieval Maharashtra.

According to the "Introduction" written by Stephens, he intended to write his poetic work in Marathi:

> He saru*a* Maratthiye bhassen*a* lihile ahe. Hea dessinchea bhassabhitur*a* hy bhassa paramesuarachea vastu niropunssi yogue*a*issy diss*a*ly ...
>
> *(Stephens and Saldanha XCIII)*

> (All this is written using the Marathi language. Of all the languages of this land, this language seemed worthy to convey the things of God ...)

However, it is necessary to note that the text also contains several words from Konkani, Portuguese, and Latin, reflecting the complex linguistic scene of seventeenth-century Goa. In the text of *Kristapurāṇa*, Stephens displays a deep understanding and appreciation of the language in which he was writing. At the beginning of the narrative, he wrote a dedication to the Marathi language describing its greatness and beauty:

P*a*rama xastr*a* zaguĩ pr*a*gh*a*ttaueya	That the highest scriptures may be revealed
B*a*hutã z*a*nã ph*a*ll*a* sidhy houaueya	on earth,
Bhassa bandoni M*a*ratthiya	And bear fruit in many,
C*a*tha niropily	With the language, Marathi,
Z*a*issy h*a*r*a*ll*a*m*a*zi r*a*tn*a*quilla	The story was narrated
Qui r*a*tnã mazi hira nilla	Like gems among stones,
T*a*issy bhassã mazi choqhall*a*	Or a blue jewel among gems,
Bhassa M*a*ratthy	Among languages, luminous,
Z*a*issy puspã mazi pusp*a* mog*a*ry	Is the language Marathi
Qui p*a*rim*a*llã mazi c*a*sturi	As the *mogra* among flowers
T*a*issy bhassã mazi saziry	Or musk among perfumes
M*a*ratthiya	So beautiful among languages
(*Kristapurāṇa* 1.1.121–123)	Is Marathi

The Marathi language is compared by the poet to the *mogra* (jasmine) among flowers and to *kasturi* (musk) among perfumes. This was in the tradition of the saint-poets of the Marathi language (Malshe 1961, 425). Jonathan Gil Harris, in "Hi Mho Jhi Kudd: Thomas Stephens's translated Flesh, or, Coconuts in Goa" (2013), notes that this praise of Marathi and composition of a text in a form familiar to the locals was not simply a "hook" to attract locals. It was a translation mediated by Stephens's own experience of smelling mogra flowers in the region (Harris 497). For Harris, Stephens's body is the "point of connection between the landscape and language" (Harris 2013, 497). It was his own delight in the landscape and its language (or the language and its landscape), that was eventually reflected in his translation of the biblical narrative. It was Stephens's experience of the terrain and natural features of Goa which enabled him to provide a fresh perspective of the Christian narrative distinctive to the region. The idea of landscape as a significant aspect of cultural translation has been discussed in some detail in Chapter 4 of this book.

Kristapurāṇa is divided into two parts: the *Paillem Puranna* (*First Purāṇa*) and the *Dussarem Puranna* (*Second Purāṇa*). The *Paillem Puranna* has thirty-six Avaswaru (cantos) while the *Dussarem Puranna* has fifty-nine Avaswaru. The number of verses in each Avaswaru varies. The *First Puranṇa* begins with an invocation to the Trinity, the apostles and saints. The thirty-nine Avaswaru contain translations of all major episodes from the Old Testament. The creation; the fall of angels; the fall of Adam and Eve; the flood; stories of Abraham, Isaac, and Jacob; Joseph; slavery in Egypt; the journey to Canaan; the kings and prophets of Israel; the desolation of Jerusalem; captivity in Babylon; Daniel and other prophets are some of the Old Testament episodes translated in *Kristapurāṇa*. The birth of Christ is foretold time and again throughout the *First Puranna*.

The *Dussarem Puranna* is divided into four parts. The first part (Avaswaru 1–17) deals with the birth and childhood of Christ. This part contains striking passages describing the Virgin Mary and the birth of Christ, among other episodes. The second part (Avaswaru 18–44) describes the miracles of Jesus and his public ministry. This part also includes the description of the Apocalypse and Judgement Day. "Part Three" (Avaswaru 45–51) describes the trial and crucifixion of Christ, while the fourth part (Avaswaru 52–59) deal with the resurrection and ascension of Christ into Vaicunttha.

At several points in the text, the Padre-guru interrupts the narrative to make apologies for not being able to write about every part of the scriptures. In a passage in the *Paillem Puranna* (1.27.72–74), the reader finds the Padre-guru responding to a question from his listeners to tell them about the prophets of Israel. He tells them that if he speaks about every prophet, the book will become too large, and so he would describe the major prophets who were central to the story of Christ: "… If the story of all were to be told/The book would grow heavy/so I am unable to tell it" (1.27.72). In the next Avaswaru, the narrator stops once again to explain that all of the prophets cannot be translated in detail and the ones that "fit" the narrative best have been chosen by the author (1.28.119–122). In "Avaswaru thirty-three", the tone is apologetic as the narrator reiterates that he had a great desire to tell about each biblical episode in detail, but had to leave some out for lack of space (1.33.49). However, in "Avaswaru thirty", the narrator does walk his listeners through all the prophetic books of the Bible through short summaries.

In these instances, the translator seems to be conscious that the text he was translating had sacred value attached to it, and that omissions may not be appreciated by either the Church which was to sanction its publication or by its listeners. At the same time, Stephens enjoyed the powers of a translator who is free to choose those episodes which suit his narrative best. The inclusions and exclusions made in such a work of translation are significant while studying the process and politics of translation.

The metre used in *Kristapurāṇa* is the "ovi". An ovi is a stanza consisting of four lines, the first three of which rhyme together, while the fourth line may or may not rhyme.

This was the metre used by the poets of the region, a large volume of Bhakti[19] poetry in Marathi being in this metre:

Vo namo visuabharita	Hail omnipresent God
Deua Bapa sarua samaratha	Father God, Almighty
Paramesuara sateuanta	True God
Suarga prathuuichea rachannara	Creator of heaven and earth
Tū ridhy sidhicha dataru	You are the bestower of virtue and
Crupanidhy carunnacaru	prosperity
Tū sarua suqhacha sagharu	Fount of grace, compassionate
Adi antu natodde	You, ocean of all joy
(*Kristapurāṇa* 1.1.1, 2)	You have no beginning, no end

These opening lines of *Kristapurāṇa* in *ovi* metre are verses of praise to the Father. The *ovi* metre could either be sung in accompaniment to music or without it and gave the narrative a lilting rhythm which may have made it easier to commit the verses to memory.[20]

In his letter to Fr. Acquaviva discussed above, Stephens expressed an interest in printing in the script of the region as it was done in Malabar. *Kristapurāṇa*, however, was printed in Roman script. According to Priolkar, the reason for this could be that the printer who made the typefaces for Tamil died before he could create typefaces for Marathi and no other person skilled in the art could be found (Priolkar 1958, 18). The Roman transliteration used in *Kristapurāṇa* is "simple and, in a way, almost original" (Stephens and Saldanha 1907, XLIX). Saldanha argues in his "Introduction" that this system of transliterating Marathi/Konkani in the Roman script may have been developed by early Jesuits who worked in the region. Saldanha (1907, L–LXII) and Malshe (1961, 52–122) have conducted detailed studies of the Romanization in *Kristapurāṇa*. Both are thorough works of research and are crucial in understanding the composition of the text. There is a complete absence of punctuation marks in the text of *Kristapurāṇa*. This is in accordance with the Marathi verse that was written during the period. According to Saldanha, this may also be due to the sing-song fashion in which Marathi verse was usually read or recited (Stephens and Saldanha 1907, LXIII).

The text of *Kristapurāṇa* is a site which provides crucial glimpses into the language and literature of the period. The routes by which printing travelled were also routes closely associated with the power centres of the colonial period. A reading of *Kristapurāṇa* provides the spaces to read these relationships that existed in Portuguese Goa. The information available in the licenses of *Kristapurāṇa* and the handwritten manuscripts are the only sources of information that remain of this text that was printed in the nascent stages of print technology in South Asia.

2.4 Many Christian Purāṇas

In the year 1923, Justin E. Abbott, a Christian missionary and scholar of Marathi saint literature, announced his finding of the Marsden Purāṇa.[21] The Marsden Purāṇa is a set of two manuscripts titled the "Adi Purāṇa" and "Deva Purāṇa" are handwritten manuscripts of *Kristapurāṇa* in Devanagari script.[22] Abbot's letter reveals that he had come across the edition of *Kristapurāṇa* edited by J.L. Saldanha in 1907. When he saw the Devanagiri handwritten Purāṇa in London, he assumed that it was the "original", after a "hasty examination" (Abbot 1923, 679). The argument he proposed was that the Marsden version was written in "far purer Marathi" and used "very little of the Konkani elements in words and idioms" (Drago 1996, 895). It also uses "dignified Sanskrit formation" (Abbot 1923, 680). For Abbot, this was evidence of the fact that the Marsden version is the original written by Stephens. A reading of *Kristapurāṇa* itself and an analysis of the socio-political background during Stephens's time, however, proves otherwise. Stephens himself stated clearly in the prose introduction to *Kristapurāṇa* that he had written the text in the Marathi language and mixed it with Konkani in order to make it comprehensible to the local people living in Goa:

> … pannasudha Maratthy madhima locassi nacelle dequhne, hea purannacha phallu bahuta zananssi suphalu hounsi, caequele, maguilea cauesuaranchi bahuteque aughadde utare sanddunu sampucheya cauesuaranchiye ritupramanne anniyeque sompi brahmannanche bhassechi utare tthai tthai missarita carunu cauita sompe quele.
>
> *(Stephens and Saldanha 1907, XCIII)*

> (… but seeing that common people do not understand pure Marathi, and so that the fruits of this Puranna may be enjoyed by many, I have left out many difficult words of the past great poets, and like poets writing in the present, have replaced them with simpler words of the Brahmana language at different places, to make the poem simple).
>
> *(Translation mine)*

Stephens clearly mentioned his intention to make the poem simple, for the locals to understand it. Konkani was spoken in Goa, but Marathi was the literary language. Stephens mixed Konkani words with his Marathi, probably with a view to reach a wider audience among those who were not literate and could not understand literary Marathi. It is unlikely, therefore, that he would have used Sanskrit, as it would have made it even more difficult for the locals of Goa to understand it. Suresh Amonkar, in his preface to his Konkani translation (2017b) of *Kristapurāṇa*, is of the view that Abbot's argument does not stand in the light of the background of Stephens's times (Amonkar 2017b, 85). Since Stephens stated emphatically that he was writing in Marathi with a mix of Konkani for the local people to understand his work, it is unlikely that Sanskrit would serve this purpose. Proselytizing religions have to use popular languages (*lokbhasha*) and not "official" ones, to appeal to the most basic religious beliefs that exist in a culture (Bandelu 1956, 11; Malshe 1961, 25). This is also true in the case of the Bhakti movement in India, where a spiritual revival within Hinduism was brought about by translation of religious texts into vernacular languages. Unlike the languages of administration, the language of proselytization, of converting an individual from an entire religion and its tradition to a new religion, had to be a language that was close to the hearts of the people.

The terms that appear in Portuguese/Latin in Saldanha's version and are Sanskritized in the Marsden copy are related to liturgy and church doctrine. Some of the terms that are Sanskritized in the Marsden Purāṇa are as follows:

i.   (1.1.37) Cruci – Siluvi
ii.   (1.1.38) Bautismu – Jnanasnana
iii. (1.55.113) Martyr – Vedasakshi
iv.   (1.6.34) Sacrifisyu – Devapuja
v.   (1.8.1) Ark – Peti
vi.   (1.8.186) Profetu – Dirghadrusta
vii. (1.10.25) Patriarch – Mahapurusha
viii. (1.19.11) Igreza – Deul
ix.   (1.20.62) Altar – Devara
x.   (1.20.62) Sacerdoti – Achari

This is merely an indicative list of the Sanskritized language of the Marsden Purāṇa. Caridade Drago has provided a line-by-line comparison with the Marsden Purāṇa as an "Appendix" to his edition of *Kristapurāṇa* (Drago 1996, 755–826). The Marsden Purāṇa also leaves out an entire canto, "Avaswaru 22" of the *Dussarem Puranna*. This is the Avaswaru containing the miracle where Jesus turned water into wine. Falcao uses the Sanskritized terms from the Marsden Purāṇa for his research. The origins of the Marsden Purāṇa remain unknown until now.

It is unlikely that the Marsden Purāṇa was the first *Kristapurāṇa* as the Church was wary and vigilant about "translation" of Christian material (Long 2005, 6). The scrutiny before authorizing religious texts in regional languages is also evident in the language of the licences printed in *Kristapurāṇa*.[23] Stephens, being one of the earliest missionaries to attempt cultural translation into an indigenous genre, would have found it difficult to cross this barrier of untranslatability. It is clear from his letters to his superiors that he had difficulties in getting permission to publish a work in the regional language. Amonkar also argues that by the time *Kristapurāṇa* was published, the Portuguese had already been in Goa for ninety years. The people, therefore, were well-versed with Portuguese names and words related to Church rituals (Amonkar 2017b, 86).

Abbot's argument that the Marsden Purāṇa is the original one also seems weak because the script of the Adi and Divya Purāṇas is *Devanagari*. The Church was on a mission to wipe out local languages and its literature and replace it with Portuguese. Added to this, there was the technical difficulty of the unavailability of *Devanagari*-type fonts for printing, which has already been discussed (Priolkar 1958, 18). It is more likely, therefore, that *Kristapurāṇa* was printed in the Roman script.

The Roman script of *Kristapurāṇa* may have been one of the reasons why the text remained unread and invisible until the beginning of the twentieth century. Priolkar, in an article titled "Pitaji Stephenskrut Kristapuran" (1949), argues that *Kristapurāṇa* remained unappreciated because it was in the Roman script (Priolkar

1949, 1). Had it been in the Devanagari script, it would have been easier to read for local readers and, more importantly, easily distinguishable from the large volume of Portuguese manuscripts that can be found in the region. Bandelu writes in the "Introduction" to his Devanagari edition of *Kristapurāṇa* that he had long desired to "bring into the light of the Devanagari script, this epic text which was lying imprisoned in the Roman script" (Bandelu 1956, 2). Burnell, in his *Tentative List* (1880), echoes a similar opinion when he proposes the idea of transliterating *Kristapurāṇa* into Devanagari so that "wedding the kindred sign to the sound, will harmonize to the eye what is harmony itself to the ear" (Burnell 1880, v).

Kristapurāṇa is one of the earliest-recorded Christian works in purāṇic form. Several examples of such appropriations of regional literary genre can be seen in the Catholic tradition after Stephens. Xavier and Županov describe Stephens's *Kristapurāṇa* as a "blueprint for later Purāṇas" (Xavier and Županov 2015, 230). One such example is the *Peter Puranna* (1634) by the French priest Etienne de la Croix (1579–1643). Croix succeeded Stephens as the Rector of the Rachol Seminary. The full title of the *Peter Puranna* is *Discurso sobre a vida do Apostolo Sam Pedro em que se refuta os principaes erros do gentilismo*. It is a Purāṇa on the life of St. Peter and contains about 12,000 verses. The work is divided into three "Purannas". According to Priolkar:

> While it cannot rank with Stephens's Purāṇa for its poetic value or felicity of expression, it presents a comparatively fuller picture of the contemporary social conditions, and in particular of the Hindu religious belief then current. … as it contains valuable reference to the popular Hindu classics of the time, such as *Yogavashishtha, Ashwamedha, Bhagwat*, etc. …
>
> *(Priolkar 1971, 44)*

A manuscript of the *Peter Purāṇa* is preserved at the Krishnadas Shama Goa State Central Library. One of the major aims of this work (as is also indicated in its title) was to refute Hindu gods and point out the errors of local religious beliefs. This aspect of systematic refutation of local deities is absent in *Kristapurāṇa*. Croix uses the image of St. Peter to persuade the locals of Konkan to turn from their "false beliefs". With this end in view he refutes Hindu belief with great vehemence and pours ridicule on Hindu deities like Vishnu, Mahesh, Ganesh and Tulsi and the stories connected with these deities.

Father Antonio de Saldanha, who arrived in Goa in the year 1615, also composed a work in Marathi prose on the life of St. Anthony of Padua. The work consists of two parts, the first part written in prose in the spoken language of Goa and the second part in the ovi form of verse in Marathi. Another Marathi work by Saldanha, *Fruitos de Arvore de Vida* (Fruit of the Tree of Life), remained unprinted. He died in Rachol, Goa in 1663. A work entitled *Sarveshvaracha Dnyanopadesha* by Simao Gomes (1647–1722) was found by Priolkar in the library of the School of Oriental and African Studies (SOAS), London. The unpublished manuscript was in Devanagari script. The date of its composition is unclear.

Gaspar de S. Miguel composed a poem of 3,000 verses on the Crucifixion. There is also a reference to a book called *Vivekamala* by the same author comprising 6,000 *ovi*. A specimen of his Marathi style may be seen in the verses he wrote in praise of Stephens, which have been discussed in this chapter. Apart from these, *Jardin dos Pastores* (Garden of shepherds) (1658) by Miguel d'Almeida and *Soliloquios Divinos* (1660) by Padre Joao de Pedrosa are Christian texts which were composed in Marathi after Stephens. The fact that a majority of these texts which were published after *Kristapurāṇa* gives further strength to the argument that *Kristapurāṇa* was printed in Roman script.

Stephens was, thus, the pioneer of a literary tradition that continued in Goa and North Maharashtra until the eighteenth century. Scholars of Marathi literature accept and study the beauty of the text as a work of literature for its contribution to Marathi. *Kristapurāṇa* could be placed in the tradition of what Hephzibah Israel would describe as "creative reuse" of material, rather than a "translation proper" of the Bible (Israel 2011, 52). Stephens did not follow a method of translation adopted by the Protestants a hundred years later. Rather, he chose to retell the story in a form that was familiar and acceptable to the people of the region.[24]

While pursuing an archival study of *Kristapurāṇa*, there seems to be a marked "invisibility and fragmentation" in the trail of documents related to the text.[25] Printed copies of the work from the seventeenth century are not known to exist, in spite of the fact that the Rachol Seminary where it was printed still stands in Goa in its original form. Handwritten manuscripts of the Purāṇa can be seen in the State Central Library, Panaji, and the University Library at Goa. It is from the licenses copied out in these manuscripts that we get information about the date of its publication and reprints. All subsequent editions of the Purāṇa have reprinted these licences. Following are the manuscripts extant today:

1   The Krishnadas Shama Goa State Central Library Manuscript: *Discurso sobre a vinda de Jesu Christo Nosso Salvador ao Mundo dividido em dous tratados feito pelo Padre Thomas Estevão Ingrez da Companhia de Jesus. Impresso em Goa com licenca das Inquisicão, e Ordinario no Collegio de S. Paulo novo de Companhia de Jesu. Anno de 1654, Escripto por Manoel Salvador Rebello, Natural de Margão no Anno 1767.*
2   The Pilar Manuscript, at the Museum of the Pilar Monastery, Pilar, Goa.
3   The M.C. Saldanha Manuscript at the Thomas Stephens Konknni Kendr, Alto Porvorim, Goa. It is highly probable that this is one of the five manuscripts used by J.L. Saldanha in the preparation of his 1907 edition of the *Kristapurāṇa*.
4   Manuscript at the Thomas Stephens Konknni Kendr.
5   The Bhaugun Kamat Vagh Manuscript in the Pissurlencar Collection at the Goa University Library.
6   A Manuscript of the work written in Devanagari script is preserved at the library of SOAS in the Marsden Collection. It is referred to as the Marsden copy.[26]

The Pilar manuscript and the manuscripts at the Thomas Stephens Konknni Kendr are now available in digitized format as a part of the British Library's *Endangered*

Archives Project. This digitization project of Goan books "Creating a Digital Archive of Indian Christian Manuscripts (EAP636)" has been led by Ananya Chakravarti. Digitization of Goan texts from Stephens's time is a significant contribution to the study of Christian writings from South Asia.

In the year 1907, J.L. Saldanha brought out a printed *Kristapurāṇa* in Roman script from the handwritten manuscripts which were available. Saldanha's edition, *The Christian Puranna of Father Thomas Stephens of the Society of Jesus,* is the first modern printed edition of the text. *Kristapurāṇa* has been transliterated into Devanagari script. S.D. Bandelu's 1956 edition, *Phadara Stiphanskrta Khristapurāṇa: Paile va Dusare* and Caridade Drago's *Christapuran* (1996) are the two Devanagari transliterations which are available today.

Three full translations of *Kristapurāṇa* exist today – one each into English, modern Marathi, and Konkani. The English and Marathi translations have been done by Falcao. Falcao, a Salesian priest, has been doing significant work in studying and popularizing *Kristapurāṇa.* He is a notable scholar who has devoted several years of work to this text. Amonkar's Konkani translation has been published in the year 2017. Amonkar has transliterated the text afresh into Devanagari from the Roman script for this work. This translation is significant as it is accompanied by a three-hundred page preface (published as a separate volume entitled *Goenche Saunsarikikaran*) with contributions by Amonkar and other scholars.[27]

S.G. Tulpule, in his work on Christian writings in Marathi, describes *Kristapurāṇa* as "Murti Christachi, Mandira Hinduche" (Tulpule et al. 1954, 14). The meaning of this Marathi phrase is that "the idol in the sanctuary is that of Christ, but the temple is that of a Hindu". Stephens managed to convey Christ in a form that was acceptable to local converts. "Murti Christachi, Mandira Hinduche" is a metaphorical expression that brings to mind the anxiety evoked (both for the missionary and the native convert) when an indigenous form is used to convey the doctrines of an alien faith. When Stephens wanted to sanctify Christ as a deity in Goa, he did not choose to do it in a foreign edifice. He constructed a 'beautiful temple' similar to that of the Hindus and sanctified Christ in it. He believed that this process of bringing Christianity to local converts would require native form and acceptance. He therefore chose a form familiar to the Hindus, creating within the purāṇic genre (the metaphorical Hindu temple), a space for Christ. As such, *Kristapurāṇa* is a symbol of the various levels of translation involved in making Stephens sufficiently Hindu in order to make his Hindu audience sufficiently Christian. In the following chapter, the crucial question of genre and its relationship with translation are taken up to further situate the text as a work of cultural translation. A close-reading of verses from the text is undertaken to emphasize on the generic transformations that occur in instances of cultural translation.

Notes

1 Isaiah 28:11, *The Bible,* New International Version.
2 Southwood quotes the following recommendation of Pounde written by Stephens, dated November 1578:

I also, Thomas Stephens, your paternity's unworthy son, humbly beg this favour for my said master, conjointly with whom for two years, more or less, in the world, I entertained this same intention, of both of us going to Rome and giving ourselves up to the Society. Being well acquainted with his life and conversation, I have noted the following facts: When I first turned my thoughts to the Society of Jesus, Divine Providence so ordained it that I should become acquainted with the said Mr. Pound; and although when out of doors I assumed the character of his servant, a position better suited to my means, and chiefly useful as a blind to the inquisitive Protestants, yet indoors I lived on terms of equality as his guest.

(Southwood 1924, 233)

Southwood does not mention the source of this extract.

3 The other five Jesuits who arrived on the S. Lorenzo are: P. Fransiscus Riccius Superior (Italian), P. Iacobus de Lemos (Portuguese), P. Ferdinandus Vaz (Portuguese), Fr. Lambertus Ruscius (Flemish), and Nicolaus Paludanus (Flemish) (Wicki 1970, 571).

4 Wicki wrote: "Anglice *Stephens*, futurus celeberrimus auctor operis Purana" (Wicki 1970, 571).

5 George Schurhammer was himself a Jesuit priest. Malshe does not give exact references of the source of the table. Nelson Falcao has reproduced the table in his work, and has cited Malshe.

6 Bassein is now known as "Vasai" in Mumbai, Maharashtra.

7 The Rachol Seminary is a symbolic edifice in this evolving landscape of texts and traditions. The library of the Rachol Seminary in Goa is one of the libraries which Swami Vivekananda visited to study Christianity before his speech at the Parliament of Religions, Chicago in 1893. It is also reported that the first instance of use of telescope in India. It shows that Goa, specifically the seminary at Rachol, was a focal point in the complex network of navigational routes and colonial aspirations in South Asia.

8 Cronin, in *Across the Lines* (2000), uses this image to describe the role of the translator, one where the translator enters a new landscape and extracts meaning for her/his readers.

9 Konkani is a language spoken in the states of Goa, Karnataka, and in the western parts of Maharashtra and has always shared a complex relationship with Marathi. During the early Portuguese regime in Goa, Konkani was largely the spoken language of the area while Marathi was the literary language.

10 Saldanha includes the letter to his father dated 10 November, 1579 in his "Biographical Note" along with the letter to his brother, dated 24 October, 1583. These were the only two letters available in the year 1907 when Saldanha's edition of *Kristapurāṇa* was being published. Malshe had access to the other two letters written to Rome by Stephens which were found around the time Malshe was doing his research. They were published as "Two Recently Discovered Letters of Father Thomas Stephens" by Priolkar in 1956.

11 A copy of this letter is preserved in The National Library of Brussels (Stephens and Saldanha 1907, XXX). The present work refers to the English translation of the letter provided by Saldanha.

12 Stephens writes that they had to use whatever money was left to pay off debts of 2,000 "xerafins", which, according to Caridade Drago, is approximately 6,250 Rupees (Drago 1996, 901).

13 Translated from Malshe's Doctoral thesis which is written in the Marathi language. Translation mine.

14 According to Zwartjes, Henrique Henriques's and Stephens's grammars were composed even before similar linguistic works in Latin or English in the West (Zwartjes 2011, 24). Missionary interventions in the language of the Indian Subcontinent were primarily meant to effectively evangelize the indigenous population. They are viewed largely as Eurocentric attempts to translate Indian languages, literature, and culture to make it easier for incoming missionaries to carry on mission work. As such, they are seen as containing little literary value. The volume of such works is, however, difficult to ignore. There are missionary grammars and dictionaries for several major Indian languages. Another

aspect that is evident from the discussion above is a genuine respect and admiration for the "copiousness" and beauty of Indian languages. To dismiss them as Eurocentric and only within the narrow confines of missionary motives would not be a fair assessment of their work. Unlike colonial scholars whose aim was to compare and study languages, the missionaries who wrote in and about Indian languages had a close and working knowledge of these languages. Their purpose was not trade or scholarly comparisons. Their purpose was to appeal to the very core of a local person's beliefs in order to translate them into a Christian. For this, it was essential to possess sensitivity towards the nuances of the language. Biographers of the Tranquebar missionaries and Jesuit writings have commented on the missionaries' grasp of the various registers and dialects and an appreciation of the local cultures pertaining to these languages. This deep involvement in the languages of the subcontinent is reflected in the writings and grammars by these European missionaries.

15 The Patriarch designate of Ethiopia, who accompanied the printing press, had to halt at Goa, as was the custom for ships in the sixteenth century. The Patriarch decided to extend his stay in Goa for a while and died there in the year 1562, before he could ever set foot in Ethiopia (Priolkar 1958, 2–6). The party that accompanied the printing press included Joao de Bustamante, a Spaniard. Priolkar argues that Bustamante must be "considered as the pioneer of the art of printing in India" (Priolkar 1958, 8).

16 The English translation of the Portuguese is as follows:

> Discourse on the coming of Jesus Christ, our Saviour into the world; divided into two Treatises, by Fr. Thomas Stephens, Englishman, of the Society of Jesus. Printed at Rachol in 1616, with the permission of the Holy Inquisition and Ordinary in the College of All Saints in the Society of Jesus.
>
> *(Translated by Saldanha, Stephens and Saldanha 1907, XXXIX)*

Stephens dedicated *Kristapurāṇa* to D. Frei Cristovão de Lisboa, Primate of India.

17 This manuscript was copied by hand in 1767, by Manuel Rebello from the 1654 edition.

18 The entire poem may be found in the handwritten manuscript at the state central library in Goa. It has also been reprinted in later editions, such as Falcao's English translation of *Kristapurāṇa* (Falcao 2012, 1512).

19 "Bhakti" is loving devotion and worship of a personal God by a devotee. The Bhakti movement, the first phase of which began in Tamil Nadu in South India at the end of the first millennium AD, spread to other parts of India over the medieval period in various phases. It was characterized by intense personal devotion and fellowship with God as opposed to the importance that canonical Hinduism gave to rituals and the priestly order. This religious movement based on loving devotion gave birth to Bhakti literature. According to Sisir Kumar Das, this literature is the "supreme literary achievement of medieval India" (Das 2005, 26).

20 Stephens also used the term "abhanga" at different places in *Kristapurāṇa*. Abhanga is a metre similar to ovi, with some variations. The *abhanga* is a stanza of four lines, the first three of which consist of four six or eight letters each. The fourth line contains three four or seven letters (Stephens and Saldanha 1907, LXIV). It can be seen that the *abhanga* metre places more constraints on the poet. Malshe discusses the debate among Marathi historians about the metre of the verses and concludes that *Kristapurāṇa* is composed in the ovi metre and that "abhanga" may have been used by the poet to mean poetic composition in a more general sense (Malshe 1961, 619–622).

21 In his 1996 edition of *Kristapurāṇa*, Caridade Drago reproduces a letter written by Abbott to the *Times of India* in the year 1925 (Drago 1996, 894).

22 The Devanagari script (*deva*-divine + *nagari*-of the city), is a phonologically-based script written from left to right. It is used for languages such as Hindi, Marathi, and Nepali. It also the script used for Sanskrit in modern times (Bright 1996, 384).

23 These licenses can be seen in the handwritten manuscript at the Krishnadas Shama Goa State Central Library (Manuscript No. MS-57). All subsequent editions have reprinted these licenses.

24 There are four full-length studies devoted to *Kristapurāṇa* that exist today. The first doctoral work on this text was by Quadra Benedetta at the University of Rome in 1943 (Falcao 2003, 215). The thesis is untraceable as of now. The second thesis was in the year 1961 by S.G. Malshe at Bombay University. The thesis is written in the Marathi language and is an exhaustive linguistic analysis of the text, with a section devoted to literary features in *Kristapurāṇa*. The primary aim of this work was to study the phonology, morphology, syntax, and semantics of the text while investigating its impact on Marathi literature and language itself. The third work is by Nelson Falcao, titled *Kristapurāṇa: A Christian-Hindu Encounter: A Study of Inculturation in Kristapurāṇa of Thomas Stephens, SJ (1549–1619)*. It was published under the same title in the year 2003. Falcao studies inculturation in *Kristapurāṇa* by analyzing the use of purāṇic terms and the manner in which elements of Catholic theology and doctrine are conveyed in the language of the Purāṇas. Falcao's work focuses on the "mutual enrichment and correction" that takes place during the "Tridentine-Vaisnavite encounter" in *Kristapurāṇa* (Falcao 2003, 39). A Master of Arts dissertation, "*Mukti* in *Kristapurāṇa*: How Thomas Stephens S.J. (1549–1619) conveys a Christian message of salvation in words with Hindu connotations" (2015) by Pär Eliasson is a critical study on *Kristapurāṇa*. Eliasson's work focuses on the concept of salvation in the text and the terms used by Stephens to translate 'salvation' for his Marathi readership.

25 "Invisibility and fragmentation" is a phrase used by Xavier and Županov to describe their experience of doing archival research on Catholic Orientalist works. By this phrase they mean to highlight the gaps in knowledge and "glaring historical absences" in the study of Catholic orientalism (Xavier and Županov 2015, 288).

26 Schurhammer writes that in 1935, a Protestant version of the Christian Purāṇa also appeared in print. It is entitled *Christian Katha* (or Christian story), edited by Dr. Hivale of Pune and written in the Devanagari script (Schurhammer 1953, 209). Protestants were attracted to the literary beauty of the text but were uncomfortable with the passages about Mary and other aspects specific to Catholicism.

27 Apart from these, there are several essays and articles on *Kristapurāṇa*. Priolkar mentions the text in his book *The Printing Press in India*, as one of the earliest printed works in the subcontinent. S.G. Tulpule has done significant work on *Kristapurāṇa* in his research as a Marathi literary historian. His article "Marathica Khristi Puranika" (1954) studies Christian purāṇic works composed in Marathi while his volume *Classical Marathi Literature* (1979), locates *Kristapurāṇa* in the history of literature in the Marathi language. Georg Schurhammer S.J. is a significant scholar in the field of Jesuit biographies. His biographies of Stephens, in German and in English, are important accounts on Stephens's life, and make mention of *Kristapurāṇa* as Stephens's magnum opus. Each of these scholarly works makes significant contributions to the understanding of *Kristapurāṇa*.

3

GENRE, NOVELIZATION, AND TRANSLATABILITY IN *KRISTAPURĀṆA*

Namadeva came with Panduranga,
And roused me in a dream. "I appoint you a task,
Write poetry, do not talk of vain affairs"…
What is left undone, you must finish, O Tuka.[1]
(Tukaram, 1577–1650)

3.1 Genre in Translation

In the prose "Introduction" to *Kristapurāṇa*, Stephens stated that his composition was a "Purāṇa" containing the story of Jesus Christ:

> Believers and good Christians, the story of the Lord Jesus Christ the Saviour has been written in this Purāṇa. (Bhauarthiya baraueya Christauano, hea Purannantu Suamiya Jesu Christa Taracachy Catha lihily ahe …).
>
> *(Stephens and Saldanha 1907, XCII)*

By establishing at the beginning of his work that it was a Purāṇa, Stephens firmly located his work in the literary tradition of Marathi Purāṇas. In addition to the novelty of a Catholic missionary attempting to recreate the entire biblical narrative as a poetic work, the reader is startled by the poet's choice of genre for his epic composition. The poet-priest could have narrated biblical stories in a form familiar to the Church; for example, a Marathi translation of the Latin *Vulgate*, in prose. By choosing to compose the biblical narrative as a Purāṇa, Stephens was making a crucial translatorial decision because, in literary works, "meaning is derived from the form rather than the content" (Xavier and Županov 2015, 230). The genre of the composition is as critical as its content.

DOI: 10.4324/9781003146544-4

Stephens's composition led to cultural translation of the Bible, as well as of the purāṇic tradition. The translatorial movement in the case of *Kristapurāṇa* was not a linear one from biblical "source text" to purāṇic "target text". As biblical stories were narrated into Marathi, purāṇic terms began to be translated into Christian concepts. At the same time, biblical stories were interpreted and justified within the purāṇic tradition. The mutual transfer and appropriation of sacred concepts that occurred in this process of cultural translation of genre is a significant aspect discussed in this chapter. Genre itself, in the specific context of *Kristapurāṇa*, is discussed at length in this chapter. The purpose of this discussion is to understand cultural translation as a deep-rooted process leading to generic transformation. In the process of decoding Stephens's choice of genre, the idea of "Purāṇa" itself is explored. The present reading raises crucial questions about the genre of Purāṇa and on the manner in which it developed as a literary tradition. The critical relationship between the ideas of "genre" and "translation" is one of the aspects explored in the following sections.

"Genre" has been explained in critical thoughts as "a kind, type or class of literature" (Cuddon 1998, 289).[2] A literary work may be classified into a specific genre based on its content or its form. A genre is associated with a set of conventions or stylistic patterns to which a work must conform.[3] Genre is not to be understood as "properties" of texts. Frow argues that "Genre is neither a property of (and located 'in') texts, nor a projection of (and located 'in') readers; it exists as a part of the relationship between texts and readers, it has a systematic existence" (Frow 2006, 102). This means that a single text can be a participant in more than one "genre" of literature.

Genre is one of the factors that create the "horizon of expectations" against which any text is read (Jauss 1982, 95).[4] In other words, the genre in which a translated work is presented to readers plays a role in shaping the meaning of the content within the text. In translation, the genre chosen by the translator is a major decision that affects the literary shape and reception of the translated text. Different genres evoke different expectations and responses from an audience as they "… create effects of reality and truth which are central to the different ways the world is understood" (Frow 2006, 19). Frow argues that genre works at the level of semiosis "which is deeper and more forceful than the explicit 'content' of a text" (Frow 2006, 19). A genre that is held in reverence in a source culture may not be held in similar reverence in a target culture. The meaning ascribed to the genre itself shapes the meaning of the translated "content". The choice of the purāṇic form to convey a biblical message in the seventeenth century is significant in this context.

The aspect of genre is critical in cultural translation as it is one of the sites through which nuances of cultural transfer may be perceived. The relationship between cultural translation and genre has been given careful attention by Chatterjee, in *Translation Reconsidered: Culture, Genre and the "Colonial Encounter" in Nineteenth Century Bengal* (2010). Chatterjee views genre as a site for cultural translation (Chatterjee 47). While studying the literary scene of nineteenth-century Bengal, she discusses the manner in which literary genre such as the sonnet and the novel were appropriated by Bengali literature through translation practices while other genres, such as the epic, faced "resistance and rejection" (157). Rather than the "word" or the "content" of the novel, the genre itself is translated into Bengali literature in the nineteenth century:

> It is neither the linguistic/literary text nor the culture only that is translated, but between these two, there is the category of the genre, which has the ability of passing from one language to another much more easily and becomes the site for cultural translation.
>
> *(Chatterjee 2010, 158)*

Literary genres travel from one culture to another through the process of cultural translation. Chatterjee also states that the power of the colonized lay in accepting, rejecting, or modifying these travelling genres to suit their cultural needs: "The process of cultural translation that determined the reception of certain genres and its modifications to suit the cultural needs of the reading public is where the power of the colonized lay" (Chatterjee 2010, 157).[5] In the context of seventeenth-century Goa, the purāṇic tradition was local to the region. The power of the colonized lay in appropriating and (re)interpreting the biblical narrative through the lens of purāṇic concepts and in negotiating their religious conversion and tensions with the Portuguese colonizers.

In cases of holy-text translation, the translator has to make crucial decisions regarding the genre in which the text is produced. She/he can bring the genre of the source text(s) to the target culture. The other option available is to translate into a genre that evokes similar "expectations" in the target culture. A translator's decision to use a genre from the target culture may be read as an act of cultural translation, as the content of the source text is adapted to fit the dimensions of a new genre, along with a new language. The text is "submitted" to the generic features of a new literary tradition, in order to make it acceptable in the target culture.

Israel situated the relevance of genre in Bible translation in *Religious Transactions in Colonial South India* (2011), where she has studied the context of Bible translation into the Tamil language. She critically analyses the Protestant missionaries' choice of genre while translating the Bible in South India. The Protestants composed a significant volume of biblical translation work in Tamil Nadu, inaugurated by Ziegenbalg's translation of the Tamil New Testament. Israel argues that the local Tamils ascribed sacred value to poetic works rather than prose texts. There was no literary tradition of writing serious, religious texts in prose (Israel 2011, 171). The Protestants, however, chose to translate Christian texts into prose and had an "intriguing reticence in the matter of translating into culturally familiar genres" (Israel 2011, 181). Another instance of the Protestant preference for prose may be found in Carey's legacy. The massive corpus of biblical translations that he left behind is in prose. The Catholics who arrived in Tamil Nadu two centuries before the Protestants, however, preferred to translate Christian literature into poetic forms. Beschi's *Tempavani* (c.1796) is a classic example of this. In the *Tempavani*, Beschi translated small portions of the Bible into Tamil and modelled it after the *Kamparamayana* (Israel 2011, 175).[6] The Protestants were suspicious of this Catholic use of indigenous forms for evangelization. For them, any form that was related to Hinduism was unsuitable to the Christian message. The decision to translate the Bible into discursive prose was also to make it accessible to all classes of society and not just to the higher strata which was used to reading poetic religious literature (Israel 2011, 181).

Despite this wariness about Hindu sacred genre, Protestant missionaries who translated the Bible into Indian languages did work with indigenous concepts and lexical fields in the process of translation. Israel quotes a conversation between a Danish missionary and a local Tamil, where the Tamil points out to the missionary that all the words they used belonged to the locals and that the Protestant missionaries had no "letters" or "words" of their own (Israel 2008, 38). Israel also discusses the Tamil translation of the term "God" by Bible translators, in her volume *Religious Transactions in Colonial South India*. Protestant missionaries, while translating key terms like "God", struggled to dissociate Tamil lexical terms from their Hindu meanings and "re-make" the sacred meanings of the concepts they used in Bible translations (Israel 2011, 104, 121). As translators in foreign mission fields, Protestant missionaries had to negotiate existing religious vocabulary in the region. They had to work with locally available vocabulary and translate Christian concepts in ways that were comprehensible to the local readership. It is clear that Protestants in Indian missions undertook conceptual accommodation. However, they were wary of using indigenous literary genre to translate sacred texts. Hence, despite the fact that local Tamils ascribed sacredness to poetic forms of literature, early Protestant missionaries in South India chose to translate into prose. Here we see a marked difference in the translation strategies of the early Catholics and Protestants. Although both groups were grappling with regional vocabulary in the process of sacred-text translation at different points in time, the Catholics were more willing to locate their translations within indigenous literary systems.

De Nobili, hailed as the pioneer of inculturation in the Madurai mission, saw local Tamil culture not as heathen but as a form of "defective Catholicism" (Mosse 2012, 32). Using this argument, all he had to do was remove the "defective" Hindu meanings and replace them with Christian meanings while retaining the form.[7] This process was mediated by translation of Christian material into these indigenous forms. Translation, thus, emerges as a major process for inculturation in the Church. De De Nobili replaced the Portuguese and Latin words used by Henriques in his Catechism with Tamil and Sanskrit religious terms (Županov 1999, 79). His translation strategy was at variance with the Jesuit policy of retaining church terms in Portuguese or Latin. The transmission and "reprocessing" of local forms and culture took place through missionary attempts at translation of religious material (Županov 2012, 415). The Catholics did not have a distrust of indigenous genre like the Protestants did, two centuries later.[8] For the Catholics, translating the Christian message into poetic forms served the purpose of rendering Christianity "honourable" (Mosse 2012, 33). In addition to this, the historicity and sacredness that the local audience attributed to the purāṇic genre gets transferred to Christianity, when the Christian message is translated into a Purāṇa.

The use of vernacular languages by European missionaries was only the "first step" towards using native genre and social forms. Joan-Pau Rubies, in his work *Travel and Ethnology in the Renaissance* (2004), argues that this appropriation had far-reaching effects for European Christianity as the missionaries had to distinguish between Christianity and European civil life (Rubies 2004, 316, 317). European travellers, specifically missionaries, had to negotiate and decipher which form of Christianity was acceptable to the locals, and which local customs were acceptable to Christianity. Often, when a missionary adapted Christian practices to make it acceptable to the locals, it was opposed by other members of the clergy for departing from European notions of Christianity. This debate reached its climax during the time of de Nobili (Županov 1999, 34). Although Stephens's work never provoked the polemical debates that de Nobili's life and work attracted, Stephens was already undertaking "accomodatio" in his missionary field in the late sixteenth and early seventeenth century.

Stephens had already taken an indigenous genre, the Purāṇa, and translated the biblical message into it. His mastery over the *ovi* metre used by the Purāṇa composers in Marathi and the creative shaping of Christianity into this form is one of the important decisions he makes as a cultural translator. Stephens's choice of genre is explained in the text itself. A group of local Christians came to Stephens and requested that they should be given books in their own language to read. The reason they gave for this request was that they had been banned by the Church from reading Hindu literature after they converted to Catholicism:

Ha motta *a*bhiprauo zi mh*a*nne	He said, Sir, this is an important suggestion,
Tumĩ t*a*ri varilĩ maguilĩ purannẽ	Have you not refused us the old Purāṇas?
T*a*ri pratipust*a*quẽ amã car*a*nne	Then why do you not compose
C*a*issy n*a*c*a*rity tumĩ	Similar books for us?
(*Kristapurāṇa* 1.1.143)	

Stephens decided to write for these neo-converts in the form that they were used to reading. Brijraj Singh, in "The First Englishman in India: Thomas Stephens" (1995), writes about the significance of the purāṇic tradition in the life of these new converts. He writes that Stephens

> versified various stories from the Bible for the pleasure as well as religious instruction of new converts, who may have still felt the spell of the Hindu *Purāṇas*, though by changing their religion, had now rejected the contents of these works.
>
> *(Singh 153)*

The converts, who were banned from reading local religious works, still felt the allure of these literary works. Their request for a Purāṇa may be read as an attempt to negotiate the "break" from tradition enforced by the Portuguese administration, and necessitated by their conversion to a new religion.

This passage also gives us a glimpse of the newly converted Christians' life in seventeenth-century Goa. The restrictions placed by the Inquisitor's office and the Portuguese administration led to sites of tension, which forced missionaries to come up with creative ways of negotiating the process of translation of individuals from being a Hindu to a Christian. This is also a significant moment in the understanding of translation in the colonial context. Bassnett and Trivedi note that, in the colonial period, translation was largely uni-directional (Bassnett and Trivedi 1999, 7), with texts being translated from the languages of the colonies into European languages. The demand by the locals of Salsette for a text from the colonizer's language to be brought into their own language may be viewed as an active engagement with their colonized state and an attempt to "read" the "other" through translation.

Falcao uses the purāṇic form to argue that Stephens anticipated the need of the Church to be locally rooted or "grown from the soil" (Falcao 2003, 5) almost four hundred years before the concept of inculturation was introduced and accepted by the Roman Catholic Church. Stephens writes in his introduction that his purpose for writing the Purāṇa was to prove that the belief of the locals in idols is false. He intended to do so by presenting the biblical story clearly to the locals. He was convinced that once they read it in a form and language they understood, they would clearly see the "light" and follow Christ (Stephens and Saldanha 1907, XCIV).

Cultural translation by missionaries and their appropriation of indigenous genres for the purpose of evangelization changed the message that was being translated, while at the same time changing the local language in the process (Rafael 2012, 29). The empty spaces created behind words were replaced with Christian meaning in the course of translation, leading to a palimpsest of meanings which showed through its layers. The genre of Purāṇa into which the biblical story was narrated in *Kristapurāṇa* adds several complexities to the discussion on genre and cultural translation. Purāṇic texts were revered and were central to the religious practices of the locals of seventeenth-century Goa. The exchanges and appropriations that take place when two major sacred traditions such as the biblical and the purāṇic encounter each other in literary translation are significant in understanding the process of cultural translation. Cultural translation also provides the openings by which the development of genre such as the Purāṇa may be understood better. The questions raised by the present reading of *Kristapurāṇa* on the development of the Purāṇic tradition are crucial for making sense of the literary lineage of subcontinent. The next section analyses the features of the purāṇic tradition and its capacity to reinvent itself by accommodating new languages and their stories.

3.2 Novelization and the Purāṇa

The word "Purāṇa" means "ancient" (Hazra 1937, 240). Over the passage of time this word has come to be associated with a class of texts written in Sanskrit. A Purāṇa may be described as:

> ... a class of books written in Sanskrit, expounding ancient Indian theog-
> ony, cosmogony, genealogies, and accounts of kings and *rsis*, religious belief,
> observances, and philosophy, social and political ordinances ... the whole
> illustrated and enforced by tales, legends, old songs, anecdotes, and fables.
>
> *(Pargiter 1922, 447)*

In the framework of traditional genre theory, Purāṇas could roughly be classified as "epics".[9] Purāṇas may be treated as epics for their grand literary style, lofty subjects and heroic characters. However, these works go beyond the Western definition of "epic" genre. They are more "ancient", as their name suggests, and hold religious significance in the Indian Subcontinent. In addition to being epic poetry, they also hold the place of "scriptures" in some cultural traditions. Stephens, in fact, uses the word, "Puranna" (*Kristapurāṇa* 2.21.7) in his work to mean "scriptures", strengthening the argument that "Purāṇa" was used in the sense of "scriptures" in seventeenth century Marathi usage.

The Purāṇas, however, are more "ancient" (Hazra 1937, 240) than the quin-tessential epics of Indian literature, the *Mahabharata* and the *Ramayana* (Cuddon 1998, 383). Purāṇic texts deal with origins, destruction, and regeneration and are considered sacred, specifically in South Asian culture (Hazra 1937, 241). As a result of the sacredness and veneration accorded to the Purāṇas, they have been described as the "fifth Veda", putting them next only to the Vedas in authority. Apart from the religious veneration accorded to Purāṇas, they also influenced "early ideas of cosmography and geography" in the Indian Subcontinent and have been treated as early geographical documents (Rocher 1986, 130,131). Purāṇic texts have also been read as historical documents of dynasties and migration in the subcontinent. According to Hazra, the historicity that was attributed to the Purāṇas was because of the dynastic lists and chronicles of kingdoms preserved by these texts (Hazra 1937, 264). They have been read as important documents in reconstructing a social history of the subcontinent, due to their references to the social conditions preva-lent in ancient South Asia (Hazra 1937, 266). Whatever the "authenticity" of the historical information contained in purāṇic works, these texts are rich storehouses delineating the linguistic and cultural evolution of the subcontinent.

Purāṇas have been variously dated by scholars to have been composed in the centuries between 500 BC and 1000 AD (Rocher 1986, 100–104). Wilson argues that most Purāṇas "assumed their actual state" no earlier than the time of Shankaracharya, around the eighth century AD (Wilson 1840, ix–x). Individual Purāṇas have been dated separately while passages may have been added to early Purāṇas in subsequent centuries. In this ever-evolving purāṇic tradition, there are eighteen Sanskrit *mahapurāṇa* (great Purāṇas) and eighteen *upa-purāṇa* (sub-Purāṇas) which are accepted as the canon of purāṇic literature (Wilson 1839a, 61; Hazra 1937, 240).[10] Scholars of purāṇic literature[11] frequently emphasize on the sheer volume of works which are classified as Purāṇa. Horace Hayman Wilson, Ludo Rocher, and Rajendra Prasad Hazra, among others, begin their discussion of the Purāṇas by acknowledging the voluminous nature of the purāṇic corpus. According to Wilson, the *Vishnu Purāṇa* and *Bhagavata Purāṇa* are most frequently read among all the Purāṇas (Wilson 1839a, 62).

A Purāṇa should contain five primary distinguishing marks: *Sarga* (creation), *pratisarga* (dissolution or recreation), *manavantara* (early periods of mankind), *vamsa* (genealogies), and *vamsyanucharita* (accounts of persons mentioned in the genealogies) (Pargiter 1922, 449; Hazra 1937, 241, 242; Rao 1993, 87). These five signs are called "pañcalakṣaṇa", or five distinguishing marks of a Purāṇa. These signs, however, are not to be seen as strict "requirements" of a purāṇic text. Wilson, and Indian scholars like V.N. Rao and Pandurang Kane, among others, argue that all the five distinguishing marks may not necessarily be found in every Purāṇa. Kane writes that of the total verses of the *Vishnu Purāṇa*, only about 20 per cent verses of deal with *pañcalakṣaṇa* material. According to Hazra, the remaining verses contain,

> glorifications of one or more of the sectarian deities ... numerous chapters on new myths, and legends, and multifarious topics concerning religion and society, for instance, duties of the different castes and orders of life, sacraments, customs in general, eatables and non-eatables, and rites and ceremonies, impurity on birth and purification of things, names and descriptions deeds ... pacification of unfavorable planets, of wells, tanks, and gardens, worship, devotional consecration of temples and images of gods, initiation, and various mystic rites and practices.
>
> *(Hazra 1937, 246, 247)*

The first dateable description of the Purāṇa as scripture is found in the fifth-century text, *Amarakosa*, which defines Purāṇa as "that which has five characteristics" (Coburn 1980, 341). The Purāṇas which are available today, however, do not possess all five of these signs.[12] According to Wilson, the *Vishnu Purāṇa* shows the maximum amount of *pañcalakṣaṇa* elements among all the eighteen primary Purāṇas. The *Vishnu Purāṇa* is divided into six parts called "amsas". Each amsa contains a number of chapters. The first three amsas deal with creation, recreation, geography, atmosphere, the solar system, the fourteen *manavantara*s, duties of different castes, and funeral rites, among other subjects. The fourth part provides detailed genealogies and accounts of kings. The fifth part deals with the adventures of the divine Krishna. The final amsa deals with the types of knowledge which can lead to the Supreme hero of the text, the God Vishnu (Hazra 1937, 257).

These distinguishing signs which mark purāṇic texts may be found in *Kristapurāṇa*. It contains the story of the creation of the world (1.2.32–58), of the flood and re-creation (1.7.47–102; 1.8.1–15), the genealogy of humankind and of Jesus Christ (2.12.38–63; 2.17.41–72), stories of kings, patriarchs, and saints (1.25.1–10; 1.29.3; 2.1.32, 33). Along with this there are abundant descriptions of everyday life, church practices, prophecies, and worship, among other things, similar to Hazra's description of purāṇic subjects. According to Malshe, *Kristapurāṇa* is based on the Bible, and, as such, the Bible can also be said to hold all these distinguishing marks of a Purāṇa (Malshe 1961, 404).

Rao argues, in his essay "Purāṇa as Brahminic Ideology" (1993), that rather than constituting the actual content of purāṇic texts, the *pañcalakṣaṇa* can be viewed as an "ideology"[13] or a "worldview":

> *Lakṣaṇa* is not a definition; nor do the five *lakṣaṇas* inform us of the contents of a Purāṇa. *Lakṣaṇa*, as the dictionary tells us, is a distinguishing mark. Furthermore, *lakṣaṇas* are not necessarily objective, empirically observed facts; they could be perceived "facts" … The five *lakṣaṇas* order the events of the Purāṇa. They provide the listeners with a view of time and space in which the events narrated in the *Purāṇas* occur. In other words, the *pañcalakṣaṇas* create a world and a worldview.
>
> *(Rao 1993, 89)*

The *pañcalakṣaṇa*,[14] thus, provide a framework of time and space within which the stories contained in the Purāṇa are enacted. In the case of regional folk narratives that began to appear in the purāṇic tradition, this framework provided access to the larger worldview of Sanskrit Purāṇas and gave these folk traditions a space to locate themselves within the dominant (in this case Sanskrit) literary tradition.[15] According to Rao, purāṇic texts cannot be considered as individual bound texts. He states that "One could make sense of any of these texts only by listening to these texts as a part of this tradition" (Rao 1993, 92). Each of these texts is a part of the "totality of a text tradition with intertextual relationships and commentorial contexts" (Rao 1993, 92). The *pañcalakṣaṇa*s run like threads through these numerous texts, holding them together as a tradition marked by intertextuality.

The earliest writings in the vernacular languages of India were translations from classical languages such as Sanskrit and Tamil (Singh 1996, 12; Ramakrishnan 2009, 31). The works were translations in a "different and loose sense as they strove to translate ancient Indian knowledge … by appropriating it in various Indian *bhashas*" (Singh 1996, 12). In these early translatorial attempts, the Purāṇas appeared quite frequently (Ramakrishnan 2009, 31; Choudhuri 2010, 119). These Purāṇas told newer stories other than the traditional Sanskrit ones and took on a life of their own. They were new creations infused with the colour of the region in which they were being translated. These "transformed" texts served as harbingers of a new vernacular tradition, as means of resisting existing hegemonic literary practices. By absorbing the traditions of the regions they were translated into, these Purāṇas developed their own distinct style.

The fifteenth-century Odia text *Sarala Mahabharata* is a fascinating case in point of the travel of Sanskrit textual traditions into regional languages. In his essay, "Retelling as Interpretation: An Essay on Sarala Mahabharata", B.N. Patnaik presents a critical reading of the Odia text of Sarala Das's[16] *Mahabharata*. Sarala Das insisted on calling his Odia *Mahabharata* a "Purāṇa, a sacred text" (Patnaik 2013, 2). Sarala Das, in fact, went so far as to call it his "Vishnu Purāṇa" (Patnaik 2013, 5). This raises the question of why these regional poets insisted on calling their creations Purāṇa. It is possible that the title of "Purāṇa" ascribed certain sacredness to the narrative by placing it within the tradition of the canonical Sanskrit Purāṇas. Sarala was writing during a time when it was considered heresy to write a sacred Purāṇa without the sacred language, Sanskrit (Patnaik 2013, 5). In addition to this, Sarala took considerable liberties with the narrative of the Vyasa Mahabharata and added his own stories and local colour to it. Patnaik notes that Sarala announced that the goddess Sarala was the actual author of the Purāṇa, and said that he was merely a foolish scribe writing down what the goddess inspired (Patnaik 2013, 5).[17] According to Patnaik, Sarala may have been doing this to escape criticism for composing a sacred text in the Odia language.

Sarala Das had no narrative tradition in the Odia language as a precedent, when he wrote his *Mahabharata*, as "he was the one who created the tradition" (Patnaik 2013, 6). As a pioneer of Odia literature, when the time came for him to narrate a story in his own language, Odia, he was drawn to the purāṇic genre. He chose to name his Odia Mahabharata a Purāṇa. Stephens was in a similar position when he began missionary work in sixteenth-century Goa. He had no precedent of a Bible or any biblical narrative in an Indian language. Stephens, like Sarala Das, chose to narrate his story in verse and name it a "Purāṇa". The Purāṇa gives rise to certain expectations of sacredness and places the works in this tradition in the temporal-spatial framework of the ancient texts. It appears from an understanding of the regional Purāṇas, that authors who desired to place their stories of beginnings, genealogies, and heroic acts in the ancient purāṇic tradition named their works as Purāṇas. These poets aspired for their narratives to be more than just folk narratives. Purāṇic texts, whether Sanskrit or vernacular, are a way of tracing back the ancestry of a particular belief system. When a regional poet labelled his composition as a Purāṇa, his composition became part of an ancient tradition, adding its own cosmology to the canon of purāṇic texts. They were enfolded into the purāṇic worldview and placed in the tradition of the "dominant" narratives.

In the centuries between 1000 AD and 1500 AD, a large number of regional poets began translating Sanskrit sacred texts into vernacular languages, including Marathi (Pollock 1998, 45; Das 2005, 191; Novetzke 2016, 5). Stephens's *Kristapurāṇa* was located in this tradition of Marathi Purāṇas. Malshe points out that Stephens's inspiration for the purāṇic form comes from his reading of earlier and contemporary Marathi poets, who composed Purāṇas and undertook translations of Sanskrit Purāṇas into Marathi (Malshe 1961, 404).[18] Stephens himself mentions in his "Introduction" to *Kristapurāṇa* that he was following the style and language of the poets of the region (Stephens and Saldanha 1907, XCIII).

Vivekasindhu, written by Mukundaraja of the *Nath* sect, is considered as the first text to be written in Marathi (Tulpule et al. 1994, 159–160; Das 2005, 191). It was composed at the beginning of the twelfth century. This work is written in the form of a dialogue (Das 2005, 191). The next important phase in Marathi literature was the period of the *Mahanubhava* sect. The sect, founded by Sri

Chakradhara, contributed to the development of early Marathi literature. *Shishupala Vadha* (1292) by Bhaskarabhatta Borikar, *Rukmini Swayamvara* (1292) by Narendra, *Sahyadri Varnan* (1333) and prose works such as *Lilacharitra* are important works by the Mahanubhavas. By the end of the thirteenth century Jnaneswar (1275–1296) and Namdev (1270–1350) were composing their Marathi works. Jnaneswar's *Bhavarthadeepika* (1290), well known as the *Jnaneswari*, is his interpretation and commentary of the Sanskrit *Bhagvad Gita*. It is studied as an early work of translation from the Indian Subcontinent.

Literary production in early modern Maharashtra took place against the cultural backdrop of the religious sects that were developing in the region. Marathi saint poetry can be read as part of the Bhakti waves that were sweeping across the subcontinent, a movement that has often been characterized as egalitarian and anti-caste. However, in the case of Marathi saint poetry, this was hardly a homogenous movement with a single-minded goal of annihilating caste or other social hierarchies. The period in which these texts such as *Jnaneswari* were composed was one of developing ideas of a public that was the "body of devotion" led by leaders such as Chakradhar in the twelfth century and patronized by the Yadava rulers (Novetzke 2016, 210). Christian Lee Novetzke argues that it was this move towards the creation of a religious "public" that led to Marathi literary production, and that therefore it was not a courtly activity.[19] Multiple religious sects were competing for resources and devotees and were composing poetry to disseminate their teachings to a larger public (Ketkar 2019, 18). In Jnāneswar's work, the Sanskrit text of the Gita is placed alongside his Marathi commentary, bringing together the religious message of the Gita and the emerging idea of a "Marathi mandali", a Marathi-speaking public.

These new literary traditions in Marathi were not only travelling to different regions of Western India; they also entered the stream of global circulation with the advent of Portuguese rule. In his doctoral thesis, Malshe lists some of these early Marathi texts and their Portuguese translations which were found in Portugal. Among these are handwritten manuscripts of *Harishchandra Purāṇa* (author unknown), *Dronapurāṇa*, and Dnyandev's *Yogavasishta* among other texts.[20] This establishes the theory that Stephens had access to the works of classical Marathi poets. While there is evidence that Stephens had read Sanskrit (Zwartjes 2011, 46), his text is clearly located in the tradition of the Marathi Purāṇas listed by Malshe. According to Priolkar, Stephens's style is more in line with the older poets such as Jnaneswar or Namdev, than his contemporaries, such as Tukaram (Priolkar 1971, 43). This may be because of the texts that were available to Stephens for study, as listed by Malshe in his work. The influence of Marathi saint-poets on Stephens is evident in numerous passages in his work, specifically in passages where a deep devotion and longing for the "divine" is seen, reminiscent of the saint-poetry associated with the Bhakti movement in the region. One such passage is the description of Simeon who waited in the temple to see Christ incarnated:

Ussuassu ghaloni mh*a*nne vello vellã	He sighed and said from time to time,
Suamiya to dinu pauĩ z*ã*u*a*1lã	Lord, bring that day near,
C*a*di teya tar*a*ca m*a*z*ã* ddollã	When the saviour with my eyes,
Deqh*a*in*a* mĩ	I will see
Zetuquẽ ahe s*a*unssarantu	All that is in the world,
Yetuqueacha maza ubagu bahutu	I am weary of it all,
S*a*unssar*a* goddhiuecha suarthu	The sweetness of the world,
Sandd*a*u*a*la maza	Is lost to me
Deqhaueya Israely tar*a*cu	To see the saviour of Israel
M*a*nor*a*thu ur*a*la tochi yecu	Is the only yearning left in me,
Tennẽ aratẽ mi tuza seu*a*cu	With that one desire, your servant
Ur*a*lã s*a*unssarĩ	Lives on in this world
(*Kristapurāṇa* 2.11.42–44)	

The emptiness of the world and the longing of the devotee-beloved to see the deity is one of the predominant themes within Bhakti saint-literature.[21]

Malshe has compiled a detailed comparison of passages from *Kristapurāṇa* with these canonical Marathi texts (Malshe 1961, 424–480). A study of these comparisons reveals similarities in style and language between Stephens and other Marathi poets. Malshe compares *Kristapurāṇa* separately with each of these texts, perhaps with a view to prove that Stephens was leaning heavily on the earlier poets for inspiration. In this process, we also learn that all these poets, including Stephens, had several idiomatic usages which appear strikingly similar.[22] The Marathi Purāṇa tradition was thus developing its own distinct identity and register, of which Stephens's *Kristapurāṇa* was a part.

The genre of Purāṇa, thus, appears to provide spaces for new stories and languages to seep in, while still being recognized among the repertoire of Purāṇas. Rao argues that the Purāṇa have a quality of open-endedness and flexibility which enables them to accommodate stories from varied regions and beliefs. He makes this argument by positioning the Purāṇa against the Vedas, which are closed texts to which nothing can be added or removed. Every sound of the Vedas has to be preserved intact. In opposition to this, the purāṇic texts have a "flexibility of content" (Rao 1993, 93) with a fixed ideology. This ideology, in Rao's opinion, is manifested as the *pañcalakṣaṇa*.

The Purāṇas are "functionally open texts: they have accepted into their fold events, stories, legends, and occurrences of many regions and communities, transforming them to confirm to a fixed ideology" (Rao 94). This open-ended nature provides space for new stories and languages to enter this epic form leading to a "novelization", a renewal of the classical genre. Bakhtin (1895–1975), in "Epic and Novel" (1941), proposes the idea of the novelization of the "epic". When epic genres are novelised,

> They become more free and flexible, their language renews itself by incorporating extra literary language, they become dialogized, permeated with laughter, irony, humor, elements of self parody, and finally – this is the most

important thing – the novel inserts into these other genres an indeterminacy, a certain semantic openendedness, a living contact with unfinished, still-evolving contemporary reality.

(Bakhtin 1981a, 7)

Bakhtin proposes that "the novel" inserts "a certain semantic openendedness" into other genres. For Bakhtin, the epic genres are antiquated (Bakhtin 1981a, 13). Novelization provides the open-endedness required for such antiquated genre to come to terms with "contemporary reality". The term "novelization" is used here primarily to underline the capacity of the purāṇic genre for accommodating varied narratives and to evolve with time. The genre of Purāṇa exhibits a potential for "novelization" which made it possible for numerous regional legends to be accommodated within it. It would seem that this potential for novelization is inherent in the genre, making it open to accepting external influences. It was the regional "folk" narratives that began to novelize the purāṇic genre in the regions where they were being translated (Ramanujan 1993, 101; Rao 1993, 89). These novelized regional Purāṇas continued to call themselves Purāṇas, and in the process each region developed its own distinctive register of purāṇic texts.

Novelization can only take place when a genre provides "space" for newness to enter. Bakhtin has argued, in "Epic and Novel", that the epic genre are closed and moribund with no scope for any growth. The subjects and style of epics are predetermined and of ancient gravity. By contrast, the genre of novel is fresh, open and ever-changing.[23] Bakhtin has argued that it is the effect of the novel on literary systems that leads to the entry of new fables, language and idioms into the epic (Bakhtin 1981a, 7). It can be seen from the case of the Purāṇas that in order for novelization to take place in an epic, the epic genre should provide space(s) for new stories to enter. The novel cannot "access" an epic genre without these "spaces" into which they can seep in and imbue with newness. The Purāṇas provide these spaces where novelization can occur. Bakhtin's aspiration for the Western epic seems to be realized in the inherent potential for novelization in the genre of Purāṇa.

The inherent tendency of the Purāṇa to be novelized can also be understood in the light of Benjamin's idea of "translatability". According to Benjamin in "The Task of the Translator" (1921), "Translatability is an essential quality of certain works, which is not to say that it is essential that they be translated; it means rather that a specific significance inherent in the original manifests itself in its translatability" (Benjamin 2012, 254). The text holds the seeds of its translation in itself. Benjamin argues that certain texts call to be translated. It is not necessary that these texts must be translated in practice, but they possess an innate feature which invites translation. It is possible that this nature of translatability within the Purāṇas was one of the reasons, in addition to the religious significance enjoyed by them, which made them among the first texts to be translated from Sanskrit to the vernaculars. As they began to be translated and came into contact with regional "folk" narratives, they became open to "novelization", giving rise to a new and vigorous purāṇic tradition in the vernacular languages of the subcontinent. Cultural translation into the vernaculars was one of the major ways in which Sanskrit Purāṇas were novelized.

The Purāṇas were harnessed by missionaries to narrate Christian scriptures to the people they intended to convert to Christianity. On the one hand, there were measures to wean the local population away from Hindu texts, while on the other hand, a literary tradition such as the Purāṇa, which was sacred to Hindu beliefs, was appropriated by missionaries to translate liturgy and biblical narratives. Missionaries like Stephens fully understood the high value of poetic traditions in conveying religious truths as opposed to the prose in which European texts were composed. *Kristapurāṇa* of Stephens is a site which opens up questions on and provokes inquiry into the genre of Purāṇa. As a literary text, *Kristapurāṇa* enables an understanding of the translatability of the purāṇic genre and its potential for "novelization". As a translator, Stephens wanted his narrative to be considered sacred and given the reverence that was given to Hindu religious literature. By choosing to translate the story of the Bible into a "sacred" tradition such as the Purāṇa, Stephens changed two traditions: (a) the biblical tradition which got transformed when it was recited as a Purāṇa, and (b) the purāṇic genre which got "translated" and "novelized" in its encounter with Christian scriptures. Cultural translation is one of the ways in which these spaces for novelization within the purāṇic tradition are exposed and "new fables" are able to enter these spaces in order to novelize the tradition.

One question that calls to be raised is that of the intention of the locals when they asked for a "Purāṇa". The several senses in which the term "Purāṇa" is used in the text is significant in this context. This is also significant to the various meanings attributed to the term "Purāṇa" in the vernacular languages into which they were translated. Stephens uses three important terms throughout the text: "Grantha" (1.20.36), "Shastra" (1.20.36), and "Purāṇa". "Grantha" is used to mean a physical book. For example, in verse 1.20.36, the Padre-guru mentions "xastracha granthu", the book containing the law. "Shāstra" is used to mean law, or scriptures. Thirdly, "Purāṇa" is used to describe the text that the Padre-guru was narrating. Purāṇa is also used to mean scriptures at several points in the text. This term is used both while referring to the ancient prophets and the Padre-guru's retelling of the Christian narrative (1.36.138; 2.21.7, 26). These usages are complex and require a separate study to understand the full import of the term "Purāṇa" as it was used in seventeenth century Goa.

The Purāṇic tradition, which has been studied to date in the context of the *pañcalakṣaṇa*, as classical sacred works, and as important links in the Sanskrit literary tradition, requires much deeper study as to the specific ways in which these texts are received and interpreted in regional traditions. According to Patnaik, Sarala Das's Mahabharata was "essentially the puran style; what Sarala did was explore its limits in creative terms" (Patnaik 2013, 26). Patnaik's statement may be applied to other regional "purankaars", including Stephens, who took the classical genre of Purāṇa and explored its translatability and potential for novelization to the fullest.

3.3 Dialogic Nature of *Kristapurāṇa*

The dialogic nature of texts is one of the distinctive generic features of the purāṇic tradition. Purāṇas are composed as a dialogue or question-and-answer format. In a Sanskrit Purāṇa, dialogue is used to build the narrative:

> The invariable form of the Puráñas is that of a dialogue, in which some person relates its contents in reply to the inquiries of another. This dialogue is interwoven with others, which are repeated as having been held on other occasions between different individuals, in consequence of similar questions having been asked. The immediate narrator is commonly, though not con-stantly, Lomaharshaña or Romaharshaña, the disciple of Vyása, who is sup-posed to communicate what was imparted to him by his preceptor, as he had heard it from some other sage. Vyása, as will be seen in the body of the work, is a generic title, meaning an 'arranger' or 'compiler'.
>
> *(Wilson 1840, xi)*

The *Vishnu Purāṇa*, for example, begins with a dialogue between Maitreya and his teacher, Parasara, after verses of adoration to Vishnu:

> OM! GLORY TO VÁSUDEVA. –Victory be to thee, Puñḍaríkáksha; ado-ration be to thee, Víswabhávana; glory be to thee, Hrishikeśa, Mahápurusha, and Púrvaja. ...
>
> Maitreya, having saluted him reverentially, thus addressed Paráśara, the excellent sage, the grandson of Vaśishṭha, who was versed in traditional his-tory, and the Puráñas; who was acquainted with the Vedas, and the branches of science dependent upon them; and skilled in law and philosophy; and who had performed the morning rites of devotion.
>
> *(Vishnu Purāṇa 1–3, Wilson 1840)*

Kristapurāṇa, similarly, begins with an invocation to the Trinity and the saints before beginning the dialogue between the Padre-guru and his listeners, the new Christians of the region (1.1.126). In the following sections of this chapter (Sections 3.4 and 3.5) on the concept of Vaicunttha, it will also be argued that dialogue is one the key features that shaped the direction in which the text evolved. The dialogic nature of *Kristapurāṇa* is twofold: (a) the conversational tone and the development of the nar-rative through dialogue, and (b) a more complex dialogic relationship where texts from diverse traditions such as the biblical and the purāṇic, "speak" to one another.

The dialogic tone of the Purāṇa is also critically connected to its "orality". Patnaik argues, in the context of the Sarala Mahabharata, that the "oral" nature of purāṇic texts is vital to the way the narrative develops (Patnaik 2013 2). In Sarala's case, he was narrating the Mahabharata to an audience who were unlearned in Sanskrit. The question of what to be included and what to be excluded, for Sarala, would have been decided on the basis of how well it could hold the attention of his listeners (Patnaik 2013, 1–3). This would mean that Sarala's retelling would have some portions and characters developed more than they were in the canonical *Mahabharata*, producing a text which was the Mahabharata, but was new at the same time. The genre of Purāṇa, with its dialogic narrative style, its digressions, and framed stories, is shaped by its orality. It is indicated in *Kristapurāṇa* that it "given" to the people on a Palm Sunday was narrated over the course of subsequent Sundays (*Kristapurāṇa* 1.1.169).

Kristapurāṇa is composed in a dialogic format, as a discussion between the narrator, Padre-guru, who is a priest of the Catholic Church, and the converts in seventeenth-century Goa (*Kristapurāṇa* 1.1.129–146). The conversations are often between the Padre-guru and his listeners, that is, between the characters of the story. The text displays the characteristic digressions of Purāṇic texts, and the unfolding of the narrative is determined by listeners who may intervene from time to time, influencing the way the Padre-guru developed his narrative. At different points in the narrative, the narrator enters the story and addresses one or more of the characters. In the final chapter of the text, after Christ's resurrection from the dead and ascension back into Vaicunttha, the narrator addresses the angels:

Vaincunttha prauessu santã samagamĩ
Zo caritaye Christu suamy
Tethila vartamana bhodduue ho tumĩ
Niropize amã
(*Kristapurāṇa* 2.59.1)

Christ the Lord enters Vaicunttha
In the company of the Saints
Oh angels, send us
News about it from heaven

The narrative voice implores the angels in Heaven to describe the victorious entry of Christ into Vaicunttha for the benefit of his readers. The Son of God, who had come down from Vaicunttha to save mankind, had now ascended back to his abode having completed his mission on earth. The tone of the Purāṇa in these verses is that of a dialogue between the narrator, the *padre-guru* (1.1.128), and other characters in the story. Here, the narrator speaks to the angels in Heaven, while at other places in the Purāṇa he addresses a group of local Christians who are his listeners in the narrative. Stephens' Purāṇa has these features of a dialogic format, a central narrator, a group of listeners whose questions the Purāṇa answers, and it is also interwoven with dialogues with other characters who appear from time to time in the narrative.

Traditional Purāṇas were disseminated by their recitation or *pathan* by purāṇic scholars (Patnaik 2013, 27). The very act of listening to Purāṇas was considered blessed. *Kristapurāṇa* participates in this oral tradition of purāṇic dissemination. In the text the padre-guru urges his listeners to give ear to his narration of the scriptures, and be blessed: "So you listeners/Fill your minds with joy/and listen to these scriptures/you will be blessed" (1.5.153). This aspect draws the attention of the reader to the fact that these early instances of cultural translation were oral attempts to explicate sacred texts to audiences who had no access to them in their source languages. In *Kristapurāṇa*, Christ himself does the ministry of retelling the scriptures

(2.19.10). He went about the land of Israel carrying out his task of "shastrakathana", narrating of the scriptures to those who came to listen to him (2.27.114).

Apart from the dialogue between narrator and listeners in the text, more complex aspects of dialogue among texts and cultures are revealed in a reading of *Kristapurāṇa*.[24] Dialogue with locals was one way in which missionaries negotiated local customs and familiarized themselves with the culture. These interpretations of local culture are reflected in the literature composed by missionaries. Županov writes about the dialogic method followed by missionaries:

> For the Jesuit missionaries, a dialogue was, first of all, a strategy for acquiring knowledge of geopolitics and geography, of customs and manners, of economy and bioresources, and of religious practices linked closely to the secret internal knowledge of the soul. The presence of these dialogical voices, fragmented as they were, is attested in Jesuit correspondence, where dialogues spring forth, as embedded theatre pieces, from the epistolary narratives.
>
> *(Županov 2012, 416)*

These voices are brought out clearly in *Kristapurāṇa* because of the inherent space given to dialogue in the purāṇic tradition. The "secret internal knowledge" of the soul, which could not be gathered by official administrative procedures, was crucial to the missionary enterprise.[25] The dialogue with local customs and texts composed in the region gives rise to a text such as *Kristapurāṇa*, which is constantly "speaking to" local cultures and is in turn "spoken to" by these cultures. The resultant text is a cultural translation that transforms all the texts and traditions involved in the dialogue, and leads to a "creative Christianity" suited to the intricacies of the region in which the text was being composed. The purāṇic concepts that enter the biblical narrative in this creative retelling are spaces which provide insight into the manner in which translators such as Stephens negotiated the complex process of cultural translation of religious texts. One such purāṇic term "Vaicunttha" is taken up for analysis in the following section.

3.4 Culture, Translation, and Vaicunttha

In *Kristapurāṇa*, Vaicunttha is transformed into a Christian heaven through Stephens's cultural translation of the biblical narrative. Diogo Ribeiro, editor of Stephens's *Doutrina Christa*, comments on Stephens's use of the word "Vaicunttha" in Christian writings. Ribeiro writes in the introduction:

> ... this word (vainkuttha = vaikuntha) is used among the Heathens and in *Canarim* language means Heaven, inhabited by their Gods (pagodes); although already today in the same language among the Christians it is used and means our Heaven of glory and blessedness.
>
> *(Xavier and Županov 2015, 227)*

Vaicunttha is firmly established by Stephens as the abode of the Trinity. The throne of the creator God is set there and that is where all humans return after that they have attained *moksha*, to become one with their Creator. The grand plan of God for humankind is formulated and orchestrated from this central site, Vaicunttha. The deity ascribed to the ruler of Vaicunttha, Vishnu, is transferred to the Christian godhead through translation. Christ, then, becomes *Vaicunttha-nayak* (Leader of Vaicunttha), *Vaicuntthasabhecha kaanti* (light of the Vaicunttha assembly), *Vaicunttha raya* (king of Vaicunttha). The gospel enters the culture while the culture enters the gospel and both stand transformed, creating a new, third space within contested sacred spaces of Catholicism and Hinduism. Ribeiro's comment is testimony of the power of translation in grappling with the sacred – that the Vaicunttha that was once inhabited by "heathen Gods" now means "our Heaven of glory and blessedness".

In the following close reading of passages from *Kristapurāṇa*, an attempt is made to investigate early missionary interventions into the religious space(s) in India and understand how translation was used as a process of grappling with the cultural complexities of such "sacred encounters". The idea of "Vaicunttha" is analysed in order to bring out the relationship between the sacred and cultural translation.

In his introduction to *Kristapurāṇa* Stephens wrote that his aim was to convince the locals in Goa that Christ was the saviour of humankind and the only God worthy of worship (Stephens and Saldanha 1907, XCIV). He expounded the Trinity of the Father, Son and the Holy Spirit and introduced Christ as the Son who would lead humankind to the Creator, to his abode in heaven. *Kristapurāṇa* begins in its first chapter with the creation of heaven by the Creator and ends with the victorious re-entry of Christ into heaven.

In all these episodes, Stephens uses Vaicunttha and *suarga*[26] interchangeably to describe the abode of God. *Vaicunttha* is the abode of the Hindu God Vishnu (Wilson xx). Vaicunttha is also known as *Vishnupada* or the "feet of *Vishnu*". Its location has been variously described in different Purāṇas as set on Mount Meru or to the north of the Himalayas (Williams 290). In Hindu mythology, this is the celestial home inhabited by Vishnu and his consort Lakshmi (Bane 147). Vaicunttha is distinct from the other 'spheres' or *lokas* of the heavens. Wilson (1786–1860) explains, in his summary of the *Padma Purāṇa*, that Vaicunttha, the abode of Vishnu, is placed above all the other spheres or *lokas* of suarga. "The Swarga Khaṅḍa describes in the first chapters the relative positions of the Lokas or spheres above the earth, placing above all Vaikuṅtha, the sphere of Vishṅu" (Wilson 1840, xx). It has also been described as "the highest of regions, the blessed abode of Visnu" (Raychaudhuri 1937, 78).

The supreme position of Vaicunttha in the heavenly spheres has special significance for *Vaishnavism*, a sect of Hinduism where Vishnu is worshipped as the supreme God. In fact, the growth of *Vaishnavism* in several regions of the Indian Subcontinent gave rise to Vishnu-worship and led to the consecration of Vaicunttha as the highest abode of God (Karmarkar 1937, 83, 84). An analysis of this concept of Vaicunttha in Stephens's text leads us to a clearer understanding of how translation plays a role in disseminating the sacred and in the process, transforms it.

The word *Vaicunttha* has been used about three hundred and twenty-two times in *Kristapurāṇa*, in different forms. Four of these episodes have been chosen to study the aspects of translation of sacred texts in the seventeenth century. In this process, we read Stephens himself as a translator and attempt is made to decipher the dilemmas and anxieties of a translator-priest in a cross-cultural mission, as reflected in the text.

While translating his protagonist, Christ, for a Marathi readership, Stephens may have had to decide what figure of Jesus he wanted to construct for his readers, the newly converted Christians of Goa. These Christians were Brahmins who had read the Hindu Purāṇas and understood the hierarchy of Hindu deities. Christ had to find a space above all the other Gods that they had worshipped until then. Stephens's aim was to convince the local readers that Christ is the only true Saviour. He was fully confident that once the locals read the whole story of Christ, they would be persuaded that the Christian "shastra" (sacred text) is different from all the other "shastra" they had read until then. He wrote in his introduction to the Purāṇa:

> Yetuquẽ amanchea xastra anny anniyeca xastra bhituri *antara* ahe *ai*ssẽ mhannaunu s*a*m*a*sta deqhaty. Mhann*a*unu ami hea amanchea Purannantu teanchẽ xastr*a* l*a*ttic*a* anny am*a*nchẽ s*a*te *ai*ssẽ mhann*a*unu daqh*a*unssi nahĩ c*a*sttau*a*tõ; cã tẽ ap*a*issẽ s*a*m*a*stanssi drustty p*a*dd*a*taye; Christau*a*nchẽ xastr*a* ap*a*nn*a*pẽ sobh*a*taye, mir*a*u*a*taye, va tenchi b*a*r*a*ue mhann*a*unu ap*a*nn*a*pẽ daunu dentaye; vachileya aiquileya pure.
>
> *(Stephens and Saldanha 1907, XCIV)*

All can see that there is a difference between our sacred text and other sacred texts. Therefore no effort has been made in our Purāṇa to prove that their texts are false and our text is true; because it is evident to everyone on its own. The sacred text of Christians shines beautifully on its own and shows that it is the excellent one. It is enough that it is read or heard.

Stephens comes across in this passage as completely self-assured and certain that the "truth" of the Christian message could be conveyed, even if the genre of Purāṇa in which he chose to compose in was distinctly Hindu in its form and essence. His conviction is clear in his introduction. It is necessary, therefore, to understand where Stephens places Christ in relation to the Hindu Gods of the Purāṇas to convince people of his deity. The Purāṇa begins and ends with *Vaicunttha*. The first Avasvaru introduces *Vaicunttha* as the abode of the Trinity, the Almighty Creator, while in the final Avaswaru Christ victoriously enters *Vaicunttha* after conquering death on the cross.

At the beginning of the *Paillem Puranna*, Stephens gave a description of *Vaicunttha*:

Hẽ yetuquẽ n*a*pure z*a*halẽ	And as if all this were not enough
Anny suamiyẽ c*a*e quelẽ	Again the Lord made
Su*a*rga v*a*rutẽ r*a*chilẽ	Above the heavens,
V*a*incunttha sthan*a*	The place called Vaicunttha
C*a*e v*a*rnũ tea v*a*incuntthassi	O, how should I describe this Vaicunttha
Yeu*a*ddy m*a*ti qh*a*inchy amanssi	Do I have the wisdom for describing it?
Up*a*ma dentã su*a*rga pr*a*thuuissi	If I compare it to all the heavens and the earth
Thoddy hoe	It will not suffice
(1.2.60, 61)	

On reading these verses, *Vaicunttha* seemseen to have created by the "Christian" God. It is significant that Stephens uses both "swarga" and "Vaicunttha" in the same sentence, indicating that he makes a distinction between the two. *Swarga* is translated as heaven. Stephens, however, seems to have been aware that in the Hindu Purāṇas the lesser deities inhabited the spheres of swarga while Vishnu, the supreme deity, dwelt in *Vaicunttha*. Wilson explains, in his summary of the *Padma Purāṇa*, that Vaicunttha, the abode of Vishnu, is placed above all the other spheres, or 'lokas', of 'swarga'. It seems from the text that Stephens wanted to ascribe to Christ the highest power among the Gods and placed him in *Vaicunttha* so that there was no doubt in the minds of the readers that the "Christian" God reigned supreme above all other Gods that the local Christians had ever heard about, or worshipped, before.

Translation has been vital in grappling with ideas of the sacred and in disseminating religious texts to cultures beyond their origin. However, the relationship between the sacred and translation has always been a strained one. The reason for this may be the inherently heretical nature of translation. Translation lets the 'foreign' enter a culture and imbues it with newness. The Garden of Eden, which is depicted as Paradise on earth, is described by Stephens as *Bhumivaincunttha*, or '*Vaicunttha* on earth'. This was the place where God came down to speak to his creation, the first humans, Adam and Eve.

M*a*nuxu r*a*chileya v*a*ri	When man was created
Deuẽ teya *a*u*a*su*a*ri	God, on that occasion
Neuni bhumiv*a*incunttha bhituri	Took him to Bhumivaicunttha
Ttheuila teathẽ	And placed him there
(*Kristapurāṇa* 1.3.42)	

After describing the creation of man and Eden, Stephens goes on describe the beauty of this *Bhumivaicunttha*, the Garden of Eden:

Z*a*issea gaghanĩ tara zh*a*ll*a*caty	As the stars that shine in the sky
T*a*isse te m*a*idhanĩ puspẽ sobh*a*ty	So the flowers filled the garden
Zai zui mog*a*ry sẽu*a*ty	Jasmines and chrysanthemums of every kind
Mir*a*ue p*a*rompari	Adorn the place
(1.4.100)	

Eden transforms into *Bhumivaicunttha*, a term used to depict holy sites of Hinduism, places on earth where God is known to reside. Tropical flowers like *zai, zui,* and *mogra* grow in this Bhumivaicunttha. In Stephens's translation of Vaicunttha, it transforms into a space which contains the throne of the trinity. Wherever the presence of the Trinity exists, takes on the significance of Vaicunttha. In the *Dussarem Puranna*, Mary's womb is visualized as a microcosm of Vaicunttha by Stephens: "Now the womb of the Virgin/Is Vaicuntthanagara (city of Vaicunttha)" (*Kristapurāṇa* 2.5.78). Christ, who was enthroned in Vaicunttha, is now enthroned in Mary's womb. When his throne is placed in Mary's womb, her womb transforms into a microcosmic Vaicunttha. The cultural translation that occurs here is not just of the Christian theology, but also of purāṇic cosmogony. Vaicunttha stands transformed into the abode of the trinity in this process of cultural translation.

The genre of Purāṇa that Stephens used to translate his message for Marathi readers adds newness to the existing Christian imagery. Translation transforms the message and imbues it with newness. This newness is not necessarily always in the interest of the "patronage" (Lefevere 2012, 206) that validates a translated work, in this case the Catholic Church. This is because translation has the potential to become a means of social change and aids in reorientation of religious hierarchies. A close reading of the idea of Vaicunttha in *Kristapurāṇa* brings to light the ways in which the purāṇic genre has been appropriated by Stephens to evangelize the new community of local Christians in Goa. The genre, taken by Stephens and transformed into a receptacle for Christian meaning, transforms the message itself. The messages were invested with meanings and imagery other than the ones intended by the poet in addition to his intended message.

In this process, the characters and their actions are localized. For instance, in *Kristapurāṇa*, the biblical Isaac touches the feet of his father, Abraham, as a mark of respect to him (1.9.71). This distinctly regional gesture of respect to elders is used by Stephens to portray Isaac's obedience to his father. *Ghee* (clarified butter) and milk are served by Abraham to the guests who arrived at his door (1.9.29). Other purāṇic concepts enter the Christian narrative in this text. John the Baptist does a "pradakshina" around his parents before leaving to live in the wilderness (2.14.36). ("Pradakshina" is a purāṇic term which means "to one's right" and involves walking around a holy place or person as a symbol of prayer (Bowker 224).) He also worships God by joining both hands and bowing down ("kar sampushti pranipatu kela") (2.18.36). The psalms that the Israelites sang to celebrate the crossing of the Red Sea were "ovi" and "pouadde", traditional Marathi panegyrics sung to celebrate someone's greatness or power (1.17.49, 53). After his temptation by Satan, Christ is served a meal on "patraval" by angels, a traditional plate made of leaves in which food is served (2.20.141). These local details used beautify the text and follow in the tradition of traditional saint-poets are intermingled with more complex theological decisions in the cultural translation of church concepts. The figure of Christ, for instance, is carefully crafted as the only saviour and as the deity who rules from Vaicunttha.

Stephens's Christ is addressed as "Vaicunttha *nayeca*" by his mother Mary, whose eyes are compared to lotuses:

Sadagdita zahalẽ cantthanalla	Her throat choked up
Gahĩuaralẽ hrudaye camalla	Lotus-heart overwhelmed
Praghattalẽ ananda zalla	Waters of joy appeared
Nayena camallĩ	In the lotus eyes
Mhanne mazea suamiya mazea ballaca	And said, My Lord, My Child
Manuxã carannẽ vaincunttha nayeca	O Lord of *Vaicunttha*
Manuxe zanmu visuataraca	Saviour of the world, for humankind
Ghetalassi tuuã	You took human-birth
(*Kristapurāṇa* 2.7.68, 69)	

The Virgin Mary addresses infant Jesus soon after giving birth to him. She addresses him as both her child and as "Lord". The picture of Mary and the scene depicted here has a distinctly "Indian" imagery. This is an example of 'inculturation' where the gospel enters the culture and the culture enters the gospel (Phan 2003, 6). Mary's address to Christ as "Lord of *Vaicunttha*", as Saviour, and at the same time as her "child" underlines the divinity of Christ as well as his human form. Mary, "Vaicunttha ranny" (Queen of *Vaicunttha*) (1.1.43), expounds the theological complexity of the divinity and humanness of Christ. Christ's incarnation as man opens the way for humankind to enter *Vaicunttha* and become one with God, completing the circle of events that began with God's creation of *Vaicunttha*.

Amonkar, in his Konkani translation of *Kristapurāṇa*, proposes the "Vaicunttha model" to explain Stephens's strategy to disseminate the Christian message (Amonkar 2017b, 79, 81). In *Goenche Saunsarikikaran*, Amonkar proposes what he calls the "Vaicunttha model" (*Vaicunttha praroop*) of Stephens. He argues that Stephens used the term Vaicunttha, and used the structure of Vaicunttha to describe the heaven of Christianity so that local Hindus could be convinced of the truth of Christianity. He further argues that in order to refute Hindu beliefs and convince the locals that their religion is false, missionaries had to first read the Purāṇas themselves. After understanding the basic tenets of Hinduism from the sacred poetic texts of the Hindus, the missionaries use the same genre to translate the Christian message and refute Hinduism. Amonkar considers the composition of *Kristapurāṇa* as a well-thought-out strategy by the Church so that the Vaicunttha model could be used to entice the Hindus of Goa into Christianity: "The religious administration saw that it would be easy to entice the *Vaishnavite* Goan Hindus into the fold of Jesus Christ by translating 'God' as 'Vaicunttha-nath', 'Jesus Christ' as 'Vaicunttha-putra', 'Vaicunttha-mauli' and 'heaven' as 'Vaicunttha'" (Amonkar 2017b, 81).[27] Amonkar argues that the "*Vaicunttha* model" was a strategy to convert locals to Christianity by composing texts that were similar to their sacred texts.

The Vaicuntthanayak (leader of Vaicunttha) of the text, Christ, is described as the rising sun. Christ's arrival into the world is described by the narrator as the gradual rising of the sun, shedding light on the world (2.4.7). He is also praised as the foremost among mankind: "As the moon among stars /or the wish-fulfilling tree among trees /the Son of God shines/among the children of men" (2.15.65). His words are "*amrut-dhara*" (nectar-stream) and like *agnibana* (fiery arrows). The

Padre-guru exhorts that faith in this Vaicunttharao (King of Vaicunttha) leads to the ultimate peace, which is salvation by gaining entry into Vaicunntha (*Parama* sukha Vaicunttha mukti) (2.28.16).

Stephens's intricate knowledge of Hindu cosmogony and hierarchy of Hindu heavens places Christ in Vaicunttha, rather than in any lower sphere of *suarga*, placing Christ on the same pedestal as Vishnu. His use of purāṇic genre transfers sacredness to the Christian message and renders it "honourable" (Mosse 2012, 33). He superimposes Christian meaning(s) on to Hindu signs and uses pre-existent sacred vocabulary to pour out Christian meanings into the sacred space(s) that existed before the arrival of Christianity. An analysis of Vaicunttha in *Kristapurāṇa* reveals the complex transactions that took place when the biblical and purāṇic traditions were brought together by Stephens in his poetic work.

3.5 A Sacred Vocabulary

The encounter between gospel and culture in seventeenth-century Goa brought the problems of cross-cultural translation to the fore. On the one hand, there was the understanding that the "Word of God" was pure and powerful, hence the danger of heresy in translation. On the other hand, there was the overwhelming need for large scale translation since the beginning of colonial missions, as "translation defined to an important degree the limits and possibilities of conversion" (Rafael 2012, 21). Through translation a text could be "subverted" and meaning unintended by the original begin to surface. This process of translation would mean destabilizing cultural and religious codes.

In the twentieth century, the Catholic Church came to the realization that "culture" and "mission" could not be kept separate and that heresy had to be redefined. Missionaries had to deal with local cultures and find ways of adapting the message to suit local sensibilities. The intense scrutiny with which missionary practices of Stephens' period were viewed was made more flexible to accommodate cultural variations in spreading the gospel message. The Catholic Church accepted "inculturation" as a method of grappling with cross-cultural spaces in evangelization. The acceptance and propagation of inculturation within the Catholic Church signified a shift from the prevalent "Eurocentric" view of evangelization to a Church characterized by "cultural and religious pluralism" (Phan 2003, 3).

The translation that is seen here is not a mere linguistic transfer of Christian words into the language of the Hindus. It is a cultural transaction, a moment in translation when the culture becomes an inseparable part of the message that is conveyed during evangelization. The culture that the missionaries intend to replace with a Christian one is now harnessed to convey Christian meanings. Rafael, in his volume *Contracting Colonialism*, writes:

> Translation is then a matter of first discerning the differences between and within social codes and then of seeing the possibility of getting across those differences. To do so is to succeed in communicating, that is, in recognizing

and being recognized within the intelligible limits of a linguistic and social order. Hence if translation is to take place at all, it must do so within a context of expectation: that in return for one's submission, one gets back the other's acknowledgement of the value of one's words and behaviour.

(Rafael 2012, 210)

Rafael writes about translation in the context of conversion of the Tagalog society in Philippines into Catholicism and the nuances of translation in this religious encounter between disparate cultures. In order to get an "acknowledgement of the value of one's words" from the target audience, the translator must "submit to the conventions of a given social order" (Rafael 210). In other words, the translator must first be translated by submitting to the conventions of the target culture. Only then effective communication can take place through translation. Stephens is transformed from an English Jesuit who arrived in India with the aim of preaching Christianity, to a Marathi-speaking priest well versed in the cosmogony of the Hindu Purāṇas. He underwent a transformation while acquiring a deep understanding of the existent social order and developed an appreciation of the linguistic and literary complexities of the region in which he worked. Translation emerges as more than mere linguistic transfer, as "records of cultural contestations and ideological struggles" (Tymoczko 2015, 443) which take place when the sacred is translated in cross-cultural encounters.

Although Stephens, in his introduction to *Kristapurāṇa*, is confident of the truth of the Christian message, his "ideological struggles" as a translator are reflected in the text. In Avasvaru 1 of the first *Puranna*, he describes the Trinity of the Father, Son and the Holy Spirit:

Pita Putru dog*a*i z*a*nn*a*	Both the Father and the Son
Anny Spiritu Sanctu ap*a*nn*a*	And the Holy Spirit himself
Z*a*ri zahale teg*a* z*a*nn*a*	Though they are three persons
T*a*ri teg*a* Deu*a* nh*a*u*a*ty	Yet they are not three Gods
Teg*a* z*a*nnanchẽ yec*a*chi t*a*tu*a*	The three are made of one matter
Yequi pr*a*cruti yec*a* suamitu*a*	One nature and one lordship
Yec*a*chi Deu*a*pann*a* yec*a* z*a*nn*a*tu*a*	One godhead, one knowledge
Mh*a*nnoni teg*a*i z*a*nn*a* yecuchi Deuo	Therefore the three are One God

(Kristapurāṇa 1.1.17, 18)

In this passage, the Padre-guru explains the concept of "Trinity" to his listeners. We sense an anxiety in the tone of the narrator that the Hindu converts may assume that Christians believe in three Gods. So, Stephens quickly clarifies that the Father, Son and Holy Spirit, "Though they are three persons/Yet they are not three Gods" ("Z*a*ri zahale teg*a* z*a*nn*a*/T*a*ri teg*a* Deu*a* nh*a*u*a*ty"). They are made of one substance and share one godhead. The apprehension of a Catholic priest translating the biblical narrative into a form sacred to the Hindus of the region can be clearly seen here. While he admirably adapts the Christian message to fit into an ancient poetic genre, we see in passages like the one quoted above that he hastens to make a distinction between the many Gods of the Hindus and the "triune" God of Christianity. *Pita*, *Putru*, and *Spiritu Sanctu* are three but their essence is one and they are "one God".

These dilemmas faced by a missionary undertaking cultural translation of the Bible are evident in several other passages in the text. In the part where the Padre-guru narrates the life of Joseph, he tells his listeners about Joseph's dreams, their interpretation, and how they were fulfilled (1.12.62–87). However, he is quick to emphasize that not all dreams are from God and that they should not put too much trust in traditional, local interpretations of dreams. Throughout the text, the strategy is to translate the biblical story and at the same time emphasize the difference of the Christian story from Hindu ways of life.

Stephens' anxiety can be understood against the background of the restrictions placed on translation of Catholic literature into regional languages.[28] Lynne Long quotes from the *Liturgiam Authenticam*, a document of the Catholic Church created after the Second Vatican Council (1962–1965), giving instructions on the use of the vernacular in liturgy:

> … it is to be kept in mind from the beginning that the translation of liturgical texts of the Roman Liturgy is not so much a work of creative innovation as it is of rendering the original texts faithfully and accurately into the vernacular language.
>
> *(Long 2005, 6)*

The distrust of the inherently heretical nature of translation existed in similar intensity during Stephens' times. Translations of Christian texts into vernacular languages had to be cleared by the Inquisitor's office and "creative innovation" was generally discouraged. Hence, the anxiety of the translator as there is the danger of the text assimilating into the indigenous literary tradition (Xavier and Županov 230) and the anxiety of the "translated", the local audience, of seeing a foreign message delivered in a form familiar to them.

In placing the Christian God in Vaicunttha, Stephens trod the fine line between heresy and cultural translation. He submits to existing social conventions in order to effectively communicate with his readership. His use of the idea of Vaicunttha is an example of this cultural submission. Simultaneously, he had to make a decision to leave terms like "Spiritu sanctu" and "trindad" untranslated in order to guard against the danger of the narrative slipping back into the repertoire of Hindu beliefs. The study of Vaicunttha in *Kristapurāṇa* sensitizes a reader to the balance between "heresy" and "accuracy" that a translator had to maintain while translating a sacred text.

Important Christian terms in *Kristapurāṇa* remained in Portuguese or Latin and were not translated into the target language. In the verse on Trinity quoted above, it is significant that the term for Holy Spirit, "Spiritu Sanctu" remains untranslated into Marathi. Untranslatability helped translators of sacred texts to maintain the 'purity' (Rafael 2012, 29) of sacred terms. Core terms like *Spiritu Sanctu* (Holy Spirit), *prophetu* (prophets), and *trinidad* (trinity) have been retained in Portuguese or Latin in *Kristapurāṇa*. While writing about similar untranslated Catholic concepts in

Tagalog society, Rafael argues that it may also have served the purpose of standard-izing the Catholic faith that was spreading across several geographical boundaries.[29] Translation was unavoidable because the extent of evangelization and conversion was determined by translations of Christian texts. At the same time, untranslatabil-ity was used as a guard against the dangers of translation.

The purāṇic genre, of all other Hindu literary genres, must have seemed suitable to Stephens as the Purāṇas primarily dealt with individual deities.

> But besides these and other particulars, which may be derivable from an old, if not from a primitive era, they offer characteristic peculiarities of a more modern description, in the paramount importance which they assign to individual divinities, in the variety and purport of the rites and observances addressed to them, and in the invention of new legends illustrative of the power and graciousness of those deities, and of the efficacy of implicit devo-tion to them. Śiva and Vishńu, under one or other form, are almost the sole objects that claim the homage of the Hindus in the Puráńas; departing from the domestic and elemental ritual of the Vedas.
>
> *(Wilson 1840, iv, v)*

The "paramount importance" that Purāṇas "assign to individual deities" as opposed to the Vedic emphasis on rituals, provided a suitable space for Stephens to replace the figure of Vishnu with Jesus Christ in his *Vaicunttha*. It is significant to note that even though Stephens appropriated the space of Vaicunttha as the abode of the Trinity, he does not use the name "Vishnu" to mean the Christian God. In a conscious translatorial decision to empty a space of its pre-Christian meaning and invest it with Christian ones, Vaicunttha and the sacredness attributed to it is retained, while Christ is enthroned as the ruler of Vaicunttha. The purāṇic genre becomes the metaphoric temple in which the deity of Christ is sanctified in seven-teenth-century Goa, just as Vishnu's *Vaicunttha* becomes "our heaven of glory and blessedness". The Jesus of the Bible becomes *Jeju-Swami, Kristu-Swami, Vaikunth-raja, Vaikunth-nayak*, completely translated into a form with which the readers could identify. Israel, in her article "Words … Borrow'd from Our Books", quotes a con-versation in Tamil among a Danish missionary and the locals of Tamil Nadu. The locals accused the missionary of borrowing from the very books they criticized:

> "… your books have no letters, but ours; and no Words, but what are bor-row'd from our books, and from our language." The missionary replies saying, "tho' your Words are very good, yet what you mean by them is Falshood [sic] and Vanity".
>
> *(Israel 2008, 38)*

For these early missionaries, the existing sacred vocabularies were icons which could be emptied of their meaning and filled with the meanings of their choice by cultural translation. There is a deliberate cultural politics involved in this emptying and refilling of meaning into existing sacred vocabularies. Long notes, in her edited volume *Translation and Religion* (2005), that one of the major challenges in translating holy texts is to negotiate the already existing 'sacred' vocabulary. "… the holy resists translation, since the space it needs in the target language is often already occupied; available vocabulary is already culturally loaded with indigenous referents" (Long 2005, 1). Early Catholic missionaries took existing vocabulary and invested them with Christian meanings to aid in the conversion of locals to Christianity.

The neo-Catholics of seventeenth-century Konkan were undergoing a process of translation, breaking away from their own lineage of faith and rituals to become members of a new tradition. This text, written in the tradition of regional poets, and containing the "new" story of salvation, may have provided the historical and doctrinal background of their new faith by expressing "the Christian experience in a language familiar to the Hindus" (Falcao 2003, 39). *Kristapurāṇa* can be seen as a monumental effort by Stephens in his attempt to translate the local Konkani man/woman, into a worthy member of the kingdom of God. Stephens seemed to have been creating novel literary and cultural "spaces", while combining two different "sacred" cultures and in this process, rewriting both the traditions involved in the cultural encounter.

Cultural translation is one of the channels through which novelization of the epic genre such as the Purāṇa occurs. In this process, new literary traditions are created in the culture of the target text. A work like *Kristapurāṇa* was not meant to be a single piece of literature to preach the gospel. The entire literary culture of the region was to be revolutionized in order to establish Christianity in the region and wipe out the memories of the old religious texts of Hinduism. The translation and untranslatability in *Kristapurāṇa* modified the language in the process of translation, introducing into Marathi literature terms such as *Spiritu Sanctu* and *Trinidad*. Stephens was, thus, taking far more effective steps in spreading and establishing his religion than other methods of forced conversion.

The translation and untranslatability that occurs during the cultural transmission of scriptures is evident in readings of *Kristapurāṇa*. Missionaries who worked in cross-cultural missions were well aware of the power of indigenous languages and literary traditions in converting people to a new religion. This process of inculturation, though undertaken with the primary, practical purpose of converting people, gives a whole new shape and essence to both the cultures involved in this process. It would not be inaccurate, then, to describe Stephens as the "father of inculturation in India" (Falcao 2003, lxv) and his *Kristapurāṇa* as one of the earliest examples, in South Asia, of a text that embodies this process of cultural translation and generic transformation. Through Stephens's cultural translation, the purāṇic genre was transformed and a new literary tradition of Christian Purāṇas was created. In this process, spaces such as Vaicunttha were transformed into Christian places, and became part of the spiritual landscape of the new converts in Goa. The transformation of landscapes and creation of novel geographical terrains through cultural translation in *Kristapurāṇa* is analysed in the following chapter.

Notes

1 *Medieval Indian Literature: An Anthology*, edited by Ayyappa Panikker, translated by Nelson Frazer and K.B. Marathe, p. 561.

2 The criteria for classifying works in to genre have evolved over time beginning from Plato who identified three genre – lyric, epic, and drama – to present times when genre is used as a mode for reading film and New Media. Derrida argued, in 'The Law of Genre' (1980), that literary texts 'participate' in several genres rather than 'belonging' to any particular genre. According to Hans Robert Jauss, in *Towards an Aesthetic of Reception* (1982), genres are not logical classes, but "groups or historical families" (Jauss 1982 80; Frow 2006, 70). Gerard Genette, in *Paratexts: Thresholds of Interpretation* (1987), writes about the external signs that surround a work of literature. Even before a book is read, the "paratexts" such as the title of the text, or its size and preface give an indication of its genre and affect the reception of the text. Georg Lukács, in his 1969 work *Probleme der Ästhetik*, argues that artistic genres "grow out of the concrete determinacy of the particular social and historical conditions. Their character, their peculiarity is determined by their capacity to give expression to the essential features of the given socio-historical phase" (Lukács 1969, 118; Frow 2006, 135).

3 John Frow writes, in *Genre: The New Critical Idiom* (2006): "Genre … is a set of conventional and highly organized constraints on the production and interpretation of meaning. … Generic structure both enables and restricts meaning, and is a basic condition for meaning to take place" (10).

4 Hans Robert Jauss, in his *Towards an Aesthetic of Reception* (1982), coined the term "horizon of expectations" that forms the background of the reception of any text (Jauss 95).

5 Miriam Salama-Carr, in "Translation and the Creation of Genre: The Theatre in Nineteenth Century Egypt" (2006), argues that literary translation is one of the key channels of cultural transfer which leads to the creation of new genre (314). She points out that the introduction of French plays in Egypt and their translation into Arabic led to modes of adaptation as well as the subversion of European source texts. The first phase of this process of translation was a straightforward enactment of European plays in their source language(s) on the Egyptian stage. Eventually, these plays began to be translated into Arabic, and "showed varying degrees of adaptation and acculturation" (315). These plays were "subverted" and integrated into local forms as folk drama and shadow theatre, leading to the creation of new genre. The translation of these plays also revealed the tensions between "classical" Arabic and the Egyptian vernacular, which was the preferred language for the translation of these plays (316). As a part of the Arabic renaissance, the European plays "engaged, via translation, with local forms of representation and migrated to a new genre, which contributed to the construction of national identity" (Salama-Carr 2006, 323).

6 The *Kamparamayana* is a telling of the *Ramayana* in Tamil, composed by the poet Kampan (Das 2005, 60).

7 In his Latin writings, de Nobili argued that

> just as Christianity legitimately adopted many of the local customs and even religious practices of The Greco-Roman world and successfully endowed these with 'Christian significance', it is equally legitimate to practice this adaptation when Christianity encounters other great civilizations beyond the boundaries of Europe.
>
> *(Clooney 2020, 51)*

8 There are later examples of poetic retellings of the Bible within the Protestant tradition as well, in languages such as Tamil, Bengali, and Marathi, among others, beginning in the nineteenth century. A significant Marathi example from the early twentieth century is the *Khristayana* (1919), a poetic retelling of Christ's life in the style of Marathi saint-poetry. *Khristayana* is attributed to Narayan Waman Tilak (1861–1919) and completed by his wife Lakshmibai Tilak (1868–1936) in 1919.

9 An epic is a work of literature that deals with great subjects and is centred around the figure of a "hero" whose actions have momentous effects on the human race. "Primary" epics like Homer's *Iliad* and *Odyssey* or South Asian epics such as *Ramayana* and *Mahabharata* developed from oral traditions whereas "secondary" or literary epics are in the written form from the start (Cuddon 231). Mikhail M. Bakhtin, in "Epic and Novel" (1941), notes that the epic is an antiquated genre. It requires a "national past" and an "epic distance" from the present (Bakhtin 1981a, 13). Lukács views the epic as a genre of the past, of a 'not-so-fragmented world':

> Many thinkers, notably Georg Lukács, have seen the epic form as the product of a relatively early and harmonious civilization, a form which is no longer feasible in a modern world riven by various modes of fragmentation. Lukács sees the novel as the epic of a world abandoned by God.
>
> *(Cuddon 1998, 241)*

10 The eighteen Mahapurāṇa are:

> Vayu Purāṇa; Brahmanda Purāṇa; Markandeya Purāṇa; Visnu Purāṇa; Matsya Purāṇa; Bahagavata Purāṇa; Kurma Purāṇa; Vamana Purāṇa; Linga Purāṇa; Varaha Purāṇa; Padma Purāṇa; Naradiya Purāṇa; Agni Purāṇa; Garuda Purāṇa; Brahma Purāṇa; Skanda Purāṇa; Brahmavaivarta Purāṇa; Bhavisya or Bhavisyat Purāṇa.
>
> *(Hazra 1937, 240)*

11 Owing to an inability to understand the primary Sanskrit texts well, all the scholarship on Purāṇas presented in this chapter is drawn from Indologists and Indian scholars who have written about Purāṇas in the English and Marathi languages.

12 One possible explanation suggested by scholars for the absence of all five of the distinguishing marks is the question of the "authorship" of Purāṇa. The eighteen great Purāṇas which are available currently are not the first Purāṇas. The theory of the divine origin of Purāṇas is that the first Purāṇas emerged from the fifth mouth of the god Brahma. These one billion *slokas* were arranged by Vyasa, "the Arranger", into eighteen Purāṇas for the mortal world (Coburn 1980, 344).

13 According to Rao,

> ...*pañcalakṣaṇa* is the ideological frame that transforms whatever content is incorporated into that frame. Since the ideas of *pañcalakṣaṇa* are tacitly assumed in the Brahmanic worldview, they do not appear in every Purāṇa and do not constitute a sizeable length of the text even when they appear.
>
> *(Rao 1993, 87, 88)*

14 V.N. Rao argues that the ancient Purāṇas were known to have not five, but ten distinguishing marks, or *dasalaksana* (Rao 1993, 89). I am indebted to B.N. Patnaik for pointing out the concept *dasalaksana*. Many of the questions discussed in this chapter, specifically the complexities of *pañcalakṣaṇa* and translations of Purāṇas into vernacular languages, were opened up in a conversation with him.

15 Rao discusses the "Puranization" of the folk story of *Kanyaka* in the Kannada language and elaborates on how it attained the position of a Purāṇa in the *Vasava Kanyaka Purāṇa* (Rao 1993, 89, 91).

16 Sarala Das was an Odia poet who lived in the fifteenth century AD. He is widely regarded as the originator of Odia literature. A digital copy of Vol. 3 and Vol. 4 of Sarala's Odia *Mahabharata* may be found on the following link: http://sites.iitgn.ac.in/digitalstudies/digital_repository/. This website is an initiative of the Digital Humanities group at the Indian Institute of Technology Gandhinagar.

17 V.N. Rao makes an interesting distinction between scribe and poet, between literate and illiterate. Rao notes that until the nineteenth century, there were traditional scholars who could not write. Though they could not write, these

Purāṇa scholars had all the sophistication of the language scholar, with a complete awareness of grammatical organization. Therefore, he set himself apart from the illiterate oral poet who not only could not write but also lacked any awareness of the grammar of his language.

(Rao 1993, 95)

18 S.G. Malshe's unpublished doctoral thesis "Father Stiphanschya Khristapuranacha Bhasik aani Vangmayina Abhyasa" (1961), is a voluminous study composed in Marathi and contains a chapter that provides a detailed comparison of *Kristapurāṇa* with other Marathi works that he considered to be inspirations for Stephens' work.

19 For Sheldon Pollock, the court was the epicentre of the process of vernacularization in many regional Indian languages (see Pollock 2006). Novetzke argues that in the case of Marathi, vernacularization took place in the field of everyday life, the "quotidian", outside of the royal courts (Novetzke 2016, 2). He defines vernacularization as "the strategic use of the topos of everyday life within a social, political, artistic, linguistic, and cultural process in which the quotidian ("ordinary", "everyday") expands at the center of a given region's public culture" (Novetzke 2016, 10). For Novetzke, vernacularization is a process that displays the nexus between power, language, and place in its relationship to a "public".

20 Marathi texts found in Portugal, as noted in Malshe's doctoral thesis:

Krishnacharitrakatha (Krishnadasnama); *Prahladcharitra* (Vishnudasnama); *Harishchandra Purāṇa Katha* (Vishnudasnama); *Vasishtayogu* (Jnandeo); *Garudachi Katha* (Sivdas?); *Balkreeda* (Simpnama); *Harnichi Katha* (Author unknown); *Rajneetichya Ovya*; *Bhagvad Gitechi Teeka* (Nivruttidev); *Ramacha Ashwamegh*; *Sukhdev Charitrakatha*; *Gurushishya Samvad*; *Madalsa*; *Rukmini Swayamvar*; *Dharmacha Aswamegh* (Vishnudasnama); *Varna Parva* (Vishnudasnama); *Seetaharan*; *Krushnarjunacha Samvadu*; *Mrugarajachi Katha*.

Marathi texts translated into Portuguese:

Yograj Tilak; *Viveksindhu* (Mukundraj); *Jnaneswari*; Poetry of Vishnudasnama; *Anadi Purāṇa*. Malshe had created this list based on a 1953 essay by Prof. Panduronga Pissurlencar describing the finding of early Marathi texts in Portugal. It is argued that some of these handwritten Marathi texts are in Stephens's handwriting.

(Malshe 1961, 425, 426)

21 The following *abhanga* by the Marathi saint-poet Namdev (c.1270–c.1350) echoes similar feelings of love for Vitthala:

I shall never budge from your feet
I swear by you, O Lord of Pandhari
Your name on my lips
And our interminable constant love shall remain forever.

(From Ayyappa Panikker, Medieval Indian Literature: An Anthology,
trans. Pradeep Gopal Deshpande, p. 501)

This is an indicative example from the vast corpus that includes Marathi saint-poetry. The verse quoted at the beginning of this chapter is a translation of an *abhanga* by Tukaram, from this same tradition of saint-poetry. Tukaram and Stephens were contemporaries. The extract has been translated by Nelson Frazer and K.B. Marathe (see Panikker 1999, 561).

22 The phrase "Ghrute simpila vaisuanaru" (1.12.33) has been used in *Kristapurāṇa* several times to describe anger, which flares like fire when *ghee* is poured into it. This is compared by Malshe to "Zaise ghrute simpila agni" from a Marathi text known as *Mahimchi Bakhar* (c.1500) (Malshe 1961, 461). This phrase, however, is a common one used by Marathi poets before and after Stephens to describe anger. Malshe's comparative reading of passages from *Kristapurāṇa* and Marathi Purāṇas is a rich study which reveals the manner in which Marathi Purāṇas were developing their own distinctive style.

23 In "Discourse in the Novel" (1934–1935), Bakhtin writes that "In the poetic image narrowly conceived [in the image-as-trope), all activity-the dynamics of the image-as-word-is completely exhausted by the play between the word [with all its aspects1 and the object (in all its aspects). The word plunges into the inexhaustible wealth and contradictory multiplicity of the object itself, with its 'virginal,' still 'unuttered' nature; therefore it presumes nothing beyond the borders of its own context (except, of course, what can be found in the treasure-house of language itself)" (Bakhtin 1981b, 278). As opposed to this, in the novel, "an image can fully unfold, achieve full complexity and depth and at the same time artistic closure …" (Bakhtin 1981b, 278).

24 "Dialogue", here, is taken to mean both the words exchanged between the characters of the text, as well as moments wherein diverse texts and traditions speak to one another in the process of cultural translation. In the "Introduction" to the work *In Dialogue with Classical Indian Traditions: Encounter, Transformation and Interpretation* (2019: Introduction), Brian Black and Chakravarthi Ram-Prasad note that dialogue forms a "recurring and significant component of Indian religious and philosophical literature". This dialogue could be a "a language-loaded encounter between two or more interlocutors whether these interlocutors are people – real or imagined – or texts – either contemporaneous or of different historical periods". The articles in this volume study different aspects of dialogue in various Indian classical texts.

25 It is significant to note here that the catechism of the Catholic Church also followed the format of a dialogue between the priest and the confessor. Stephens's Konkani Doutrina Christa, a translation of Marcos Jorge's catechism, was written in this format. Jorge's Portuguese catechism, also known as the "Big Catechism", was written in similar question-and-answer style (Županov 2012, 422). This a spect of dialogue among priests and converts requires further study in the context of *Kristapurāṇa*.

26 The spelling of "suarga" (heaven) is as per Stephens's Romanization in *Kristapurāṇa*, except in quotations where individual authors have used other spellings.

27 Translated from Amonkar's Konkani work. Translation mine, in consultation with Amonkar.

28 The aversion to translation of religious texts extended to all religions and their sacred texts. Steiner writes, in *After Babel*, "To mutilate a single word in the Torah, to set it in the wrong order, might be to imperil the tenuous links between fallen man and the Divine presence" (63). Translation of sacred texts was, thus, approached with caution in all religions through the ages.

29 One of the significant moves towards standardization in the Catholic Church was the "Council of Trent". The Council of Trent (1545–1563) was held in Trent and Bologna, Northern Italy. It is considered as one of the most important ecumenical councils of the Catholic Church. The Council was a reaction against the Reformation movements (Rafael 2012, 29).

4

(RE)PAINTING LANDSCAPES, (RE)INVENTING TRADITION

> For it seems to me that neither the frontiers between the wild and the cultivated, nor those that lie between the past and the present, are so easily fixed. … The sum of our pasts, generation laid over generation, like the slow mold of the seasons forms the compost of our future. We live off it.[1]
>
> *(Simon Schama,* Landscape and Memory*)*

4.1 Geography, Memory, and Cultural Translation

The Tower of Babel has long been used as a metaphor for translation. The act of translation was viewed as a constant endeavour to reconcile the scattering of languages that took place at Babel. In this chapter, the scene is invoked for its striking visual quality and to underscore the nature of spaces in the scene. Babel, in this context, conjoins the metaphorical image of translation with the symbolism associated with landscapes:

> Now the whole world had one language and a common speech. As people moved eastward, they found a plain in Shinar and settled there. They said to each other, "Come, let's make bricks and bake them thoroughly." They used brick instead of stone, and tar for mortar. Then they said, "Come, let us build ourselves a city, with a tower that reaches to the heavens, so that we may make a name for ourselves; otherwise we will be scattered over the face of the whole earth." But the Lord came down to see the city and the tower the people were building. The Lord said, "If as one people speaking the same language they have begun to do this, then nothing they plan to do will be impossible for them. Come, let us go down and confuse their language so they will not understand each other." So the Lord scattered them from there

DOI: 10.4324/9781003146544-5

over all the earth, and they stopped building the city. That is why it was called Babel—because there the Lord confused the language of the whole world.

(NIV, Gen. 11:1–9)

The land that the tower stood on and its relationship to the aspirations of the people setting out to build it have been under-explored themes in the field of Translation Studies. The Tower of Babel was firmly situated in the plains on which it stood. The people set out to build the tower to "make a name" for themselves, and out of the desire to be rooted in a land rather than being "scattered". They travelled eastward, surveyed the landscape of Shinar and decided to build their city on the plains. This scene opens up questions of the ties between geography, travel, and memory – themes that also emerge from a reading of the translated landscapes in *Kristapurāṇa*. The fateful tower situated on the plains of Shinar is an image that symbolizes the "need" for translation, a tower that has its foundations in tropes of culture(s), topographies, and the desire for rootedness.

This image of Babel may also be seen as a metaphor for the "spatial turn" in Translation Studies. Federico Italiano, in *Translation and Geography* (2016), discusses the "spatial turn" in Translation Studies (Italiano 3).[2] The study of translation in the context of geography is an important exercise in thinking beyond the linguistic confines in which translation has been studied. It places translation within the framework of the geographical settings in which knowledge and power were transacted through acts of translation.

The critical analysis in this chapter grapples with the vocabulary of geography and translation in order to locate the relationship between translation and the representation of landscapes in *Kristapurāṇa*. In addition, this discussion also brings to fore the complexities that arise when translated landscapes were part of sacred texts and were meant as an alternative to the religious landscape of the region. The aspect of early Portuguese colonialism, and the accompanying transformation that took place in the topography of colonies like Goa, as reflected in *Kristapurāṇa*, is another focal point in this chapter. The transformation of Stephens into a translator, who could enter Hinduism through its texts and introduce Christianity to the locals, is a crucial aspect of cultural translation. By deciding to "enter by the door of the other in order to make them come out" (Županov, *Disputed Mission* 126), Stephens used local customs and landscapes as a door to enter the world of the locals and lead them out to Christianity. Cultural translation may also be read in the transformed biblical landscapes of *Kristapurāṇa*. Rather than just creating "linguistic equivalents" of the places of the Bible in Marathi, Stephens was carefully painting regional nuances from Goa in his text. *Kristapurāṇa* therefore appears as a Christian narrative with distinct South Asian visual characteristics.

This idea of space and cultural translation gains special significance in the context of a text such as *Kristapurāṇa* which was composed within the Portuguese colonial context. Discovery of new lands was one of the driving factors in early imperial expeditions and the translational encounters that took place as result of these colonial missions. These ideas of land, conquest, memory, and translation are intertwined in the narrative of *Kristapurāṇa*.

Kristapurāṇa has a distinct visual quality, bringing to mind the transformations that were underway in seventeenth-century Goa. Rather than being a text with specific scenes of natural beauty, it comes across as a dynamic creative force, calling into existence new topologies. *Kristapurāṇa* is dense, with vivid descriptions combining biblical landscapes with the natural, social, and cultural landscape of Goa. In the following sections, the abundance of landscape writing in the text is located and analysed in some detail. The geographical and cultural terrain of Goa is intricately woven into the text, resulting in a large number of passages in which landscape can be read. Episodes with vibrant landscapes can be seen in Stephens's descriptions of the Garden of Eden (1.3.46–93), the Great Flood (1.7.47–52), the Promised Land (1.22.14–18), and the Virgin Mary's beauty (1.2.150–152), among numerous other such passages. The scope of this discussion is vast and difficult to be encapsulated in one study. In this chapter, a close reading of the text is undertaken to illustrate the use of landscape in the text and to explore whether a critical relationship between translation, cultures, and landscape exists.

Stephens's *Kristapurāṇa* can be read as a site where Christianity and indigenous literary practices come together to form a "creative" expression of Christianity strongly reminiscent of the region in which it was produced. The word "creative" has been used here in two senses: (a) the use of imagination to conceptualize a novel form of literature; and (b) the power of a work of translation to call into existence new topologies. As readers enter the narrative of this text, biblical lands unfold before them. These lands are wondrous terrains where ancient places/spaces from the Bible merge into the social and geographical terrain of seventeenth-century Goa. In *Kristapurāṇa*, descriptions of ancient Egypt and Palestine abound with flora and fauna from Konkan while discussions on the divinity of Christ are set alongside examples of caste and "idol worship" of the Konkan region.

The term "landscape" may be defined as "a natural scene mediated by culture" (Mitchell 2002, 5).[3] W.J.T. Mitchell argues, in *Landscape and Power*, that landscape is a cultural construct. It is closely tied up with an individual's sense of place and identity. It is interpreted and created by the human mind. Rather than a mere physical, geographical space, it denotes mental and cultural representations of space. The portrayal of a landscape in a certain light, the attribution of sacredness (or profaneness) to them, are all creative of human agents. Barbara Bender, in "Time and Landscape" (2002), argues that landscapes are not objective.

> Landscapes are created out of people's understanding and engagement with the world around them. They are always in process of being shaped and reshaped. Being of the moment and in process, they are always temporal. They are not a record but a recording, and this recording is much more than a reflection of human agency and action; it is *creative* of them.
>
> *(Bender 2002, 103)*

Nature exists outside of human beings, but its interpretation and categorization takes place through humans (Bender 104). There exists a physical, natural world which is the geographical aspect of landscape while at the same time there is a cultural aspect that is manifested in literature, paintings, and other cultural artefacts. Hubert Zapf argues that "literature is a cultural form where culture and nature meet" (Zapf 2017, 3). As a cultural form, literature embodies the "interconnectedness" (Zapf 2017, 11) between humanity and nature. The "aesthetic" (Zapf 2017, 5) of literature does not merely use landscape as an adornment or setting. They are a "vital mode of ecological knowledge and transformation" (Zapf 2017, 5).

In "Invention, Memory, and Place" (2002), Said states that memory and geography are imagined spaces, that are "constructed" by the human mind (Said 2002, 243). Thus, landscape emerges as both a physical space as well as a space in human memory. Said further argues that "Geography stimulates not only memory but dreams and fantasies, poetry and painting, philosophy …, fiction …, and music …" (Said 2002, 247). The collective memory of communities is tied with the terrain of the land they inhabit. A disruption of this relationship creates a rupture in the tradition of the region. Simon Schama, in *Landscape and Memory* (1995), argues that "… landscape is the work of the mind. Its scenery is built up as much from strata of memory as from layers of rock" (Schama 1996, 7). Schama's voluminous work on landscape emphasizes that landscape is a repository of human memory, "obsessions" (Schama 1996, 18) and cultural imaginations. Landscapes are invested with the memories and aspirations of communities which call them their own. An unsettling of the landscape of any region, such as in colonial contexts, would have implications on the cultural memory associated with the landscape.

Land was the tangible, visual element in imperial ventures and their encounters with conquered regions. In his article "Invention, Memory, and Place", Said describes the relationship between land and conquest as the "hold of geography and memory on the desire for conquest and domination" (Said 2002, 247). While examining the construction of Palestine as a historically significant landscape, Said notes the "powerful hold" that "locale" had on Western crusaders despite their "enormous distance" from Palestine (246). The idealized landscapes of Palestine that were represented in Renaissance paintings reinforced the Western perception of the "Holy Land". The ownership that the crusaders felt over the Palestinian landscape is an example of the allure of imagined geographies. He argues that geographical imagination and conquest go hand in hand:

> It is easy to see the fact of displacement in these colonial enterprises, which at the bottom is the replacement of one geographical sovereignty, an imperialist one, by another, native force. More subtle and complex is the unending cultural struggle over territory, which necessarily involves overlapping memories, narratives, and physical structures.
>
> *(Said 2002, 247, 248)*

The contests for dominion over territory lead to "complicated memories" (247) and a palimpsest of complex narratives and traditions. Given the centrality of landscape in the colonial narrative and the vital relationship between translation and conquest, not much thought has been given to representation of landscapes in works of translation.

In order to deal with the "locational disrupture" (Bassnett and Trivedi 1999, 13) in colonial narratives, a new landscape must be created. Said argues that literature is one of the ways in which traditions are "invented" (Said 244). Since traditions and geography are closely linked, the invention of tradition also involves the invention of new landscapes, and terrains where the locals can reimagine[4] their identity. Bella Brodzki, in *Can These Bones Live?* (2007), argues that translation is one of the routes through which survival is ensured: "Translation is the mode through which what is dead disappeared, forgotten, buried, or suppressed overcomes its determined fate by being borne (and thus born anew) to other contexts across time and space…" (Brodzki 2007, 6). She further notes that "Through the act of translation, remnants and fragments are inscribed – reclaimed and reconstituted as a narrative – and then recollected collectively" (6). Translation may thus be seen as one of the routes through which the invention of tradition takes place in sites of rupture and fragmentation. The present reading of *Kristapurāṇa* argues that cultural translation aids in this "invention of tradition"[5] by creating new landscapes for the colonized to reimagine their identities. These landscapes provide an anchor to the colonized in the context of the loss of their land and their traditions.

The landscape writing in *Kristapurāṇa* draws attention to the cultural translation undertaken by Stephens in composing this text. The novel terrains which rise out of the narrative are indicative of the careful painting of landscapes by the translator. As Stephens attempts to negotiate Goan customs and the locals attempt to make sense of the Christian way of life, they meet in a mediating landscape of cultural translation which is neither completely biblical nor completely Goan. The present chapter reads these landscapes to understand their position in such encounters of cultural translation.

Landscape is a major thread that weaves its way through the entire narrative of *Kristapurāṇa*. The term "landscape", here, is used to mean both Stephens' depiction of the natural world as well as the socio-cultural landscape of the region. It is used in the sense of the natural, geographical imagery of flora and fauna described by Stephens in the text. It is also taken to mean the social and cultural details that are woven into the text that lend a unique "local" texture. The natural world, trees, animals, and flowers specifically from South Asian regions, provide local colour to the narrative while the socio-cultural landscape that emerges from *Kristapurāṇa* familiarizes readers with seventeenth-century Goa. In the following sections, the themes of travel, conquest, literary symbolism, memory, and the creation of new topographies are drawn out of the text in order to understand the place of landscapes in cultural translations. Each of the following sections deals with one of these several layers of landscape writing in *Kristapurāṇa*.

4.2 Travel, Landscapes, and Cultural Translation

Stephens and his relationship with the land of Goa can be read along two lines: (a) Stephens as a European traveller who marvelled at the landscape of sixteenth-century Goa, and (b) Stephens as a poet-priest and author of *Kristapurāṇa*, who had to take into consideration local cultures and cultural landscape in order to have been able to compose a literary work of epic proportions. Stephens's transformation from a traveller to a poet and translator emerges as we study his poetic work, *Kristapurāṇa*.

In the letter to his father in 1579, Stephens recorded his first impressions of the Goan landscape:

> The first signs of land were certain fowls, which they knew to be of India; the second, boughs of palms and sedges; the third, snakes swimming on the water, and a substance which they call by the name of a coin of money, as broad and as round as a groat, wonderfully painted and stamped by nature, like unto some coin. And these two last signs be so certain that the next day after, if the wind swerve, they see land, which we did to our great joy, when all our water (for you know that they make no beer in those parts) and victuals began to fail us; and to Goa we came the 24th of October, there being received with passing great charity. The people be tawny, but not disfigured in their lips and noses, as the Moors and Kaffirs of Ethiopia. They that be not of reputation, or at least the most part go naked, saving an apron of a span long and as much in breadth before them, and a lace two fingers broad before them, girded about with a string, and no more. And thus they think themselves as well as we with all our trimming.
>
> *(Stephens and Saldanha 1907, XXIX)*

In the passage quoted above, Stephens had to "translate" the appearance of the local population into terms that were familiar to his father, a London merchant. Stephens' description of the locals is from the point of view of a traveller. They are described as "tawny" and compared to natives of Africa. Their dress and appearance is interpreted within a British framework by Stephens, the traveller. The descriptions of Goa in Stephens' letters bring out the difference of the "other" as he attempts to convey his first impressions of the region to his father. This epistolary representation of the Goan landscape brings out what Said, in his *Orientalism* (1978), explains as "the difference between the familiar (Europe, West, "us") and the strange (the Orient, the East, "them")" (Said 1978, 51). The image of the "tawny", "almost-naked" Goan portrayed by Stephens reinforces what Said describes as the stereotypical representation of the "Orient" by colonial writers. Early travel writings contain some of the best examples of such orientalist descriptions of the inhabitants of "other" lands.

Casey Blanton, in *Travel Writing: The Self and the World* (1997), writes that the travel writer has a desire to "mediate between things foreign and things familiar" (Blanton 2). Several levels of translation are required to "mediate" the languages, customs, and other cultural nuances of a new landscape. This involves basic negotiation of day-to-day needs in a foreign language, to more complex transactions of travel writing where the "foreign" is translated into terms that are familiar to a home readership (Cronin 2000, 35). The process of translation for a traveller begins as soon as he departs for foreign shores. The early impressions formed by the traveller are a part of the process of negotiating the unfamiliar landscape of a geographical region. In the case of travel writing, these early impressions of the traveller are documented, and determine the ways in which these foreign lands are conveyed to readers back home. In the letter to his brother, Stephens gives a detailed description of the coconut palms that grow abundantly in Goa:

> We have here a tree oftener seen than the elm or the vine, called the Palm on account of its likeness to it, or perhaps because it is really so, if you admit that palm is a generic word and consists of two species. It gives oil, liquor (vinum), toddy (lac), syrup (mel), sugar and vinegar. Coir-rope is also made from it to tie with, and its branches are used to protect huts from rain. It gives fruit all the year round, which are rather nuts than dates, resembling a man's head. When the exterior rind has been removed, they equal the size of two fists. Inside, the fruit contains water like light beer and good to quench one's thirst. It is so plentiful that, after drinking from one fruit, you would not look for another. In the interior of the nut is a kernel lining it all over like a covering and forming a prized article of food. The shell furnishes the blacksmith with charcoal. Those that live near the sea not only load their boats with the tree, but also utilise it for making ropes and sails. You will find hardly any piece of writing except on its leaves. Those that live on land invariably make use of them to shelter themselves from rain.
>
> *(Stephens and Saldanha 1907, XXXIV)*

Stephens presents a detailed description of the coconut palm and its uses. He enumerates that every part of the tree is used in the region in one form or the other. The coconut palm and its uses in India have been a subject of wonderment for European travellers through the ages. The ways in which these early travellers depicted landscape affected the way in which readers in their homelands perceived the region. The Orient was long seen as an exotic, unconquerable realm inhabited by fantastic creatures.[6] According to Xavier and Županov, the Orient was considered a symbol of the lost Biblical Eden (Xavier and Županov 2015, 14).

A study of Stephens' writings is a study of how he evolved from these descriptions of the landscape to a participant in the landscape and its literary traditions. From the initial wonderment of the traveller and Eurocentric descriptions of the Goan landscape, Stephens progresses during his four decades of missionary life in India to be a poet-priest who was aware of the literary conventions of the Marathi language of his period.

Stephens' life, and the Christian message that he carried with him, were both transformed in the process of cultural translation that began as soon as he set foot on Indian shores. In his essay "Hi Mho Jhi Kudd: Thomas Stephens's translated Flesh, or, Coconuts in Goa" (2013), Harris argues that Stephens underwent a bodily transformation just as the bread in the Catholic Eucharist is believed to transform into the body of Christ.[7] According to Harris, Stephens was "altered by his exposure to new cultures and a radically new climate" (Harris 2013, 492). Harris discusses two kinds of transformation: (a) transformation of the flesh due to the climate and food of the region, and (b) transformation due to the language(s) of the region. In the first instance, the heat and tropical weather in the region altered the bodies of early European travellers. The food that they ate in these tropical climates added to the understanding that their bodies were hardly unchanging. Stephens' body was altered by his physical absorption of the elements of the land:

> Traveling and feeding in India, then, meant absorbing the matter of India into one's body. This entailed becoming other than what one had been. For Thomas Stephens's passage to India was inseparable from the transformative passage of India's physical elements through his flesh.
>
> *(Harris 2013, 494)*

In addition to this, Stephens was also learning the languages of the region. He was well versed in Portuguese, the language of the colonial administrators of Goa. He knew Konkani well enough to compose the first grammar of the language and Marathi, in which *Kristapurāṇa* was composed. Harris argues that this is bound to have changed Stephens's "bodily habits" in the way he spoke:

> Pronouncing Marathi's different consonants and vowels, and what he calls its "liquids" and its "mutes," would have required him to transform how he used his facial and labial muscles. His eccentric yet systematic Romanized spelling of Marathi in *Kristapurāṇa*, with its use of italicization and diacritical marks to distinguish between different vowel sounds and its meticulous distinction between different dental consonants that sound identical to most English speakers (d, dd, dh, ddh, t, tt, th, tth), shows how much attention Stephens had paid to the nuances of Marathi pronunciation and to getting these right. Speaking Marathi also changed the Christianity he sought to bring to his readers.
>
> *(Harris 2013, 497)*

The language changed Stephens' bodily behaviour as well as the text he was translating, and, in the process, creating a unique form of Christianity in the region. Stephens had to "use" his body differently once he reached Goa, leading to "an ongoing process of fleshly transformation", which is a part of the process of "cultural translation" that takes place in migration to colonial settings (Harris 2013, 492). This in turn added local colour to the cultural translation of the biblical narrative that Stephens wanted to convey to the locals of Goa.

As a translator attempting to transform the "spiritual landscape" of a region, Stephens had to be well versed with the physical landscape of the region which inspired his work. The sights and sounds of seventeenth-century Goa became an integral part of Stephens' translation of the Biblical narrative, as will be seen in the following close reading of passages from *Kristapurāṇa*. These verses display an appreciation of the language and the literary traditions of the saint-poets of the region. The representation of landscape thus becomes a lens for the reader through which he/she can watch the evolution of Stephens from an "Orientalist" traveller to a participant of the saint-poet tradition in Marathi. In the next section, landscapes in *Kristapurāṇa* are situated through the framework of literary symbols and images.

4.3 Symbols, Images, and Landscapes in *Kristapurāṇa*

In *Kristapurāṇa*, the culture(s) of the target audience is deeply woven into the biblical story, thereby transforming biblical landscape(s). The most striking and frequent use of landscape in *Kristapurāṇa* is as "symbol" for events in the narrative. Mitchell notes in his edited volume *Landscape and Power* (2002) that landscape may be used as symbols:

> It is clear that landscape can be deciphered as textual systems. Natural features such as trees, stones, water, animals and dwellings can be read as symbols in religious, psychological, or political allegories; characteristic structures and forms can be linked with generic and narrative typologies such as the pastoral, the georgic, the exotic, the sublime, the picturesque.
>
> *(Mitchell 1)*

Landscape is analysed by Mitchell, not just as a picturesque space. It is a "body of symbolic forms capable of being invoked and reshaped to express meaning and values" (Mitchell 2002, 14). It is understood as a space which has cultural and symbolic value for individuals associated with the landscape.

Stephens made use of the natural features of the Konkan region as "concrete images" (Cuddon 1998, 699) to convey the emotions and ideas that are central to the text. The "trees, stones, water, animals and dwellings" of the region are used by Stephens as symbols while narrating *Kristapurāṇa*. The presence of familiar symbols gives readers an experience of walking through familiar terrain while attempting to comprehend a completely unfamiliar religious tradition like Christianity. This provides a route for the "local" to enter Stephens's Christian narrative and leads to a transformation of the biblical narrative.

Kristapurāṇa begins with praises to the "Almighty God" (1.1.1) and goes on give its readers a description of a "prelapsarian" Eden. Stephens described the Garden as "anandasthan",[8] "place of joy". It is an idyllic setting, where the lamb does not fear to lay down with the lion (1.4.84). The birds make "poetry" in their various languages. A river and its tributaries flow musically through the garden. The landscape in these passages reflects the situation of humankind in Eden before the fall. The harmony is reminiscent of humankind's position of supremacy in the scheme of creation and their favour in God's sight. Stephens paints an ideal scene of a beautifully created garden and God himself is portrayed as an artist who painted the beautiful landscape (1.2.58). The landscape portrayed here is "innocent", "the harmless place where violence is unknown" (Mitchell 261):

Anny teyã vanantarĩ	In that wood
Barauy nizhrodacachy zhari	There was a spring of sweet water
Phunttoni paruatachy phatari	It broke out of mountain rocks,
Maha lahari vahantasse	And flew out with great waves
Tiye zhary passoni	From that spring,
Yequi nadhi umattaly tethouni	A river emerged
Bhumiuaincuntthĩ maidhanĩ	And spread itself
Prassãualy (1.4.90, 91)	On the plains of *Bhumivaicunttha*
Tetha mandu sitallu pauanu	The gentle, cool breeze
Yento puspauassu gheunu	Came, carrying the fragrance of flowers
Camallẽ pracassalĩ deqhunu	And seeing the lotuses in bloom
Zhempauita	Danced towards them
(*Kristapurāṇa* 1.4.96)	

This "tropical" Eden has lotuses growing in the pools and the breeze carries the fragrance of tropical flowers. This idyllic scene is in contrast with the scene in which Lucifer is plotting against God, giving rise to chaos in Vaicunttha. There is darkness and thunder and the atmosphere in Vaicunttha changes from one of harmonious worship to one of revolt and downfall:

Vaincuntthĩ zahala budabudacaru	In Vaicunttha there arose a murmur,
Zaissa uchamballe sagharu	As of a rising sea,
Yecade samaĩ utthila garzharu	And sometimes there arose thundering
Choũ meghancha	Of the four clouds
Qui Ganguecheya voga mazari	Or as if in the Ganga,
Gundda silla baissalea vari	A great rock had been set,
Viscattuni dõ tthaĩ zae lahary	And the waves split and flowed in two
Pannĩ vaze baddabaddã	directions,
(*Kristapurāṇa* 1.2.95, 96)	The waters rumbling thunderously

The image used here is of a river, Ganga, whose serene flow is disturbed by the rock that falls into it and cleaves its stream into two, symbolic of the angels' division into two bands. It has to be noted here that Stephens, while narrating the story of the angels' fall, uses tropical climate markers such as the thundering monsoon clouds to convey his message. The grim events that took place in Vaicunttha are reflected in the landscape painted by Stephens. The "good" angels, led by Michael, try to reason with Lucifer and his comrades, but when Lucifer refuses to acknowledge the greatness of the "Creator", God himself pronounces judgement:

Dauadda dauadda re ya Luçifera	Trample, trample this Lucifer
Nedaua vaincuntthĩ thara	Do not give him place in Vaicunttha
Ghala suargouni yemapura	Throw him from heaven into hell,
Mellicarã sahita	With his accomplices

Zaissa varussa calla auasuarī	As in the time of rain
Vizu paddale tallapuni ambarī	Lightning falls, flashing from the sky,
Taisse te nitidharmache ary	So those enemies of righteousness,
Suargouni paddale	Fell from the sky
(*Kristapurāṇa* 1.2.104, 106)	

God's wrath at Lucifer's rebellion and the enormity of Lucifer's fall are reflected through the grim scene painted by Stephens in these verses. When God himself rose out of his throne to pronounce judgement, Lucifer lost his place in Vaicunttha forever.

Another route through which the landscape enters the narrative is through the replacement of specific referents in the source texts with familiar alternatives from the local environment. In cases where a local equivalent for a natural feature was not available, Stephens used terms from the natural features around him. Adam and Eve, after eating the forbidden fruit, discovered that they were naked. After recovering from the shame of this new-found knowledge, they look for ways to cover their nakedness. Instead of the proverbial fig leaf, Stephens's Adam and Eve clothe themselves with banana leaves:

Tāua adipurussanche lochana	Then the original man's eyes
Taissechi ugaddale zanna	Opened and he knew
Ugaddī deqhoni apanna	He saw that they were naked
Lazea paualī	And withered in shame
Lagu veguẽ dhauinalī	Running in haste
Cadally patrẽ caddilī	He broke off banana leaves
Siuanni ghaloni pairilī	And sewed garments
Zhanquilẽ anga	To cover their bodies
(*Kristapurāṇa* 1.5.4, 5)	

The translatorial decision of using "banana" in place of "fig" is uniform throughout the text.[9] In a later episode from the New Testament where Nathaniel met Jesus, Nathaniel was standing under a banana tree (2.21.46) instead of the fig tree mentioned in the Bible (John 1:48). Stephens makes deliberate use of nature to reflect the mood of the narrative. Nature in *Kristapurāṇa* reflects the action that is taking place. Flowers and idyllic landscapes are symbolic of peace and obedience to God while fire and barrenness are portrayed as punishment for sin. Abstract ideas are conveyed poetically through the use of "concrete images" from the surrounding scenery. It brings events that occurred in faraway settings into the immediate environment of the listeners, enabling them to empathize with the action in the narrative.

Zaissy coquilla duqhẽ zhallambaly	Like the koel, overflowing with grief
Ti champeya chhaî baissaly	Sits in the shade of the *champa*
Pilẽ sanddalī apulī	And cries
Mhannauni rudhaty	Because her nestlings are lost

Nistturẽ camattiye dattunu
Tyechy poqharanny guiuassunu
Nelĩ ghontterichĩ pile chorunu
Paqhẽ nathilĩ

Searching out her hollow
With ruthless sticks
Her nestlings were stolen away
Leaving the bird deprived

Mhannauni ty coquilla
Rudhana cary ratrichã vellã
Duqhẽ zahaly veaculla
Pileyã laguy

So the koel
Cried in the night-hours
And was troubled with grief
For her babies

Baissoni xaqha vari
Duqhachẽ gayena cary
Allauity nana suarĩ
Viyoguẽ caroni

She sings songs of grief
Sitting on a branch
She intones various notes
To grieve their parting

Taisse Iaco bhacta zahalẽ
Iose Beiamichẽ duqha paddalẽ
Mhannoni rudhana manddilẽ
Ratri dinu
(*Kristapurāṇa* 1.14.1–5)

So the devout Jacob
Drowning in grief for Joseph and
    Benjamin
Set up a lament
Day and night[10]

Jacob's sorrow on the loss of his sons Joseph and Benjamin is compared to the wailing of a koel bird on the loss of her nestlings. The koel's mourning, here, is used as a metaphor for Jacob's grief. The depth of Jacob's grief and his helplessness is brought out effectively by comparing him to a koel. The sights and sounds of a Goan evening, the trilling of the koel, and the fragrance of the *champa* is infused into Jacob's mourning.

The motifs of the koel and champak trees are recurrent in the text. Another passage where it can be found is in the song that Mary sang after she saw the resurrected Jesus. After the laments of the crucifixion came the joyful songs of resurrection. Stephens paints a picture of all nature rejoicing at the resurrection of Christ. The koel sings in celebration while sitting on the champak-flower tree. The winds from the hills of Malabar in the south bring the sweet perfume of lotuses. The entire scene that is painted by Stephens here is that of an Indian spring, a time for new birth and celebration:

Mhannaty atã varussauo guela
Maguileã casttancha puru sunttala
Apadecha moddaua bhangala
Ala anandu guimalla

Now the rains are gone
The flood of sorrow has receded
Calamities are broken
Now summer is here

Amanchea banasthalla
Phanconi alĩ puspẽ phallã
Sussara sabdẽ ganty coquilla
Champaca vari

In our garden
Flowers and fruits have blossomed
The koel sings sweetly
On the *champak* tree

Amanchea malleyantu malleyanillu
Puspa camallancha parimallu
Gheuni yento sitallu
Acassa marguĩ
(*Kristapurāṇa* 2.52.48–50)

The winds from the south
Bring to our garden
Sweet perfumes of lotuses
Through the sky

While in the story of Jacob the koel and the *champak* sang plaintive tones to join in his grief, in Mary's case the koel sang songs of victory. This introduction of Goan landscape into the biblical narrative is a major translatorial decision. In the verses quoted in the "Introduction" of this book, the listeners expressed their concerns about the authenticity of the Padre-guru's narrative. This reveals that the translator was conscious of the fact that he was about to compose a text by adding poetic adornment to scriptures. He was well aware of the questions that would be asked of the "faithfulness" of such as composition. As a part of his explanation to the questioner, he says that a painter of portraits paints faces, and adds trees and other natural features in the background to beautify the picture. That does not make the portrait a false one (2.2.108). Similarly, he clarifies that the landscape that he paints in *Kristapurāṇa* is meant to beautify, but does not mar the "truth" of the text.

The use of images derived from the natural features of the region to describe the mood and events of the narrative is an effective literary tool. It impresses in the minds of the readers the depth of feeling experienced by characters like Jacob who lived in another time and another place. As these characters are placed in the tropical landscape of Goa, the locals identify with them and recognize the familiar themes of sorrow and fear that are experienced by the characters as the story progresses. This technique also creates a lasting impression in the mind and appeals to the cognitive faculties of listeners so that they remember verses of *Kristapurāṇa*. In this process, the imagery of the Bible transforms into a local one with banana leaves, koels and the flowering *champa*, making the landscape a medium through which local culture blends with the biblical narrative and gives rise to novel terrains. These passages from *Kristapurāṇa* reveal a continuous two-way process of translation. The Christian story is brought into the landscape of the Marathi language through translation while the Marathi landscape enters into the Christian story, transforming it.

4.4 Everyday Landscapes

The landscape portrayed by Stephens in *Kristapurāṇa* depicts the "everydayness" of the life of a convert in Goa. In the first chapter of the *First Puranna*, the narrator, the Padre-guru, describes his motivation for reciting the Purāṇa. On a Sunday evening in Goa, young Brahmin boys were gathered around the padre in a church to recite the catechism. As the sound of the recitation rose to the sky, a Brahmin arose and asked the Padre-guru a question (1.1.143). The Brahmin reminded him that they were forbidden by the Catholic Church to read the Hindu Purāṇas. They were curious about the stories written in the land of the "firangis". He suggested that the Padre should write a Purāṇa for them so that they could spend their time "profitably" by reading it (1.1.131–145).

The scene depicted by Stephens evokes in the reader's mind a picture of Goa dotted with churches and the converts actively trying to locate themselves in their new faith. *Kristapurāṇa* comes across as the result of a dialogue between the priest and the locals. In one such dialogue, the narrator attempts to explain the concept of "original sin" stemming from the fall of man in the Garden of Eden. One of the new Christians questions the padre about why a just God would impute Adam's sin on all his descendants. He observes that, "we were not even born then" (1.4.35). The priest goes on to explain the idea that all men are of the race of Adam, and they have fallen short of the glory of God. All those who are born of Adam have sin in them:

Anny to honta nardaiuu zaissa	And as he was unfortunate
Taissĩ lencuruuẽ zalmalĩ vanssa	So were the children born in his race
Pahepã putru hoe piteya sarissa	See, the son becomes like his father
Nachuqhe uchita bapacheya	And does not lose the father's reward
Bramhacullĩ hoe bramha ballacu	In a Brahman family a Brahman child is
Sudra upaze sudradicu	born
Matongacha anamicu	A Sudra gives birth to a Sudra
Taissachi hoe	A Matang's child
(*Kristapurāṇa* 1.4.55, 56)	Is like him

Stephens explains Adam's sin by using the caste system prevalent in seventeenth-century Goa as an example. These verses provide a glimpse into the Catholic Church's interpretation of the caste system. The Matangs were an "impure" caste, untouchables. Stephens' easy depiction of the caste system connotes an acceptance of caste as a social system of the region.[11] In Avaswaru 1 of the *Dussarem Puranna*, Stephens poetically invites all people to listen to the story of Christ: "So all you listeners/ Brahma, Kshatriya Vaishya, Shudra, and all…" (2.1). As a translator, Stephens places Christian ideas in the framework of Indian social norms in order to elucidate them to his readers. Caste enters Stephens' "Christian" text as a result of a dialogue with the natives. In this process Christian imagery is transplanted into the Marathi language while at the same time indigenous Hindu images begin to appear in Stephens' "Christian" story. As Stephens appropriates indigenous sacred forms to translate the Christian message, readers respond by actively "interpreting" it through their own worldview. This may lead to interpretations that are not necessarily desired or expected by the translator.

At other places in the text, Stephens uses natural imagery to elucidate the concept of original sin. Cain's murderous rage in killing his brother Abel is attributed to the sin of their parents, Adam and Eve. Stephens explains the situation with the image of a plant which had been injected with poison in its roots. The poison which entered the roots and pith (Adam and Eve) flourished in the branches and fruits (Cain). It seems from these verses that caste is accepted as a given in Goan society by the missionaries. However, in other passages in the text, the Padre-guru tries to impress on his listeners that all humans are created equal (1.3.64). The process of cultural translation seen in *Kristapurāṇa* is a constant balancing act between maintaining the "purity" of the Christian message and incorporating local aspects to make the story familiar to readers.

Texts which were written to justify Christianity and refute Hinduism distinctly reflected the local religious landscape. In order to refute the basic tenets of

Hinduism and establish Christianity as the "truth", Catholic priests had to study Hindu texts and practices. Croix's *Peter Purāṇa* may be considered as a strong refutation of the idolatrous practices of the Hindus of Goa. Croix extensively lists the deities worshipped by the Hindus of Goa and refutes their divinity one by one (Henn, *Encounters* 75). The snake-god *Nageshi*, *Ganesha*, and the goddess *Sateri* are among the deities listed by Croix. In comparison to Croix's Purāṇa, Stephens's *Kristapurāṇa* has a more "literary and theological" focus (Henn *Encounters* 75). Stephens did not harshly refute Hindu deities but used a far subtler approach and attempted to place Christianity as the way to salvation.

In Stephens's description of the fall, Satan comes to Eve in the form of a snake. The snake is described by the Padre-guru in elaborate detail:

Dirgha serira zeyachẽ	Whose body was long,
Nana parincheya ranganchẽ	And had colours of all kinds,
Zaissẽ dhanuxe gaghanichẽ	As if a rainbow
Mirauatu asse	Was shining in the sky
Cupantunu thembe gallatã	As the sun shines through
Teyã mazi bimba tallapata	Water droplets falling from the clouds,
Taissẽ serira mirauata	So his body shimmered,
Pahantã teyachẽ	If you looked at it
Qui mayora pichẽ nilla	Blue, like the feathers of a peacock,
Qui vanaparuueachẽ cantthanalla	Like the neck of a forest-bird,
Taissẽ anga disse sacalla	That is how the body looked,
Teya azagarach	Of that serpent
Quele ractauarna ddolle	He had eyes of the colour of blood,
Gunziyã sariqhe calle	Black like berries,
Te pahaueya te velle	To look at that sight,
Adaõ canta nigaly	Adam's wife set out
(*Kristapurāṇa* 1.4.105–108)	

Stephens' snake is a wondrous creature. It had all the colours of a tropical landscape. This is the snake that deceived Eve and led to the fall of humankind. A question which arises in the readers' mind while reading this description is about Stephens' reasons for describing the serpent, the "enemy", in such resplendent language. It may be argued that Stephens was refuting the divinity of the snake-gods of Goan Hindus by painting an image of the snake as the devil and an enemy of humankind. In another passage, the translator reinforces the image of the serpent as an enemy and advises against its worship: "The snake deceived us all/Do not worship him" (1.6.64). Herod's evil wife, Herodias, who plotted the beheading of John the Baptist is also described as a venomous, hissing snake (2.23.87). Stephens adopted a subtler approach while condemning the deities of Goa and displayed a fine understanding of the religious imagination of the target audience for whom he was writing. These verses are evocative of episodes from the *Bhagavata Purāṇa* where the encounter between Krishna and Kaliya the serpent are elaborately discussed (canto 10, chapter 16).

The elaborate portrayal of episodes such as the meeting between Eve and the serpent provide evidence of Stephens's acquaintance with purāṇic stories.

Stephens emerges as both poet and translator in *Kristapurāṇa*. As a poet, he composes a poem of epic proportions for the Christians of seventeenth-century Goa. As a translator, he translates biblical events and concepts for the converts. Landscape, here, functions both as a part of the poetic imagination as well as an integral part of the process of cultural translation. Landscape is a medium through which the culture enters the translated work.

The everydayness of life in Goa enters the Christian story and transforms its landscape. At the same time, the transformation that occurs in the region as the biblical story emerges through the narrative. The temples in the region slowly began to be replaced by churches. It is in such a church, a "devmandir" (temple of God), that *Kristapurāṇa* was first recited:

Sass*atty* dess*ī* yeque Deu*a*m*a*ndhir*ī*	In a *devmandir* in Sasati,
Astamanī aditeuar*ī*s	One Sunday evening,
Christauanche cum*a*ra ritu s*a*ry	The sons of Christians, according to their
Doutriny b*a*iss*a*le	custom,
(*Kristapurāṇa* 1.1.126)	Sat down for the *Doutrina*

The verse mentioned above provides us a glimpse from a church in Salsette in seventeenth-century Goa. Stephens uses the term "devmandir" to mean a Christian church. In this passage, we get a glimpse of the changing physical landscape of Salsette, along with its changing linguistic and religious landscape. The term "devmandir" (temple of God), which could have meant a Hindu temple in pre-Portuguese Salsette, transforms into a Christian church. As Stephens translates the Christian story, the traditional biblical landscape transforms into one that is imbued with local colour, while at the same time changing the landscape of the region in which this text was composed.

The image of the church, both metaphorical and physical, is an important part of the changing landscape of *Kristapurāṇa*. The scene that opens before the Padre-guru begins his narration is that of a church adorned for Palm Sunday in seventeenth-century Salsette. The narrator describes the awe experienced by converts as they entered the church, lined with images of saints, the golden retable and the adorned altar (1.1.172, 175). As they walk into the church, the southern breeze (*maleyanilu*) wafts across the landscape and the fragrance of incense rises up (1.1.176). It is after this that the Padre makes the sign of the cross (1.1.179) and begins reciting the Purāṇas. The mellow tones of a coastal Goan morning are captured by Stephens in these descriptions, while placing the church at the centre of the new Christian's everyday experiences.

We see that *Kristapurāṇa* is born in a *devmandir* in Salsette, in seventeenth-century Goa (1.1.126), when young local Christians gathered to recite the catechism on a Sunday evening. The text grew out of the local soil in a physical sense. It originated out of the physical space of a Goan church and the minds of new converts searching for new Purāṇas, in the absence of their old ones. The Padre-guru gave his word (*bhassa*) to the Brahmins that he would compose a Purāṇa for them (1.1.170). As the Padre-guru gives "language" (*bhassa*) to the Christian experience of the converts in Goa, a new Christian landscape emerges. The word "bhassa", used by Stephens, can be taken to mean both "language" and "promise". As the translator enters the polyphony of the Goan linguistic scene and extracts hitherto-unheard stories for his listeners (Cronin 2000, 66), the Christian story enters Goa, creating new landscapes. The multiple layers of complexities in cultural translation are revealed in this process of extracting new stories for the new Christians of seventeenth-century Goa. In the process of extracting these new landscapes for his readers, the translator himself undergoes cultural translation, and stands transformed by the temporal-spatial travel undertaken while composing narratives for a local audience.

Biblical landscapes have been transformed over the centuries as Christianity travelled across time and space. The places/spaces kept evolving and shifting shape based on the cultures with which they came into contact. This shape-shifting took place primarily through the translation of Christian texts into newer languages. The place/space that emerges in Stephens's poetic version of the Bible is somewhere between ancient Palestine and seventeenth-century Konkan. Stephens travels both in time and in space throughout the narrative, "to-ing and fro-ing between specific geographical locales and the human imagination" (Said 246). The constant back-and-forth travel between biblical places and Konkan create the spaces in which Stephens's landscapes are located. This process of translating places, rather than being a linear linguistic travel, is a continuous process of temporal and spatial travel.

As Stephens attempts to weave together a Christian narrative for the new Christians, the Brahmins interject from place to place, adding their own detail and colour to the story.[12] The detailing in the landscape is influenced not just by the translator's interpretation of the story, but also by the converts' interpretation of it. As the Padre-guru translates biblical episodes for the new Christians, they "translate back", leading to the creation of places/spaces that have Palestinian names, with distinct geographical features from coastal Konkan. A discussion on "landscape" in *Kristapurāṇa* must take into account both a "sacred landscape", which emerges out of Stephens's translation of the biblical story into Marathi, as well as the local, Goan landscape that invariably seeps into biblical spaces, with or without the translator's consent. The following sections deals with the relationship between Goan villagers and their land, and the role of cultural translation reinventing these relationships which were disrupted by colonial ventures.

4.5 Landscape, Identity, and Cultural Translation

In the first letter to Father Claudius Acquaviva written in the year 1601, Stephens noted with satisfaction that the people of Goa were slowly but surely forgetting the idols of their Hindu past:

... the little chapels which Fr. Provincial Nuno Rodrigues ordered to be erected in remote villages ... In them there are series of pictures portraying lives of saints, an altar and a cross; and thus the memory of the idols which were formerly in each village is gradually being wiped out.

(Drago 1996, 898)

Stephens' description brings to mind an image of the changing landscape of Goa. The idols of "pre-Christian" Goa were being wiped out and the region was beginning to be dotted with Catholic chapels. The physical transformation that took place in the landscape of seventeenth-century Goa brings into focus the way in which the topography of the region changed along with the translation of the Church's message into regional languages.

In the "Dussarem Puranna" of *Kristapurāṇa*, the Padre-guru narrates a scene in which the idols of Egypt toppled and fell, as the infant Jesus entered Egypt with Joseph and Mary:

Aissa cramauniyã panthu	So they made their way,
Maga patalĩ Egipta antu	And reached Egypt,
Tethẽ acharye vrutauantu	Listen to the miraculous events
Vartala aica	That happened there
Lingã patmanchiya muhurty	Idols of *linga* and false gods,
Tethila zanu zeyã bhazaty	Worshipped by the people of that land,
Tedhauã ulanddoni paddaty	Toppled and fell
Bhumy vari	To the earth
(*Kristapurāṇa* 2.12.64, 65)	

After the birth of Jesus Christ in Bethlehem, Joseph and Mary were warned by an angel to flee King Herod's evil plans to kill the infant Jesus. They took the child and travelled to Egypt. The verse quoted above describes the dramatic entry of Jesus into Egypt, leading to the downfall of the Egyptian Gods. Christ's physical entry into Egypt led to the downfall of Egyptian idols and places of worship. When early missionaries brought Christianity to Goa, traditional places of worship began to fall, in both the physical and spiritual senses (Henn 2015, 4). This scene is symbolic of the transformations that occurred when Christ entered seventeenth century Goa.

The Hinduism practised by the locals in Goa was specific and unique to the region and was encapsulated in their "Concannepanni" (Henn 2015, 3). Alexander Henn argues, in "Kristapurāṇa: Translating the Name of God in Early Modern Goa" (2015), that this *Concannepanni* or "Konkanness" was "distinctly void of any reference to religion". The cultural practices of these locals emanated from their relationship to the region rather than from their religious identity. The religious identity and practices of these locals was subsumed within their Konkanness. As such, separating them from their religion would require a reinventing of their Konkanness and their relationship to the environment that contributed to this identity.

Henn, in his volume *Hindu Catholic Encounters in Goa* (2014), describes the close relationship that Goans had with their land or the *ganv* (village) (Henn 2014, 83). The layout of village spaces was closely associated with the way in which the locals perceived and related to the world around them. With the destruction of temples and seizing of lands by the Portuguese, the locals faced a major rupture in their relationship with the land and the cultural memory associated with the land. In order to deal with this erasure of the past, the new converts had to invent/create a new history. The acceptance of Christianity by these subjects of the Portuguese crown, whether willingly or otherwise, led to restrictions on reading texts in the regional languages, including Hindu religious texts.

The locals in seventeenth-century Goa conceived a Christian Purāṇa out of their longing for a sense of belonging in this new-found religion. *Kristapurāṇa* emerges from these spaces created by this cultural "rupture". The Christian story had to be translated for these locals to claim it as a part of their identities. The narrative of *Kristapurāṇa* is significant as it gives us glimpses into the lives of newly converted locals grappling for their own roots in the process of transforming from Hindus to Christians. Cultural translation becomes a process to re-read and reinvent the narrative to help the locals navigate the unfamiliar terrain of Christianity:

Mhannoni he cathechy vitpati	So tell us this story from the beginning
Arambî sanguize amã prati	How it originated
Yeuaddẽ suarga ratna udayalẽ qhity	How this precious heaven-gem
Cauanniye pary	Appeared on earth
Tẽ samagra caraueya srauanna	Our minds are thrilled
Ulassataye amanchẽ mana	To hear it all,
Jesu suamiyachẽ cathana	To listen to the story of Lord Jesus,
Sauistara aicaueya	Spread out in details
Cahĩ yequi catha paricari	Some stories from the beginning
Xastrachy adî veri	Of the shastra,
Zaguî praghatta queleya vari	Reveal it to us,
Suqha hoe sacallã	So that we may have joy
Hẽ xastra sate aisse deqhatila ddollã	Seeing that this book is true,
Vollaqhaty bhauarthachî adimullã	Devotees will recognize their original roots,
Bhacti pracassu yeila agalla	And receive a new light of devotion
Suargouni amã	From heaven
Deuachea utamy vastu aicaty	As we hear excellent things of God,
Tari tachi suamy aissẽ manity	We will accept him as Lord,
Teacha prati moho carity	And have love towards Him,
Bhaye dharity teachẽ	And fear him
Mhannoni guru ya carannẽ	For this reason, guru,
Prassidha hoe veri xastrapuranna	Till the Purāṇa are revealed,
Cahĩ yeca xastrachẽ veacranna	Bring some words of the book,
Annize mana	To our mind

Dessaparinche bhasse caroni	Bring the blessed story of the Lord
Suamicatha punne pauani	Into the languages of this land,
Amã agneananthẽ niropuni	And tell it to us,
Suqhiya quize	Making us joyful
(*Kristapurāṇa* 1.1.155–161)	

These lines reveal the condition of the locals as they grappled for roots in their new-found religion. They plead with the Padre-guru to bring the "blessed story" to the language of their land. They would "recognize" their roots as they heard the words of the scripture. It is critical to note, here, that the "blessedness" attributed to the Christian scriptures by the locals in these lines is the aspiration of the missionary translator. The discontent and uprootedness that the locals experienced in the absence of the old Puranas has been discussed earlier in this narrative. The locals display a longing for a deeper connection with Christianity, and for a "tradition" to replace the one that had been erased by Portuguese invasion. In order to provide this rootedness, Stephens had to depart from the "original" and paint his poetic imagery with local colour. Cultural translation is used by poets like Stephens as a countermeasure to the effects of the break from tradition caused by Portuguese imperialism.

In order to "narrate" the places of the Bible to the people of Goa, Stephens used the process of translation. In the process of this narration, new landscapes are born. Translation gives colonized communities a landscape to imagine. In contexts such as Portuguese Goa, translated landscape provides a history and memory to newly displaced communities. The new converts desired a sense of belonging in the vacuum that was created by the erasure of millennia-old memories by imperial powers. These had to be replaced with new myths, new places, and new chronologies. Stephens was catering to this need while composing his Purāṇa.

Landscapes from disparate cultures entered each other in the text and contributed to the ways in which these cultures were shaped. The "Christian God" began to live in Vaicunttha and the new converts' religious imagination was re-shaped, with the figures of "new" lotus-eyed Gods introduced into their religious landscape. *Kristapurāṇa* reflects a transition in the identities of the new converts of Goa: Just like the changing geographical, socio-political and literary landscapes of the region, these converts were being transformed from being Hindu to becoming Christian in their identities. Stephens captures these moments of transition in the landscapes of his *Kristapurāṇa*.

4.6 The City and the Wilderness

The relationship between humans and nature is dependent on the worldview of the human beings who inhabit a particular geographical region (White 1967, 3, 5). Prior to the arrival of the Portuguese, the inhabitants of Goa had a worldview influenced by the traditions that had been practiced in the region for centuries. The distribution of village land and preservation of sacred groves were dictated by local customs. With the arrival of a new worldview, in this case a Portuguese, Catholic one, the locals had to recalibrate their relationship and responses to the natural features around them.

In *Kristapurāṇa*, human actions have ecological implications that lead to the transformation of the natural terrain. Stephens' Eden, an idyllic *anandasthan* with gurgling streams and tropical flowers, became a desolate place robbed of all beauty with the fall of man. Human beings are portrayed as directly responsible for the garden being stripped of its beauty and harmony. Before Adam and Eve ate the fruit, all the animals and birds of Eden lived in complete kinship with them. As soon as they sinned and lost their glory, the behaviour of these creatures changed:

Zeya monazaty anny paqhuruuã	Those animals and birds
Maguilã diuassî vollaqhuni Adãua	Who recognized Adam in the past
Manu denta hontî baraua	And revered him
Sadã callî	At all times
Tẽ azi uparatthẽ houni	Now that things are overturned
Pallatati patthi deuni	They turn their backs on him
Teachẽ suamitua vissaruni	And forget that he was lord over them
Maguilẽ sacalla	In the past
(*Kristapurāṇa* 1.5.15, 16)	

Nature itself is put off by the sinful selves of Adam and Eve. The animals were bound to revere Adam and Eve only until they were in their sinless form. As soon as sin entered, Adam became one with the other creatures, their equal. Lynn White, in his article "The Historical Roots of Our Ecological Crisis" (1967), argues that the Western Christian tradition placed humans above the rest of nature and not as a part of nature (White 4). Stephens, on the contrary, places the fallen man on an equal footing with other created things.

Adam and Eve cannot continue being in a "mood of indifference" (White 4) to the changes taking place in nature after their disobedience. They are immediately held responsible for the havoc they have wreaked on the harmony of Eden. Their actions lead to the banning of the human race from Eden. Human actions have effects on the natural forms on earth. For Stephens, desolation is the direct outcome of sin. Destruction is a result of sin, a form of divine correction for the disobedience of humans. Flourishing greenery and cool breezes abound when man is at peace with God (1.4.96), while fire and destruction are brought on by disobedience and when people depart from the commandments (1.6.41). At every instance of sin, the land is afflicted with famine, flood, or sieges by foreign kings. Stephens portrays these scenes of destruction in great detail, giving rise to some of the most poetic and striking passages in the narrative. The relationship between sin and nature is highlighted in the cities where an abundance of human habitation leads to the abundance of sin. The cities flourish or become desolate depending on the people inhabiting the cities.

When the Israelites of the Old Testament sinned and refused to turn back to God, the Babylonian king Nebuchadnezzar attacked their holy city, Jerusalem, and took the people captive. On returning from captivity after seventy years, the Jews saw the ruins of what was once their glorious city:

Ierusalea nagarĩ patale	They reached the city of Jerusalem
Samagra nagara vossa deqhilẽ	And found the whole city desolate
Templĩ nagarĩ vaddhale	The temple and the city overgrown
Vanaspaty bahuta	With shrubs
Aisse stamba paddale hati	The pillars were fallen
Vari chaddaly vallambeanchy maty	Anthills rose above them
Bhramara runnazhunnacara carity	Bumble bees hummed
Te cantity stambanthẽ	And invaded the pillars
Gharõ gharincheã cuddĩ	The shells of houses
Condalĩ mahunddallanchi zoddĩ	Were filled with pairs of snakes
Maha naga uchaloni phanny	Great cobras lifted their hoods
Phumphuuity dhuducarẽ	And hissed fearsomely
Baĩ poqharannichẽ zalla	Waters of wells and reservoirs
Sihallẽ nassalẽ sacalla	Were fouled with algae
Vari babulli bhuzaly vissalla	Babul grew over them
Tennẽ cahĩ nadisse	And hid them from view
Bhõuatea malleyanchea bhinty	The fences of fields around
Ulanddoni paddaliya hati	Were fallen over
Teyã mazi viuare dissaty	Through it were seen
Quiradduuanchĩ	Holes of little snakes
Mandhirancheã callassã vari	On the tops of houses
Ghumadde ghumughumity bharĩ	Owls hooted incessantly
Salluue zhombaty paqhiyã vari	Mynahs fought other birds
Copata ghality qhucara	Hissing with anger
Gharẽ guidẽ bahutĩ	Kites and vultures were plenty
Yecamecanthẽ zhombaty	Picking at each other
Ddolle caddoniyã qhanty	Prising out each others' eyes
Yecamecanche	For food
Draqhe vely puspa taru bhina zahale	Trees, vines, and flowering plants
Zuna taddamadda bhumy paddale	disappeared
Teanche tthaĩ vruqhe vaddhale	Ancient palm trees toppled to the ground
Apaisse	In their place wild trees grew
	Of their own accord
Bhituri paqhepilanchẽ bhirẽ radde	In them, birds cried in their nests
Templĩ angannẽ vossa zhaddẽ	The temple courts were full of trees
Dutare yerandda zahale gaddhe	Devil's weed and castor-seed flourished
Vissalla thora	Great and strong

*A*isse Iudeuĩ n*agara* deqhilẽ	The Jews saw the city
Zunẽ n*agara* vossa p*a*dd*a*lẽ	Their ancient city lay waste
Deqhoni rudh*a*na c*a*rũ lag*a*le	And seeing this
Iudeu*a* sam*a*sta	They began to weep
(*Kristapurāṇa* 1.33.7–18)	

The Jews stood grief-stricken at the desolation of their holy city. The local Konkani must have found this especially poignant as they had witnessed large-scale destruction[13] of their traditional monuments and artefacts by the Portuguese administration (Henn 2015, 4). The passage is especially evocative as it captures the angry humming of invading animals among the silence of the ruins. The weeds that grew in the ruined temple of Jerusalem were *datura* and *babul*, shrubs specific to Western India. The snakes that hissed in the houses and fields were ones with which the locals were familiar. Jerusalem was overgrown by the same weeds that the locals of Goa fought to keep away in their own farmlands. The distance between Goa and Jerusalem is traversed by Stephens through cultural translation. In the process, Goan plants and animals begin to grow in Palestine, creating a new topology which was neither completely Middle Eastern, nor completely Goan. It is the third, new place created in the process of translating the biblical narrative for a local audience. Or rather, the unique landscape that emerges in *Kristapurāṇa* is born in the "third space" (Bhabha 1994, 55) that is created in the constant back and forth travel between ancient Palestine and seventeenth-century Goa in the narrative. The places narrated by the Padre-guru are microcosms where time and space converge.

In passages like the one quoted above, readers get insight into the ramifications of the relationship between humans and nature. The narrator emphasizes the point that the practices and beliefs of the people have implications on the goodness of their land. In the episode of the legion-possessed man healed by Jesus, the Padre-guru explains that if his listeners insisted on worshipping "devils" then the devils would take control of their lands and rule them (2.26.57). The possession and prosperity of their land was tied to their beliefs and practices.

Apart from the abovementioned lines on the destruction of Jerusalem, there are elaborate verses on the great flood, the famine during Joseph's time, and Pharoah's killing of Hebrew children, among other passages. These passages are used to highlight the implications of human sin on the environment and the necessity of recognizing and submitting to divine will.

Cities like Jerusalem were full of sin due to the disobedience of the people. The wilderness, however, is portrayed in *Kristapurāṇa* as a pristine space, untouched by human trespasses. While it is a place for penance and suffering, it is also a space for renewal and strengthening (*Kristapurāṇa* 2.18.11). According to David Henderson in "American Wilderness Philosophy" (2014), the "wilderness is at once a place of divine revelation as well as temptation and punishment" (online). Mortals who enter the wilderness return from their sojourn there as enlightened beings. In his essay "Walking" (1862), Henry David Thoreau, while reflecting on the significance of the wilderness, notes that out of the "wilderness comes the Reformer eating locusts and wild honey"[14] (Thoreau 1914, 57). Many of Thoreau's works, most notably *Walden* (1854), dwell on the theme of leaving the city and retreating into nature in order to be rejuvenated.

Similarly, the characters of Jesus and John the Baptist in *Kristapurāṇa* spent time in the wilderness before they started their public ministry. Stephens portrays these periods as times of intense meditation and connection with God. The wilderness is portrayed as a space which is far away from human habitation. In *Avaswaru* 18 of the "Dussarem Puranna", John the Baptist is instructed by an angel to return to Jerusalem and start preaching (*Kristapurāṇa* 2.18.11) what he has "received" in the wilderness. While destruction and disintegration are the effects of human sin on the environment, the wilderness is untouched by human savagery. As John the Baptist prepares to leave the his solitary life in the forest and return to the inhabited world, he speaks to the animals that he had been living with for years, telling them that he is going back to a people "worse than the desert /harder than stone /crueller than wild beasts" (*Kristapurāṇa* 2.18.39).

According to Stephen Siddall in *Landscape and Literature* (2009), the Christian tradition always placed an emphasis on "solitude to refresh the world-wearied soul" (Siddall 52). The pristine quality of the wilderness is a shadow of Eden and portrays the "presence of God" that was lost by the first man. Leaving the inhabited world and going into the wilderness, is a way of distancing oneself from sinful desires and inching closer to the divinity of the Creator. Stephens' ecology holds humankind as directly responsible for the destruction of the environment around them. At the same time, he paints the wilderness as a space where the distance with the Creator can be bridged, much like his work *Kristapurāṇa*, where readers can catch a glimpse of the *Vaicuntthanath* (2.2.81), the creator God.

As the biblical Joseph and Mary travelled to Egypt along with the infant Jesus to hide from King Herod, they crossed an expansive desert. This journey into Egypt is portrayed by Stephens as a "reverse journey" of the exodus from Egypt by ancient Israelites. Stephens paints a vivid picture of Joseph leading the way through this desert with his family. As they cross the sands, Joseph points out various sites from Israel's history to Mary (*Kristapurāṇa* 2.12.38–63). He points out the places where the Israelites spent forty years on their long journey to the Promised Land. This journey is significant as it is a point where the sands of time converge with the desert sand, a journey into the cultural memory of a community that had travelled through the same deserts centuries ago. The Old Testament of the Jews and the New Testament that is to be ushered in by Christ symbolically intersect in this desert scene. Through this reminiscence, the newly converted Christians of the Konkan region in the Indian Subcontinent become participants in a tradition that played out in Palestine thousands of years before their time.

This is one of the ways in which translation and landscape are inextricably linked. People who experience an "uprooting" from traditions located firmly in their geographical terrain, need an alternate topography to regain their identity and sense of belonging. In sites of rupture like colonized regions, translation performs the important task of creating a landscape for the colonized to locate themselves in and to "reimagine" their traditions.

As a translator, Stephens had to engage with the locals in order to convince them that his *shastra* was the true one. The colonized are rarely passive recipients of the translations that are created for them. They actively "translate back" (Rafael 2012, 50), bringing out unexplored meanings of the translated work and, in the process, creating a novel form of the source texts. Translation itself means "locational disrupture" (Bassnett and Trivedi 1999, 13). When a text like *Kristapurāṇa* is composed, it is not only the regional location that is disrupted. The locals "translate back" leading to a "disrupture" in the "original" biblical landscape as well.

Stephens' translation of the biblical narrative changed the locals' relationship to their landscape. Objects that were considered sacred could no longer be held in reverence. The snake which was worshipped as *Nageshi* (Henn 2015, 7) was now the very symbol of Lucifer and had to be viewed as the enemy. Customs that were followed had to be given up in order to adopt practices ushered in by the new order. The cultural translation of the Bible into Marathi changed the way they interacted with their surroundings. By becoming Christian, they were made members of a Judeo-Christian tradition that was played out in another place and another time. Cultural translation is the process through which Stephens mediated these temporal and spatial divides. The landscapes in *Kristapurāṇa* are frozen moments, providing glimpses of "events" (Rath 2010, 61) where time and space meet.[15]

The new Christians of seventeenth-century Goa can be compared to "weary travellers" in their journey into a new religion. Robbed of their roots and artefacts that were markers of cultural memory, they grappled for solid ground to form the bedrock of their new faith. The Portuguese and Latin used in Church rituals may have echoed strangely on their ears, refusing to sink into their souls. Add to this the ban on reading regional texts, and one is led to wonder whether the allure of *Kristapurāṇa* was that it provided them with "pagefuls of familiar language" (Cronin 2000, 39), of their own language, to drink in.

As we study Stephens' telling of the Bible and the topographies that he (re) invented in the process, we see more inclusive definitions of translation emerging. Simon writes, in her article "Rites of Passage" (1990), that "Translation is not only an operation of linguistic transfer, but also a process which generates new textual forms, which creates new forms of knowledge, which introduces new cultural paradigms" (Simon 96, 97). To this list this book may add "novelized genre", "reinvented traditions", and "(re)created landscapes".

Notes

1 Simon Schama, *Landscape and Memory*, p. 574.
2 Italiano's work could be considered as one of the first book-length works dealing with the relationship between translation and geography. The idea of the "spatial turn" has been discussed by Italiano with reference to *The Spatial Turn* (2009), edited by Barney Warf and Santa Arias. Warf argues that "Geography matters, not for the simplistic and overly used reason that everything happens in space, but because *where* things happen is

critical to knowing *how* and *why* they happen" (Warf and Arias 2009, 1). Italiano marks a difference between the two approaches that he names the "geography of translation" and the "translation of geography". The first, "geography of translation", may be seen in Sherry Simon's work on urban spaces as translation zones, where she identifies a geographical city and goes on to explore the process of translation within these multilingual urban spaces. Italiano places his work in the second category, by focusing on texts and how space has been translated in them. His central aim is to inquire "how and to what extent Western spatial imaginations, in particular those constructed by literary works, have been translated across languages, media and epochs" (Italiano 2016, 4).

3 Landscape, in the sense of "a scene of natural beauty", has been a trope in poetry since time immemorial. Stephen Siddall, while drawing a historical trajectory of literary landscapes in *Landscape and Literature* (2009), writes that "the *Idylls* of the Greek poet Theocritus are generally taken to be the source of the Pastoral in English literature" (Siddall 11). The word "idyllic", which means "full of nature's charm" (Siddall 11), has roots in Theocritus' *Idylls*. The portrayal of nature in literature, however, can be seen even before classical Greece. The Christian Bible, a work of world literature, begins with the "creation" of heaven and earth by God and contains a description of the Garden of Eden, its trees, rivers, and animals. Apart from this, many other examples exist from world literature, such as the *Vedas*, where natural features have been used as a setting for the narrative to unfold. Woodworth argues that "landscape is as fundamental to literature as setting is to theatre" (Woodworth 2003, online). However, the use of landscape in literature goes beyond its usage as a setting for human action. The definition of what the term "landscape" encompasses has evolved since the beginning of these studies until the present day. Landscape was considered as an inscription, a "record" of the natural environment by human beings. From this initial understanding, the definition of landscape has evolved from being a mere imprint of natural surroundings to a dynamic interaction between human agents and natural surroundings.

4 Benedict Anderson, in *Imagined Communities* (1983), proposes the idea that nations or communities are "imagined" by its members, rather than being natural entities. The feeling of "belonging" to a community of a "nation" is influenced by several characteristics such as the decay of sacred dominions, the development of the printing press, and colonial ventures.

5 Said writes that "The invention of tradition is a method for using collective memory selectively by manipulating certain bits of national past, suppressing others, elevating still others in an entirely functional way" (Said 245). Said borrows the term "invention of tradition" from *The Invention of Tradition* (1983), edited by Eric Hobsbawm and Terry Ranger. Hobsbawm argues, in his "Introduction" to the volume, that certain traditions which seem ancient are actually constructed in the recent past. In the present study, the term "(re) invention of tradition" is used to signify the break from tradition caused by colonial ventures and how landscape writing in a work of cultural translation reinvents a tradition for culturally displaced communities.

6 The fascination of Europe with India as an "exotic" land is summed up in the story of Annone the elephant. Annone was an elephant sent as a gift to the Pope from India in the sixteenth century. The elephant, painted by Raphael, became the symbol of oriental "possibilities" (Xavier and Županov 2015, 4). India was seen as the land which even Alexander the Great could not subjugate. As such, the establishment of the *Estado da India* in the early sixteenth century was seen as an imperial victory for Portugal.

7 Stephens is one of the "foreigners" whose life is featured in Harris's work *The First Firangis* (2015), a volume that sketches brief biographies of individuals who travelled to India and made it their home. "Hi mho ji kudd" is Konkani for "This is my body", the formula for the Catholic Eucharist. Harris writes:

> In its more familiar Western guises, whether English or Latin, the words spoken by the priest supposedly induce the miracle of transubstantiation, translating the communion wafer into the flesh of Jesus. This first translation enables a second. Once the

consecrated wafer has been placed in the mouth of the Christian believer, she receives the grace of God and becomes part of the spiritual body of Jesus. The transformative power of the Eucharist is thus a doubly oral one. Spoken words translate dead matter into living flesh; eating living flesh translates an individual into a member of a spiritual community.

(Harris 2015, 491–492)

8 Then at that time
Adam's wife
Went into the place of joy *(anandasthan)*
To pass time.
(1.4.78)

9 It is significant to note that the same referent is used by Ruyl in his 1629 translation of the gospel of Mathew into Malay. Ruyl replaces "fig tree" with "banana tree" in his translation (Bellos 2011, 174). As Bible translations moved out of European languages, accommodation was used to translate the "message" clearly to readers.

10 For a translation of the verses describing the fate that befell Jacob's son Joseph in Egypt, see Appendix 2.

11 This acceptance of caste could be seen in other Catholic missions in India as well. Clooney writes that in the Madurai mission, de Nobili defended caste "forthrightly and without embarrassment as a legitimate and reasonable hierarchical structuring of society" (Clooney 2020, 4, footnote). De Nobili considered caste an essentially social, rather than a religious matter. He defended the view that Christianity was a religion for all castes and one need not lose one's caste on becoming Christian. This position taken by de Nobili has been criticized in modern times with reference to the prevalence of caste in the Catholic church.

12 One example of this would be the discussion on caste in the *Kristapurāṇa* that emerges from a Brahmin's question about Adam and the "original sin" (*Kristapurāṇa* 1.4.55, 56). This has been discussed in detail in the previous section on landscape.

13 Henn describes the violence of the Portuguese campaign: "It was not only that this campaign destroyed with determined iconoclastic violence all Hindu temples, shrines and images throughout Goa and systematically replaced the Hindu monuments with Christian churches, chapels and crosses" (Henn 2014). He further states: "Archaeological findings indicate that some of Goa's oldest churches were also at least partly built from the very rubble of the destroyed temples that they replaced" (Henn 2015, 4). The grief of finding an ancient monument desolate and fallen from glory may not have been lost on a local from sixteenth- or seventeenth-century Goa.

14 Thoreau, while writing of the Reformer who eats locusts and wild honey, alludes to the biblical character of John the Baptist who lived in the wilderness and survived on locusts and wild honey (Thoreau 1914, 57).

15 In "Knots of the Narrative: A Bakhtinian Analysis of Chronotopes in the Fiction of Amitav Ghosh" (2010), Rath studies the Bakhtinian concept of "event" as an important aspect of chronotopes. An event is a point where time and space intersect (Rath 61, 134). The event may be "unfinalizable" in life, "whereas in literature and art it may enter into a state of completion" (Rath 61). In *Kristapurāṇa*, each of the landscapes is a captured event from the time-space continuum.

5
SPEAKING AFTER

"...Tarhi anuvadalo dheetapane..."[1]
(Yet I have translated audaciously)

—Jnāneswar (1275–1296)

5.1 Translated Worlds

The metaphorical "wilderness wanderings" in the preceding chapters have endeavoured to locate translation as a crucial thread in the literary-cultural fabric of a region. Stephens' *Kristapurāṇa* provided the routes for these wanderings. The voices that may be heard in this text are not clear notes of a single source text and a resultant target text. Multiple voices emerge in the text, from local interventions in the narrative, to purāṇic concepts and local landscapes which reflect the translated worlds of the biblical narrative. The present reading of *Kristapurāṇa* has demonstrated how disparate traditions come together in a work of translation to produce a work that is unique to its setting and *skopos*.

Kristapurāṇa is a text which may be classified as a rewriting of the biblical narrative, as it is not a "translation proper" of the Bible. In *Translation and Rewriting in the Age of Post-Translation Studies* (2017), Edwin Gentzler writes that these texts which are referred to as "rewritings, adaptations, and furtherings ... tell us more about the nature of translation than the central paradigm" (Gentzler 2017, "Introduction"). *Kristapurāṇa* has provided such rare insight into the workings of translation in sites such as Goa. This reading has brought to the fore transmissive practices that existed during the period of vernacularization and has argued that it is crucial to study these translation practices as a part of the discourse on translation in South Asia.

South Asian cultures have traditionally followed their own translation practices. Though they were not theorized upon as translation practices, texts (specifically Sanskrit texts) were disseminated through genre such as *teeka* or *bhashya* (Singh 12).

DOI: 10.4324/9781003146544-6

Teeka and bhashya were essentially commentaries meant to explicate the meanings of Sanskrit texts to a wider audience. The first of these commentaries were intralingual, from Sanskrit into Sanskrit. During the centuries of vernacularization, regional poets used these genres to bring Sanskrit texts into their own languages. Sanskrit texts began to travel to the Marathi language through bhashya and teeka beginning in the twelfth century. Stephens absorbed these approaches to translation prevalent in Western India during his time and used them for telling the biblical story in seventeenth-century Goa.

Travel and transformation emerge as key concepts that are entwined with the idea of cultural translation. Travelling individuals are important conduits in the network of literary transmission. The physical act of transcribing and printing early texts such as *Kristapurāṇa* was coincident with the physical transformation of the translator-figure. *Chambers 21st Century Dictionary* defines transformation as "a change of form, constitution, substance, etc.". It also defines it as "metamorphosis" in the sense of organisms which change their physical appearances at different stages of life. Transformation, in this book, has been used in these two senses, where individuals metamorphose into newer physical appearances and behaviour, and when texts and traditions change their forms, constitution and contents in the process of cultural translation. Travel to distant lands, specifically with colonial ventures, necessitated translation to negotiate the details of daily life. These basic efforts at translating the new culture for themselves eventually led to deeper entanglements with local culture for early Catholic and Protestant missionaries. When missionaries such as Ziegenbalg sent meticulous records of Tranquebar to the Halle mission, these remained in history as the earliest representations of the region for the European world. By observing details of the landscape and cultural practices and writing about them, Ziegenbalg was undertaking "cultural translation" in the more ethnographic sense of the term. He was translating a foreign culture for his home readership. Stephens's letters to his family reveal a similar mediating position, where the missionary translated the culture of his mission field for his home culture. The division of the subcontinent into linguistic fields by missionaries could also be read as an attempt to make sense of the landscape with which these missionaries were dealing. By dividing the Indian Subcontinent into linguistic fields, they created units similar to monolingual European regions, presumably marking clear targets for their literary translation efforts.

The missionaries themselves seemed to have been translated in this process. From the lives of individuals such as Stephens, de Nobili, and Ziegenbalg discussed in this book, it is clear that the lives of these individuals and their worldviews began to transform once they started engaging with the cultural nuances of the region. What began as observation and recording of local features soon culminated in an appreciation for local literary and cultural forms, and a desire to harness these forms in their efforts for evangelization. This transformation in the missionaries, however, was not easy nor was it always welcomed by their European superiors. Once the engagement with local cultures began, these "translated men" were instantly set apart from those missionaries who refused to engage with local forms in any manner. The stock image of the missionary as someone who loved the gospel in all its "purity", and had a healthy indignation for all things local, is demolished by a reading of figures such as Stephens, de Nobili, and Ziegenbalg. The discontent of Ziegenbalg's superiors with his interest in local practices, de Nobili's trial by the Roman Catholic Church, and Stephens' struggle to print texts in the local language are testimony to the discomfort that Europeans had with the cultural translation that these missionaries were undergoing. Nevertheless, the study of these figures in the context of cultural translation has demonstrated that it is their experiments with cultural translation that makes these individuals stand out as important figures among their contemporaries. By translating Christianity for their specific microcosmic settings, they led to the creation of new literary traditions and unique local interpretations of Christianity.

In Stephens' case, this experiment involved the placing of Christianity in the context of purāṇic Hindu worldview. In order to do this, Stephens had to create a system of Romanization suited to the sounds of Marathi. Early missionaries such as Stephens were recording the structure of the language and adapting their evangelization to fit into the spaces provided by the language and culture. The transliteration of *Kristapurāṇa* into Devanagari may be read as another layer of "rewriting". The earliest Devanagari version is the Marsden Purāṇa, which has been discussed in Chapter 2 It is significant to note that this version completely leaves out the episode where Christ turned water into wine. After the Padre-guru had narrated the story of Christ's wine-making miracle, a local questioned him about the propriety of drinking wine (2.22.28). The Padre-guru immediately launched into a lengthy defence of different dietary practices of different lands. He argued that people who lived in "Hindustan" did not need to drink wine as they had access to plenty of good water. He also pointed out the ill-effects of alcoholism, pointing to the social conditions existent at the time. The writer of the Marsden Purāṇa, then, was involved in a kind of translation where the text was being manipulated (Hermans 1985) in order to give it a desired shape. The Marsden Purāṇa may also be read as a further translation of the manuscripts found in Goa because of its use of Sanskritized terms in place of the Latin/Portuguese terms found in other manuscripts. In this context, the complex relationship between the text and its script is a thread that requires further study.

The generic features of Stephens' narrative have special significance in the contemporary understanding of the act of translation. The transformation that occurs in this cultural translation is multi-layered. The conscious use of purāṇic terms and concepts in *Kristapurāṇa* is a site which reveals the intricacies of cultural translation of sacred texts. Instead of steering clear of Hindu referents, core purāṇic terms such as Vaicunttha were taken by Stephens and transformed into Christian spaces.

This book has argued that cultural translation is one of the ways in which ancient genre such as the Purāṇa are "novelized". It has also been argued that the Purāṇas inherently provide these spaces for cultural translation by accommodating new stories, languages, and cultures. The orality inherent in the purāṇic genre and its dialogic nature provided spaces for Stephens' listeners to influence the development of the narrative. In *Kristapurāṇa* the listeners do this by intervening in the telling of the story and clarifying doubts and suggesting ideas to the narrator. This makes the text a critical site for reading conversion experiences and for understanding how new Christians negotiated their new faith in the seventeenth century.

A large volume of Portuguese administrative documents are available in libraries worldwide, documenting the establishment of the *Estado* in India. However, it is texts such as *Kristapurāṇa* which provide rare insight into the converted individual's mind and provide the modern reader with a window into the past. The manner in which these locals engaged with and negotiated their new identities is an important aspect that emerged in this reading of *Kristapurāṇa*. The Jesuit records, which show that *Kristapurāṇa* was recited by locals in the seventeenth century and sung during church services, reveal the manner in which the locals appropriated this text in their everyday lives. This also leads a reader to wonder why a text which gained instant popularity after its publication lay in oblivion for centuries until Saldanha resurrected it in the early twentieth century through his printed edition.

Translation as it emerges from a reading of *Kristapurāṇa* is not a one-way process beginning with the colonizer-translator and stopping at the colonized-translated target audience. It is a complex network of transactions where the target audience's interpretation of the translated work is as critical to its form as the translator's interpretation. *Kristapurāṇa* also questions traditional ideas of a single, unmoving "original" text in translation. In *Kristapurāṇa*, the source material is as much the purāṇic tradition as the Christian narrative.

For the readers of seventeenth-century Goa, one of the reasons for being attracted to *Kristapurāṇa* was the thrill of hearing a new story in a familiar language and style (1.1.141). The inherent affinity of humans for new stories is one of the reasons that continue to draw newer generations of readers to a text such as *Kristapurāṇa*. The "newness" it imparts to the biblical narrative, the creative ways in which it explores the purāṇic tradition, are all factors that make the text relevant to the present day. The complexities of translation of sacred texts in a "microcosmic" setting such as seventeenth-century Goa also provides insight to the uses of translation in the contemporary world. Questions of sacredness, translating "back", and newer ways (or, as this book has attempted to demonstrate, older ways such as South Asian approaches) of translation are crucial in rethinking the translation of texts in today's world.

The genre chosen for holy-text translation and its consequent reception by a specific target audience may be used in contexts where holy-text translations are being taken out of the enclosure of religious practices. The Bible, for example, is increasingly being envisioned as a tool for meaningful social change in areas where it is a critical text (See Esala 2015). In India, scholars such as Devdutt Pattanaik are involved in the study of Purāṇas and other sacred text with a view to popularize them and also to engage with the ethical-social questions in them which are of relevance in the subcontinent today (see Pattanaik, *Indian Mythology*). In such contexts, South Asian texts such as *Kristapurāṇa* may provide much-needed insight into alternate ways of translating sacred texts while designing them for use in specific social contexts such as de-addiction programmes and rehabilitation attempts, among others. South Asian approaches towards translation, as understood from a reading of *Kristapurāṇa*, could make critical intervention into these translation ventures. Indigenous textual traditions from the regions of South Asia have the potential to contribute to an expanding and more nuanced understanding of translation practices.

Landscapes have been read as a significant aspect of cultural translation in this book. By analysing landscapes in the text, this book has attempted to address the current "spatial turn" in Translation Studies (Italiano 2016, 4). The role of cultural translation in (re)painting and (re)inventing landscapes for communities displaced by colonial and religious violence is one of the significant additions that this work makes to the field of Translation Studies. In the present age of inter-continental travel, refugee crises, and large-scale voluntary and forced migration, new roles of translation are being brought to the fore. The role of textual translation in aiding the re-invention of identities for dislocated communities is more relevant today, than it has been in any other age. The (re)creation of landscapes in/for areas which have been ravaged by war and migratory practices is a role that translation can play in the present age. The migrants struggle for "renegotiating cultural signs" and "translating space into place" may be better understood through the cultural translation of landscapes that take place in these contexts (see Inghilleri 2017, 143).

In the "Introduction" to her volume *Religious Transaction in Colonial South India*, Israel points out that the study of the sacred remains underexplored in the field of postcolonial studies (Israel 2011, 2). Translations of biblical texts in South Asia have rarely been studied in the light of cultural politics and identity formation. Even among the extant studies on translation in South Asia, the Portuguese period has largely remained in oblivion as far as critical studies of translated works from the period concerned. This area of study has found renewed interest among scholars and has been discussed in forums such as "Philosophy and Literature Meeting: The West(s) and the East(s)" (19–20 March 2018), a conference convened by the Goa University and the University of Porto. Portuguese-South Asian texts from the sixteenth and seventeenth centuries were highlighted through the deliberations in this conference. The present study is an attempt to address this gap in the study of sacred-text translation in the subcontinent and attempts to add *Kristapurāṇa* into the scholarship on the translation history of the region.

A study of sacred-text translation is not merely casting a glance at the ways in which texts travelled. It provides insight into the basic ways in which religions were interpreted and practised. For the converts in seventeenth-century Goa, as well as for missionaries, cultural translation provided the opportunity to discover spaces in religion that had been undiscovered before. In the process of adapting a religion to fit a certain cultural context, the religion itself becomes open to study, revealing its possibilities and limits. Comparative studies of religious texts through the rubric of translation is an important way of delving deeper into discussions on religion and bringing religious studies back into the purview of scholarly attention.

5.2 (Un)charted Landscapes

Keeping in mind the volume and complexity of themes in *Kristapurāṇa*, it is necessary to mention the threads which are yet to be unknotted in the study of this narrative. Stephens, the poet and translator, has been discussed in this book as a figure who was keenly aware of the literary and religious practices of his mission field,

Goa. His acquaintance with Hindu scriptures and life in Goa is amply substantiated in his poetic composition. As a reader, one would look for an indication from such a figure as Stephens, for his reflections on the colonial machinery, of which he was a part. However, Stephens' aim (as clearly stated in his *Kristapurāṇa)* was to convince the locals of the "truth" of Christianity. Although he critiqued individual acts of violence in his letters, an overall critique of the violence of colonial missions and religious conversion is absent in the text. A critical reading of the inclusions and exclusions in the text would be a worthwhile pursuit for the future.

Deciphering the mystery surrounding Stephens as a human figure, would have been of great interest. His missing letters, and his undiscovered place of burial, are all threads that remain unknown as of today. In addition to the difficulty of finding this material, these are aspects which had to be left largely un-investigated due to the textual focus of this work. The life of Stephens that has been recreated here is based on the textual material that is available today. An in-depth biographical inquiry into Stephens' life would be an interesting pursuit for the future.

A linguistic study of *Kristapurāṇa*—its morphology, syntax, the interesting blend of languages to be found in the text—have not been analysed in-depth by scholars in the English language. Malshe's unpublished thesis in the Marathi language focuses on these aspects, giving an intricate linguistic analysis of the text, beginning with the syllables, to sentence structure and style. It would have been significant to bring these aspects into English for a wider readership on *Kristapurāṇa*.

The figure of Christ himself, as Vaicuntthanath, as a rising sun which dispels the darkness of human life and the only way to attain *mukti* (salvation) and enter Vaicunttha is a central theme of *Kristapurāṇa*. This is an aspect which has merely been touched upon in this book. Stephens devotes a significant amount of space in his text in order to depict the humanness and divinity of Christ. The *Dussarem Puranna* begins in its first verses with the adoration of Christ: "My worship, Son of God/You are the giver of *mukti*/With the father and spirita santa/you alone are God" (2.1.2). Scenes of the crucifixion and resurrection are some of the most beautifully painted and lyrical portions of this narrative. The character of Christ in the narrative could have been fleshed out in more detail within the framework of cultural translation and is an avenue for future study.

A comparative reading with the other Christian Purāṇas composed after *Kristapurāṇa* would also yield important insights into the literary practices of the period. A study of these texts such as *Peter Purāṇa, Life of St. Anthony*, and *Sarveshvarache Dnyanopadesha* which have been mentioned in Chapter 1 may be taken up for a more detailed comparative reading in order to understand how the Christian purāṇic tradition developed after Stephens. A significant volume of the secondary material on the socio-political background of *Kristapurāṇa*, specifically the Portuguese rule in Goa, is in the Portuguese language. As I cannot read Portuguese, or the Sanskrit of the Purāṇas, my search of secondary literature was limited to some extent. English and Marathi sources have predominantly been used in reconstructing Stephens' life and English translations of Purāṇas have been used in formulating the arguments of this book.

Kristapurāṇa has close to 11,000 verses. The verses which have been cited and translated in this book provide a symptomatic understanding of the entire text. Several other verses could be closely analysed or translated to enrich the critical reading of the text. In Chapter 3, for instance, several more purāṇic terms, such as *moksa*, *punarjanma*, *yemapura*, *dharma* and *karma*, could have been studied. The analysis was limited to "Vaicunntha" in order to build a focus on the arguments in this book.

A text as complex as *Kristapurāṇa* provides multiple points of entry for critical analysis. This book has been an attempt to unravel a few of these strands. In placing *Kristapurāṇa* as a vital link in the translation history of South Asia, this book has opened it up for further analysis by scholars of translation, comparative literature and religious studies.

5.3 Distant Horizons

Cultural translation is a term with growing significance and is in the process of finding its own grammar as an area of study. I have attempted to analyse a few of its aspects through travel, generic transformations, and translated landscapes. However, the idea of cultural translation as a possible way of negotiating identities in sites of rupture requires further study. Landscapes and their place in works of translation are especially significant in this context and have been introduced by this book.

Early indological translations of South Asian texts, such as William Jones's translation of Kalidasa's *Abhijnanashakuntalam* (1789), Wilson's English *Vishnu Purāṇa* (1840), and Charles Wilkins's translation of the *Hitopadesha* (1844), would be suitable texts for reading cultural translation of landscapes. Being texts with abundant landscape writing, the depiction of landscapes in these texts, which were translated with a European readership in mind, would provide critical insight into the relationship between cultural translation and literary landscapes.

The concept of "Purāṇa" itself is of great interest and value in constructing a literary history of South Asia. The massive purāṇic corpus and its potential for novelization have only been introduced through *Kristapurāṇa*. It remains an area of study that deserves much deeper introspection and scholarly thought. The manner in which the purāṇic tradition developed and evolved would be of great interest to scholars of translation and literature, in making sense of the role of translation in the inauguration and development of vernacular literary traditions.

The aspect of "bhakti" in Marathi saint-literature, glimpses of which may be seen in numerous passages in *Kristapurāṇa*, is a thread which needs to be taken up for further discussion. The interaction between the Bhakti movements and Christian traditions, both Catholic and Protestant, have been studied by previous scholars (Pinch 177). *Kristapurāṇa* could provide useful insight into this area as an early text which used elements of bhakti poetry in a Christian writing. The temporal and spatial overlap between the saint-poet tradition and Christian missions is an important area for future study.

The figure of Mary as "Swamini", and as queen of Vaicunttha, is a significant theme of *Kristapurāṇa*. Mary is one of the most intricately constructed characters in the text and opens up some critical questions on the portrayal of women in sacred translations. Key cultural texts such as the Bible have been re-translated since the 1970s in order to highlight the depiction of women and gender minorities in works of translation (von Flotow, "Gender in Translation", 130). The translation of women and translations by women are further brought into focus by recent volumes, such as *Translating Women: Different Voices and New Horizons* (2016) edited by Luise von Flotow and Farzaneh Farahzad. The figure of Mary in *Kristapurāṇa* provides spaces for the reading of such gender-oriented perspectives into early biblical narratives. Stephens's Mary is the epitome of physical beauty and moral rectitude (2.3.11–17, 2.6.34). At the same time she is depicted as a lotus-eyed goddess who wields authority in Vaicunttha. These complexities in Stephens' painting of Mary's character provide avenues for future readings of the text. In addition to this story, extra-biblical aspects, such as the apocryphal tale of the Sybils (1.36.10) and other aspects of Catholic theology in the text, are areas which are open for analysis, and have not been dealt with in this book.

Cultural translation is a concept laden with conflict, violence, and complexities inherent in inter- and intra-cultural transfer. However, it is also one of the primary ways in which cultures "read" one another and communicate beyond linguistic and geographical boundaries. Translation is one of the paths by which newness enters cultures. In negotiating texts and traditions, translation is necessary for talking to one another in the contemporary world. The Marathi words for translation, *bhashantar* and *anuvad*, are significant in this context. One way of translating bhashantar would be as "the spaces between languages" (*bhasha*-languages, *antar*-distance). Translation inhabits these spaces in-between the multiple languages and cultures of South Asia. Anuvad, or "speaking after", implies the afterlife of a text that is embodied in the retelling of texts over and over again in the spaces between the bhashas. Texts attain their afterlife and renewed existence through cultural translation, made possible in the spaces provided by the multiple languages of South Asia. The "antar", or distance, between these languages is traversed through anuvad, a "speaking after" or retelling of texts into newer languages and cultures.

Stephens remarks through *Kristapurāṇa* that the scriptures ("Puranna") are like a great Ganga, too vast to be comprehended within the spaces of a single text:

> They have written so much,
> It is difficult for me to carry,
> So much is left in the scriptures,
> If you look at them
>
> We suffice ourselves with this much,
> Just as, to recognize the value of the waters of Ganga,
> One pot of water from it
> Is enough.
>
> (*Kristapurāṇa* 1.14.56, 57)

As it was not possible to show the whole of the scriptures to his readers, he selected portions out of it to show them that its waters are good, just as one pot of water from the Ganga will prove the goodness of all its waters. Similarly, this book has attempted to give a hint of what the river of *Kristapurāṇa* is like, and what other treasures it may hold. These verses are also symbolic of the rich and unexplored texts and translations in South Asia, of which *Kristapurāṇa* is but one example.

This journey with *Kristapurāṇa* is a continuing pursuit. The temporal limitations of this study leave the reader with more possibilities and larger questions to be addressed. The seventeenth century, in which this text was set, has afforded spaces for time-travel into distant lands, diverse cultural practices, and intense sacred transactions. Several possibilities remain for future research to study Thomas Stephens and his *Kristapurāṇa* as templates of literary and cultural transactions. The challenges of meandering through the wilderness of Christian writings and purāṇic literature remain, even as this study comes to a close. There is also a sense of anticipation and the hope that future research will take up such texts of the past, which are rare, tenuous links of the past to the present, and open up avenues which could lead the way into the future.

Note

1 *Jnāneswari* Chapter 10, verse 22. See Royson, Annie Rachel, "Audacious Retellings: Multilingualism and Translation in *Jnāneswari* and *Kristapurāṇa*" (2021) for a detailed analysis of this verse in *Jnāneswari*, Jnāneswar's Marathi retelling of the *Bhagvad Gita*.

BIBLIOGRAPHY

Primary Sources

Amonkar, Suresh. *Christa Purana (Konkani Translation)*. Goa: Directorate of Art and Culture, 2017a.

Bandelu, Shantaram P. *Phadara Stiphanskrta Khristapurana: Paile va Dusare*. 5th ed. Poona: Prasad Prakashan, 1956.

Drago, Caridade. *Christapuran*. Mumbai: Popular Prakashan, 1996.

Falcao, Nelson M. (Trans.). *Father Thomas Stephenskrut Khristapuran*. Bengaluru: Kristu Jyoti Publications, 2009.

———. (Trans.) *Father Thomas Stephens' Kristapurāṇa*. Bengaluru: Kristu Jyoti Publications, 2012.

Stephens, Thomas, and Joseph L. Saldanha. *The Christian Puranna of Father Thomas Stephens of the Society of Jesus*. Mangalore: Simon Alvarez, 1907.

Kristapurāṇa Manuscripts

Stephens, Thomas. *Kristapurāṇa* (*Discurso sobre a vinda de Jesu Christo Nosso Salvador ao Mundo dividido em dous tratados feito pelo Padre Thomas Estevão Ingrez da Companhia de Jesus. Impresso em Goa com licenca das Inquisição, e Ordinario no Collegio de S. Paulo novo de Companhia de Jesu. Anno de 1654, Escripto por Manoel Salvador Rebello, Natural de Margão no Anno 1767*). 1767. MS-57. Krishnadas Shama Goa State Central Library, Goa.

Stephens, Thomas. *Kristapurāṇa* (The Pilar MS). n.d.-a. Museum of the Pilar Monastery, Pilar, Goa.

Stephens, Thomas. *Kristapurāṇa* (The M.C. Saldanha MS). n.d.-b. Thomas Stephens Konknni Kendr, Alto Porvorim, Goa.

Stephens, Thomas. *Kristapurāṇa* (MS-2). n.d.-c. Thomas Stephens Konknni Kendr, Alto Porvorim, Goa.

Stephens, Thomas. *Kristapurāṇa* (The Bhaugun Kamat Vagh MS). n.d.-d. Pissurlencar Collection, Goa University Library.

Stephens, Thomas. n.d.-e. *The Christian Purana* (Devanagari script). Marsden Collection. London: School of Oriental and African Studies.

Secondary Sources

Abbott, Justin E. "The Discovery of the Original Devanāgari Text of the Christian Purāna of Thomas Stevens". *Bulletin of the School of Oriental and African Studies* 2.4 (1923): 679–683.

Amaladass, Anand. "Nobili, Roberto de". *The Oxford Encyclopaedia of South Asian Christianity.* (Eds.) Roger E. Hedlund, Jesudas M. Athyal, and Joshua Kalapati. New Delhi: Oxford University Press, 2012, 496–498.

Amonkar, Suresh. *Goenche Saunsarikikaran.* Goa: Directorate of Art and Culture, 2017b.

Apte, Vaman Shivaram. *The Practical Sanskrit-English Dictionary.* Delhi: Motilal Banarsidass, 1965.

Ashcroft, Bill, Gareth Griffiths, and Helen Tiffin. *Postcolonial Studies: The Key Concepts.* London: Routledge, 2000.

Asad, Talal. "The Concept of Cultural Translation in British Social Anthropology". *Writing Culture: The Poetics and Politics of Ethnography.* (Eds.) James Clifford, and George E. Marcus. Berkeley: University of California Press, 1986, 141–164.

Assmann, Jan, and John Czaplicka. "Collective Memory and Cultural Identity". *New German Critique* 65 (1995): 125–133.

Baker, Mona, and Gabriela Saldanha (Eds.). *Routledge Encyclopedia of Translation Studies.* 2nd ed. Oxon/New York: Routledge, 2009.

Bakhtin, M.M. "Epic and Novel". *The Dialogic Imagination.* (Ed.) Michael Holquist. Austin: University of Texas Press, 1981a, 3–40.

Bakhtin, M.M. "Discourse in the Novel". *The Dialogic Imagination.* (Ed.) Michael Holquist. Austin: University of Texas Press, 1981b, 259–422.

Bane, Theresa. *Encyclopedia of Imaginary and Mythical Places.* Jefferson, NC: McFarland, 2014.

Bassnett, Susan. *Translation Studies.* London: Methuen, 1980.

Bassnett, Susan, and André Lefevere. *Translation, History, and Culture.* London: Pinter Publishers, 1990.

Bassnett, Susan, and Harish Trivedi. *Postcolonial Translation: Theory and Practice.* London: Routledge, 1999.

Bastin, Georges. "Adaptation". *Routledge Encyclopedia of Translation Studies.* 2nd ed. (Eds.) Mona Baker, and Gabriela Saldanha. Oxon/New York: Routledge, 2009, 3–6.

Bayly, Susan. *Saints, Goddesses, and Kings.* Cambridge: Cambridge University Press, 1989.

Bellos, David. *Is That a Fish in Your Ear?: Translation and the Meaning of Everything.* London: Penguin Books, 2011.

Bender, Barbara. "Time and Landscape". *Current Anthropology* 43 (2002): 103–112.

Benjamin, Walter. "The Task of the Translator". *The Translation Studies Reader.* 3rd ed. (Ed.) Lawrence Venuti. Oxon: Routledge, 2012, 75–83.

Bhabha, Homi. *The Location of Culture.* Oxon/NewYork: Routledge, 1994.

Blanton, Casey. *Travel Writing: The Self and the World.* New York: Twayne Publishers, 1997.

Bowker, John (Ed.). *The Oxford Dictionary of World Religions.* Oxford: Oxford University Press, 1997.

Brems, Elke, Reine Meylaerts, and Luc Van Doorslaer (Eds.) *The Known Unknowns of Translation Studies.* Amsterdam/Philadelphia: John Benjamins Publishing Company, 2014.

Bright, William. "The Devanagari Script". *The World's Writing Systems.* (Eds.) Peter T. Daniels, and William Bright. New York/Oxford: Oxford University Press, 1996, 384–390.

Brodzki, Bella. *Can These Bones Live? Translation, Survival, and Cultural Memory.* Stanford, CA: Stanford University Press, 2007.

Buchanan, Claudius. *Christian Researches in Asia: with Notices of the Translation of the Scriptures into the Oriental Languages.* New York: Richard Scott, 1812.

Buden, Boris, Stefan Nowotny, Sherry Simon, Ashok Bery, and Michael Cronin. "Cultural Translation: An Introduction to the Problem, and Responses". *Translation Studies* 2.2 (2009): 196–219. Web.

Bullard, Roger A. "Texts/mss/Versions". *Mercer Dictionary of the Bible*. (Eds.) Watson E. Mills, and Roger Aubrey Bullard. Macon, GA: Mercer University Press, 1990, 890–896.

Burnell, Arthur Coke. *A Tentative List of Books and Some Mss. Relating to the History of the Portuguese in India Proper*. Mangalore: Basel Mission Press, 1880.

Chakravarti, Ananya. "Creating a Digital Archive of Indian Christian Manuscripts (EAP636)". *Endangered Archives Programme*. British Library, 2013.

Chambers 21st Century Dictionary. (Ed) Mairi Robinson and George Davidson. Edinburgh: Chambers, 1999.

Chatterjee, Chandrani. *Translation Reconsidered: Culture, Genre and the "Colonial Encounter" in Nineteenth Century Bengal*. Newcastle upon Tyne, UK: Cambridge Scholars Publishing, 2010.

Choudhuri, Indra Nath. "Towards an Indian Theory of Translation". *Indian Literature* 54.5 (259) (2010):113–123.

Cicero, Marcus Tullius. "The Best Kind of Orator". *Western Translation Theory: From Herodotus to Nietzsche*. (Trans.) H.M. Hubbell. (Ed.) Douglas Robinson. Oxon/New York: Routledge, 2014, 7–10.

Clooney, Francis X. *Western Jesuit Scholars in India*. Leiden: Brill, 2020.

Coburn, Thomas B. "The Study of the Purānas and the Study of Religion". *Religious Studies* 16.3 (1980): 341–352.

Conway, Kyle. "Cultural Translation". *Routledge Encyclopedia of Translation Studies*. (Eds.) Mona Baker, and Gabriela Saldanha, 129–133. New York: Routledge, 2020.

Cronin, Vincent. *A Pearl to India: The Life of Roberto de Nobili*. New York: Dutton, 1959.

Cronin, Michael. *Across the Lines: Travel, Language, Translation*. Dublin: Cork University Press, 2000.

———. *Translation and Identity*. Oxon: Routledge, 2006.

———. "Double Take: Figuring the Other and the Politics of Translation". *In Translation: Reflections, Refractions, Transformations*. Vol. 71. (Eds.) Paul St-Pierre, and Prafulla C. Kar. Amsterdam/Philadelphia: John Benjamins Publishing, 2007, 253–262.

Cuddon, John A. *A Dictionary of Literary Terms*. London: Penguin Books. 1999.

Dandekar, R.N. "Indian Mythology". *The Cultural Heritage of India*. Vol. II. (Eds.) S.K. De, U.N. Ghoshal, A.D. Pusalker, and R.C. Hazra, 80–94. Calcutta: The Ramakrishna Mission Institute of Culture. 1937.

Das, Sisir Kumar. *A History of Indian Literature, 500–1399: From Courtly to the Popular*. New Delhi: Sahitya Akademi, 2005.

Davis, Kathleen. *Deconstruction and Translation*. Manchester: St. Jerome Pub., 2001.

Derrida, Jacques. "Différance". *Speech and Phenomena, and Other Essays on Husserl's Theory of Signs*. (Eds.) David B. Allison, and Newton Garver. Evanston, IL: Northwestern University Press, 1973, 129–160.

———. *Of Grammatology*. (Trans.) Gayatri Chakravorty Spivak. Baltimore, MD: Johns Hopkins University Press, 1976.

———. "Des tours de Babel". *Difference in Translation* 167 (1985a). Print.

———. "Roundtable on Translation". *The Ear of the Other: Otobiography, Transference, Translation* (Ed) Christie McDonald. Lincoln: University of Nebraska Press (1985b): 91–161.

Deshpande, Achyut. *Prachin Marathi Vangmayacha Itihas: Bhag Choutha*. Pune: Venus Publications, 1977.

Devy, Ganesh. "Translation and Literary History—An Indian View". *Postcolonial Translation: Theory and Practice*. (Eds.) Susan Bassnett, and Harish Trivedi. London: Routledge, 1999, 182–188.

Dharwadker, Vinay. "A.K. Ramanujan's Theory and Practice of Translation". *Postcolonial Translation: Theory and Practice*. (Eds.) Susan Bassnett, and Harish Trivedi. London: Routledge, 1999, 114–140.

Dingwaney, Anuradha, and Carol Maier (Eds.). *Between Languages and Cultures: Translation and Cross-cultural Texts*. New Delhi: Oxford University Press, 1996.

Disney, A.R. *A History of Portugal and the Portuguese Empire*. New York: Cambridge University Press, 2009.

Doniger, Wendy. *Purāṇa Perennis: Reciprocity and Transformation in Hindu and Jaina Texts*. Albany: SUNY Press, 1993.

Dryden, John. "From the Preface to Ovid's Epistles in the Translation" (1680). *The Translation Studies Reader*. 3rd ed. (Ed.) Lawrence Venuti. Oxon/New York: Routledge, 2012, 38–42.

D'Souza, Desmond. "Goa". *The Oxford Encyclopaedia of South Asian Christianity*. (Eds.) Roger E. Hedlund, Jesudas M. Athyal and Joshua Kalapati. New Delhi: Oxford University Press, 2012, 277–278.

Eco, Umberto. *Interpretation and Overinterpretation*. Cambridge: Cambridge University Press, 1992.

———. *Experiences in Translation*. Toronto: University of Toronto, 2000.

Eliasson, Pär. "Mukti in *Kristapurāṇa*: How Thomas Stephens SJ (1549–1619) Conveys a Christian Message of Salvation in Words with Hindu Connotations" (Dissertation). University of Goteburg, 2015.

Eliot, T.S. *The Sacred Wood and Major Early Essays*. New York: Dover Publication, 1998.

Esala, Nathan. "Ideology and Bible Translation: Can Biblical Performance Criticism Help?". *The Bible Translator* 66.3 (2015): 216–229.

Even-Zohar, Itamar. "The Position of Translated Literature within the Literary Polysystem" (1978). *The Translation Studies Reader*. 3rd ed. (Ed.) Lawrence Venuti. Oxon: Routledge, 2012, 162–167.

Falcao, Nelson M. *Kristapurāṇa: As Christian-Hindu Encounter*. Gujarat: Gujarat Sahitya Prakash, 2003.

Fazl, Abul, and H. Beveridge. *Akbarnama*. Vol. 3. (Trans.) Henry Beveridge. New Delhi: Atlantic Publishers, 2017.

Feldhaus, Anne and S.G. Tulpule. *A Dictionary of Old Marathi*. Mumbai: Popular Prakashan, 1999.

Fernando, Leonard, and G. Gispert-Sauch. *Christianity in India: Two Thousand Years of Faith*. New Delhi: Viking, 2004.

Finer, Samuel Edward. *The History of Government from the Earliest Times: Ancient monarchies and empires*. Vol. 1. Oxford: Oxford University Press, 1997.

Flood, Gavin D. *An Introduction to Hinduism*. Cambridge: Cambridge University Press, 1996.

Foley, Henry. *Records of the English Province of the Society of Jesus*. Vol. II. London: Burns & Oates, 1883.

Frow, John. *Genre*. Oxon/New York: Routledge, 2006.

Frykenberg, Robert Eric. "Christian Inculturation in India. By Paul M. Collins. Liturgy, Worship, and Society". *Church History* 77.04 (2008a): 1118. Web.

———. *History of Christianity in India*. Oxford: Oxford University Press, 2008b.

———. "Beschi, Constanzo Giuseppe". *The Oxford Encyclopaedia of South Asian Christianity*. (Eds.) Roger E. Hedlund, Jesudas M. Athyal and Joshua Kalapati. New Delhi: Oxford University Press, 2012, 79.

Frykenberg, Robert Eric, and Alaine M. Low. *Christians and Missionaries in India*. Grand Rapids, MI: W.B. Eerdmans Pub., 2003.

Frykenberg, Robert Eric, and Richard Fox Young. *India and the Indianness of Christianity: Essays on Understanding–Historical, Theological, and Bibliographical–In Honor of Robert Eric Frykenberg*. Grand Rapids, MI: William B. Eerdmans Pub., 2009.

Geertz, Clifford. *The Interpretation of Cultures*. New York: Basic Books, 1973.

Gentzler, Edwin. *Contemporary Translation Theories*. London/NewYork: Routledge, 1993.

———. *Translation and Rewriting in the Age of Post-translation Studies*. Oxon: Routledge, 2017.

George, Annie Rachel and Arnapurna Rath. "Musk among Perfumes: Creative Christianity in Thomas Stephens's *Kristapurana*". *Church History and Religious Culture* 96.3 (2016a): 304–324.

———. "Translation, Transformation and Genre in the *Kristapurana*". *Asia Pacific Translation and Intercultural Studies* 3.3 (2016b): 280–293.

———. "Ângela Barreto Xavier and Ines G. Županov, *Catholic Orientalism: Portuguese Empire, Indian Knowledge*". *South Asia Multidisciplinary Academic Journal* [Online], Book Reviews, 13 June 2017, 2–7. http://samaj.revues.org/4353

Grierson, George Abraham (Ed.). *Linguistic Survey of India*. Calcutta: Office of the Superintendent of Government Printing, India, 1898–1928.

Grossman, Edith. *Why Translation Matters*. Hyderabad: Orient Blackswan, 2011.

Hakluyt, Richard. *Voyages and Discoveries*. London: Penguin, 1972.

Harris, Jonathan Gil. "Hi Mho Jhi Kudd: Thomas Stephens's Translated Flesh, Or, Coconuts in Goa". *Postmedieval: A Journal of Medieval Cultural Studies* 4.4 (2013): 491–502.

———. *The First Firangis: Remarkable Stories of Heroes, Healers, Charlatans, Courtesans and Other Foreigners Who Became Indian*. New Delhi: Aleph Book Company, 2014.

Hazra, Rajendra Prasad. "The Purāṇas". *The Cultural Heritage of India*. Vol. II. (Eds.) S.K. De, U.N. Ghoshal, A.D. Pusalker, and R.C. Hazra, 80–94. Calcutta: The Ramakrishna Mission Institute of Culture. 1937.

Hedlund, Roger E., Jesudas M. Athyal and Joshua Kalapati. (Eds.). *The Oxford Encyclopaedia of South Asian Christianity*. New Delhi: Oxford University Press, 2012.

Henderson, David. "American Wilderness Philosophy". 2014. Web.

Henn, Alexander. *Hindu–Catholic Encounters in Goa: Religion, Colonialism, and Modernity*. Indianapolis, IN: Indiana University Press, 2014.

———. "Kristapurāṇa: Translating the Name of God in Early Modern Goa". *South Asia Multidisciplinary Academic Journal* 12 (2015), 1–17.

Hermans, Theo. *The Manipulation of Literature: Studies in Literary Translation*. London: Croom Helm, 1985.

———. (Ed.). *Translating Others*. Vol. 2. Oxon/New York: Routledge, 2014.

Hobsbawm, Eric, and Terence Ranger (Eds.). *The Invention of Tradition*. Cambridge: Cambridge University Press, 1983.

Hooper, J.S.M. *The Bible in India: With a Chapter on Ceylon*. Oxford: Oxford University Press, 1938.

Horace. "Imitating in Your Own Words". *Western Translation Theory: From Herodotus to Nietzsche*. 2nd ed. (Trans.) E.C. Wickham. (Ed.) Douglas Robinson. Oxon/New York: Routledge, 2014, 14–15.

Inghilleri, Moira. *Translation and Migration*. Oxon/New York: Routledge, 2017.

Israel, Hephzibah. "Words … Borrow'd from Our Books: Translating Scripture, Language Use, and Protestant Tamil Identity in Post/colonial South India". *Journal of Commonwealth and Postcolonial Studies* 15.1 (2008), 31–48.

———. *Religious Transactions in Colonial South India*. Basingstoke: Palgrave Macmillan, 2011.

Italiano, Federico. *Translation and Geography*. Oxon/New York: Routledge, 2016.

Jakobson, Roman. "On Linguistic Aspects of Translation". *On Translation*. (Ed.) Reuben A. Brower. Cambridge, MA: Harvard University Press, 1959, 232–239.

Jauss, Hans Robert. *Towards an Aesthetic of Reception*. (Trans.) Timothy Bahti. Minneapolis: University of Minnesota Press, 1982.

Jeyaraj, Daniel. "Indian Participation in Enabling, Sustaining, and Promoting Christian Mission in India". *India and the Indianness of Christianity: Essays on Understanding–Historical, Theological, and Bibliographical–In Honor of Robert Eric Frykenberg*. (Eds.) Robert Eric Frykenberg, and Richard Fox Young. Grand Rapids, MI: William B. Eerdmans Pub., 2009, 26–42.

Jnaneswar. *Jnaneswari (Bhavarthadeepika)*. (Trans.) V.G. Pradhan. (Ed.) H.M. Lambert. New York: State University of New York Press, 1969.

Jones, Arun. "Christianity in South Asia: Negotiating Religious Pluralism". *Introducing World Christianity*. (Ed.) Charles E. Farhadian. West Sussex, UK: Wiley-Blackwell, 2012, 93–107.

Jones, William. *Sacontala, Or the Fatal Ring, an Indian Drama by Calidas Translated from the Original Sanscrit and Pracrit*. London: Edwards, 1792.

Katan, David. *Translating Cultures: An Introduction for Translators, Interpreters and Mediators*. Oxon/New York: Routledge, 2014.

Karmarkar, A.P. "Religion and Philosophy of the Epics". *The Cultural Heritage of India*. Vol. II. (Eds.) S.K. De, U.N. Ghoshal, A.D. Pusalker, and R.C. Hazra, 80–94. Calcutta: The Ramakrishna Mission Institute of Culture. 1937.

Ketkar, Sachin. "Lighting a Lamp with a Lamp: The *Bhavarth Deepika* as Translation". International Conference on Translation Studies: New Directions Savitibai Phule Pune University, Pune, 24 January 2018. Conference Presentation.

———. "Dnyaneshwar's 'Duji Shrushti:' Poetics and Cultural Politics of Pre-Colonial Translation in the Dnyaneshwari". *India in Translation, Translation in India*. (Ed.) G.J.V. Prasad, 1–28. New Delhi: Bloomsbury, 2019.

Koepping, Elizabeth. "India, Pakistan, Bangladesh, Burma/Myanmar". *Christianities in Asia*. (Ed.) Peter C. Phan. Malden, MA: Wiley-Blackwell, 2011, 9–35.

Lefevere, André. "Mother Courage's Cucumbers: Text, System and Refraction in a Theory of Literature". *The Translation Studies Reader*. 3rd ed. (Ed.) Lawrence Venuti. Oxon: Routledge, 2012, 203–219.

Locke, J. Courtenay (Ed.). *The First Englishmen in India: Letters and Narratives of Sundry Elizabethans Written by Themselves*. London: Routledge, 1930.

Long, Lynne (Ed.). *Translation and Religion: Holy Untranslatable?*. Clevedon, UK: Multilingual Matters, 2005.

Lukács, Georg. *Probleme der Asthetik, Werke*, Vol. 10. Neuwied: Luchterhand, 1969.

Maitland, Sarah. *What Is Cultural Translation?*. London: Bloomsbury, 2017.

Malshe, S.G. "Father Stiphanschya Khristapuranacha Bhasik aani Vangmayina Abhyasa" (Doctoral Thesis). Bombay: University of Bombay, 1961.

Marvell, Andrew. "Bermudas". *The Poems of Andrew Marvell*. (Ed.) Nigel Smith. Oxon/New York: Routledge, 2013, 56–57.

Merrill, Christi A. "The Afterlives of Punditry: Rethinking Fidelity in Sacred Texts". *Decentering Translation Studies: India and Beyond*. (Eds.) Judy Wakabayashi, and Rita Kothari. Amsterdam/Philadelphia: John Benjamins Publishing, 2009, 75–94.

Metcalf, Thomas R. *Ideologies of the Raj*. Cambridge: Cambridge University Press, 1994.

Mitchell, W.J. Thomas. *Landscape and Power*. Chicago/London: University of Chicago Press, 2002.

Moffet, Samuel. *A History of Christianity in Asia: Volume I*. 2nd ed. New York: Orbis Books, 1998.

————. *A History of Christianity in Asia: Volume II.* New York: Orbis Books, 2005.

Molesworth, J.T. *Molesworth's Marathi-English Dictionary.* Pune: Shubhada-Saraswat Prakashan, 1996.

Mosse, David. *The Saint in the Banyan Tree: Christianity and Caste Society in India.* Berkeley: University of California Press, 2012.

Mukherjee, Sujit. "Transcreating Translation". *Indian Literature* 40.4 (180) (1997): 158–167.

Munday, Jeremy. *Introducing Translation Studies: Theories and Applications.* Oxon: Routledge, 2001.

Neill, Stephen Charles. *A History of Christianity in India.* Cambridge: Cambridge University Press, 1985.

Nida, Eugene. "Principles of Translation as Exemplified by Bible Translating". *On Translation.* (Ed.) Reuben A. Brower. Cambridge, MA: Harvard University Press, 1959, 11–31.

————. "Principles of Correspondence" (1964). *The Translation Studies Reader.* 3rd ed. (Ed.) Lawrence Venuti. Oxon: Routledge, 2012, 141–155.

Nietzsche, Friedrich. "Translation as Conquest". *Western Translation Theory: From Herodotus to Nietzsche.* 2nd ed. (Ed.) Douglas Robinson. Oxon/New York: Routledge, 2014, 262.

Niranjana, Tejaswini. *Siting Translation: History, Post-Structuralism and the Colonial Context.* Berkeley/Los Angeles: University of California Press, 1992.

Nord, Christiane. *A Functional Typology of Translations.* Amsterdam/Philadelphia: John Benjamins, 1997.

Novetzke, Christian Lee. *The Quotidian Revolution: Vernacularization, Religion, and the Premodern Public Sphere in India.* New York: Columbia University Press, 2016.

O'Hanlon, Rosalind. "Contested Conjunctures: Brahman Communities and "Early Modernity" in India". *The American Historical Review* 118.3 (2013): 765–787.

O'Malley, John W. *The Jesuits: A History from Ignatius to the Present.* London: Rowman and Littlefield, 2014.

Otto, Rudolf, and John Wilfred Harvey. *The Idea of the Holy.* Oxford: Oxford University Press, 1926.

Panikker, Ayyappa. *Medieval Indian Literature: An Anthology.* Vol. 3. New Delhi: Sahitya Akademi, 1999.

Pargiter, F.E. "Purāṇa". *Encyclopaedia of Religion and Ethics.* Vol. 12. (Eds.) Hastings, James, John Alexander Selbie, and Louis Herbert Gray. London: Burns & Oates, 1922.

Patnaik, B.N. *Retelling as Interpretation: An Essay on Sarala Mahabharata.* Jadavpur: Department of Comparative Literature, Jadavpur University, 2013.

Pattanaik, Devdutt. *Indian Mythology: Tales, Symbols, and Rituals from the Heart of the Subcontinent.* Vermont: Inner Traditions/Bear & Co., 2003.

Phan, Peter C. *In Our Own Tongues: Perspectives from Asia on Mission and Inculturation.* New York: Orbis, 2003.

————. *Christianities in Asia.* Malden, MA: Wiley-Blackwell, 2011.

Pinch, Vijay. "Bhakti and the British Empire". *Past & Present* 179 (2003): 159–196.

Pinto, Rochelle. *Translation, Script and Orality: Becoming a Language of State.* Hyderabad: Orient Blackswan, 2021.

Pollock, Sheldon I. *The Language of the Gods in the World of Men.* Berkeley: University of California Press, 2006.

————. "India in the Vernacular Millennium: Literary Culture and Polity, 1000–1500". *Daedalus* 127.3 (1998): 41–74.

Prasad, G.J.V. "Caste in and Recasting Language". *Decentering Translation Studies: India and Beyond.* (Eds.) Judy Wakabayashi, and Rita Kothari. Amsterdam/Philadelphia: John Benjamins Publishing, 2009, 17–28.

Pratt, Mary Louise. "Arts of the Contact Zone". Profession, 33–40, 1991. Accessed March 4, 2021. www.jstor.org/stable/25595469.

———. *Imperial Eyes: Travel Writing and Transculturation*. London: Routledge. 1992.

Pratt, Mary Louise, Birgit Wagner, Ovidi Carbonell Cortés, Andrew Chesterman, and Maria Tymoczko. "Translation Studies Forum: Cultural Translation". *Translation Studies* 3.1 (2010): 94–110.

Priolkar, Anant Kakba. "Pitaji Stephenskrut Kristapuran: Aarambhi Thodese". *Punarutthit Yeshu*, edited by J.S. Miranda, 1–30. Vasai: Marathi C.T.S., 1949.

———. "Two Recently Discovered Letters of Father Thomas Stephens". *Journal of the University of Bombay* XXV (1956): 114–123.

———. *The Printing Press in India*. Bombay: Marathi Samshodhana Mandala, 1958.

———. "Christian Literature of the Sixteenth and Seventeenth Centuries". *Literature and Languages*. Maharashtra State Gazetteers, Directorate of Government Printing, Stationery and Publications, Maharashtra State, 1971.

Priolkar, Anant Kakba. *The Goa Inquisition: Being a Quatercentenary Commemoration Study of the Inquisition in India*. 2nd ed. Panaji: Rajhans Publication, 2008.

Pym, Anthony. *Translation and Text Transfer: An Essay on the Principles of Intercultural Communication*. Frankfurt am Main: P. Lang, 1992.

———. *Exploring Translation Theories*. Oxon/New York: Routledge, 2010.

Rafael, Vicente L. *Contracting Colonialism: Translation and Christian Conversion in Tagalog Society under Early Spanish Rule* (1988). Durham, NC: Duke University Press, 2012.

Rajamanickam, S. "The Poem Tembavani by Joseph Beschi, SJ". *Cahiers de Joséphologie* 42.1 (1994): 20.

Ramakrishnan, E.V. "Translation as Resistance: The Role of Translation in the Making of Malayalam Literary Tradition". *Decentering Translation Studies: India and Beyond*. (Eds.) Judy Wakabayashi, and Rita Kothari. John Benjamins Publishing, 2009, 29–42.

Ramanujan, Attipat Krishnaswami. "Three Hundred Ramayanas: Five Examples and Three Thoughts on Translation". *Many Ramayanas: The Diversity of a Narrative Tradition in South Asia*. (Ed.) Paula Richman. University of California Press, 1991, 22–48.

———. On Folk Mythologies and Folk Purāṇas. *Purāṇa Perennis: Reciprocity and Transformation in Hindu and Jaina Texts*. (Ed.) Wendy Doniger. New York: State University of New York Press, 1993, 101–120.

Rao, Velcheru Narayana. "Purāṇa as Brahminic Ideology". *Purāṇa Perennis: Reciprocity and Transformation in Hindu and Jaina Texts*. (Ed.) Wendy Doniger. New York: State University of New York Press, 1993, 85–100.

Rasiah, Jeyaraj. "Sri Lanka". *Christianities in Asia*. (Ed.) Peter C. Phan. Malden, MA: Wiley-Blackwell, 2011, 45–60.

Rath, Arnapurna. "Knots of the Narrative: A Bakhtinian Analysis of Chronotopes in the Fiction of Amitav Ghosh" (Doctoral Thesis). Mumbai: Indian Institute of Technology Bombay. 2010.

Raychaudhuri, Hemchandra. "The Mahabharata: Some Aspects of Its Culture". *The Cultural Heritage of India*. Vol. II. (Eds.) S.K. De, U.N. Ghoshal, A.D. Pusalker, and R.C. Hazra, 71–79. Calcutta: The Ramakrishna Mission Institute of Culture, 1937.

Reiss, Katharina, and Hans J. Vermeer. *Grundlegung einer allgemeinen Translationstheorie*. Tubingen: Niemeyer, 1984.

Rezavi, Syed Ali Nadeem. "Religious Disputations and Imperial Ideology: The Purpose and Location of Akbar's Ibadatkhana". *Studies in History* 24.2 (2008): 195–209.

Richards, John F. "Early Modern India and World History". *Journal of World History* 8.2 (1997): 197–209.

Riches, John Kenneth. *The Bible*. Oxford: Oxford University Press, 2000.

Rivara, J. H. da Cunha. *An Historical Essay on the Konkani Language* (1856), (Trans) Fr. Theophilus Lobo. Bombay: Marathi Samshodhana Mandal, 1958.

Robinson, Douglas. *Western Translation Theory: From Herodotus to Nietzsche*. 2nd ed. (Ed.) Douglas Robinson. Oxon/New York: Routledge, 2014.

Robinson, Peter. *Poetry and Translation: The Art of the Impossible*. Liverpool: Liverpool University Press, 2010.

Robinson, Rowena. "Cuncolim: Weaving a Tale of Resistance". *Economic and Political Weekly*, 1997.

Rocher, Ludo. *The Purāṇas*. Weisbaden: Harrasowitz, 1986.

Rose, Marilyn G. (Ed.). *Beyond the Western Tradition: Translation Perspectives XI 2000*. New York: University of New York, 2000.

Royson, Annie Rachel. "'Tell us This Story from the Beginning': Genre, Dialogue, and Cultural Translation in Thomas Stephens's *Kristapurāṇa*". *Nidan: International Journal for Indian Studies* 4.2 (2019): 21–42.

———. "Audacious Retellings: Multilingualism and Translation in *Jnāneswari* and *Kristapurāṇa*". *Translation Studies* 14.2 (2021): 150–166.

Rubies, Joan-Pau. *Travel and Ethnology in the Renaissance: South India through European Eyes, 1250–1625*. Cambridge: Cambridge University Press, 2004.

Rushdie, Salman. *Imaginary Homelands*. London: Granta Books, 1991.

Said, Edward W. *Orientalism*. New York: Pantheon Books. 1978.

——— "Invention, Memory and Place". *Landscape and Power*. (Ed.) W.J. Thomas Mitchell. Chicago/London: University of Chicago Press. 2002, 241–260.

Salama-Carr, Myriam. "Translation and the Creation of Genre: The Theatre in Nineteenth Century Egypt". *Translating Others*. Vol. 2. (Ed.) Theo Hermans. Manchester: St. Jerome Publishing, 2006, 314–324.

Saradesāya, Manohararāya. *A History of Konkani Literature: from 1500 to 1992*. New Delhi: Sahitya Akademi, 2000.

Sastri, K.A. Nilakanta. *A History of South India: From Prehistoric Times to the Fall of Vijayanagar*. Oxford: Oxford University Press, 1955.

Saussure, Ferdinand. *Course in General Linguistics*. 3rd ed. (Eds.) Charles Bally, and Albert Sechehaye. New York/Toronto/London: McGraw-Hill Book Company, 1915.

Schama, Simon. *Landscape and Memory*. New York: Vintage Books, 1996.

Schurhammer, Georg. "Thomas Stephens, 1549–1619". *The Month* 13 (1953): 197–210.

———. "Der Marathidichter Thomas Stephens SI Neue Dokumente". *Archivum Historicum Societatis Iesu* 26 (1957): 67–82.

Siddall, Stephen. *Landscape and Literature*. Cambridge: Cambridge University Press, 2009.

Simon, Sherry. "Rites of Passage: Translation and Its Intents". *The Massachusetts Review* 31.1/2 (1990): 96–110. Web.

Simon, Sherry, and Paul St-Pierre. *Changing the Terms: Translating in the Postcolonial Era*. Ottawa: University of Ottawa Press, 2015.

Singh, Avadhesh K. *Translation: Its Theory and Practice*. New Delhi: Creative Books, 1996.

Singh, Brijraj. "The First Englishman in India: Thomas Stephens (1547–1619)". *Journal of South Asian Literature* 30.1/2 (1995): 146–161.

Snell-Hornby, Mary. *The Turns of Translation Studies*. Amsterdam: J. Benjamins Pub., 2006.

Somaratna, G.P.V. "Henriques, Henrique". *The Oxford Encyclopaedia of South Asian Christianity*. (Eds.) Roger E. Hedlund, Jesudas M. Athyal and Joshua Kalapati. New Delhi: Oxford University Press, 2012, 298–299.

Southwood, James. "Thomas Stephens, SJ, The First Englishman in India". *Bulletin of the School of Oriental and African Studies* 3.2 (1924): 231–240.

Spivak, Gayatri. *Outside in the Teaching Machine*. New York: Routledge, 1993, 179–200.

———. "Translation as Culture". In *Translation: Reflections, Refractions, Transformations*. Vol. 71. (Eds.) Paul St-Pierre, and Prafulla C. Kar. Amsterdam/Philadelphia: John Benjamins Publishing, 2007, 263–276.

Steiner, George. *After Babel*. Oxford: Oxford University Press, 1975.

Sturge, Kate. "Cultural Translation". *Routledge Encyclopedia of Translation Studies*. 2nd ed. (Eds.) Mona Baker, and Gabriela Saldanha. Oxon/New York: Routledge, 2009, 67–70.

Sugirtharajah, Rasiah S. *The Bible and the Third World: Precolonial, Colonial and Postcolonial Encounters*. Cambridge: Cambridge University Press, 2001.

The Bible. New International Version. Oxford University Press, 1998.

Thoreau, Henry David. *Walden*. (Ed.) J. Lyndon Shanley. Princeton, NJ: Princeton University Press, 1971.

———. *Walking*. Cambridge, MA: The Riverside Press, 1914.

Toury, Gideon. "The Nature and Role of Norms in Translation" (1978). *The Translation Studies Reader*. 3rd ed. (Ed.) Lawrence Venuti. Oxon: Routledge, 2012, 168–182.

Trivedi, Harish. "Translating Culture Vs Cultural Translation". *In Translation: Reflections, Refractions, Transformations*. Vol. 71. (Eds.) Paul St-Pierre, and Prafulla C. Kar. Amsterdam/Philadelphia: John Benjamins Publishing, 2007, 277–288.

Tulpule, Shankar Gopal. "Marathica Khristi Puranika". *Pratisthan*, February 1954.

———. *Classical Marāṭhī Literature*. Wiesbaden: Otto Harrassowitz, 1979.

———. "Hagiography in Medieval Marathi Literature". *According to Tradition: Hagiographical Writing in India*. Vol. 5. (Eds.) Winand M. Callewaert, and Rupert Snell. Wiesbaden: Otto Harrassowitz Verlag, 1994, 159–167.

Tymoczko, Maria. "Translation: Ethics, Ideology, Action". *The Massachusetts Review* 47.3 (2015): 442–461. Web. 14 April 2015.

Tymoczko, Maria, and Edwin Gentzler (Eds.). *Translation and Power*. Amherst/Boston: University of Massachusetts Press, 2002.

Tytler, Alexander Fraser. "Essay on the Principles of Translation" (1790). *Western Translation Theory: From Herodotus to Nietzsche*. (Ed.) Douglas Robinson. Oxon/New York: Routledge, 2014, 209–212.

Veliath, Cyril. "Thomas Stephens – A Human Monument of Inculturation in India". *Bulletin of the Faculty of Foreign Studies*. Sophia University, 46 (2011): 153–178.

Vengco, Sabino. "Another Look at Inculturation". *Philippine Studies* 32.2 (1984): 181–196. Web.

Venuti, Lawrence. *The Translation Studies Reader*. 3rd ed. Oxon/New York: Routledge, 2012.

———. *The Translator's Invisibility: A History of Translation*. Oxon/New York: Routledge, 1995/2017.

Vieira, Else Ribeiro Pires. "Liberating Calibans: Readings of *Anthropofagia* and Haroldo de Campos' Poetics of Transcreation. *Postcolonial Translation: Theory and Practice*. (Eds.) Susan Bassnett, and Harish Trivedi. London: Routledge, 1999, 95–113.

Viswanathan, Gauri. "Currying Favor: The Politics of British Educational and Cultural Policy in India, 1813–1854". *Social Text* 19/20 (1988): 85. Web.

Visvanathan, Susan. *The Christians of Kerala: History, Belief and Ritual among the Yakoba*. Oxford: Oxford University Press, 1993.

Vitelleschi, Muzio, and Lorenzo delle Pozze. *Lettere Annue Del Giappone, China, Goa, et Ethiopia*. Napoli: Per Lazaro Scoriggio, 1621.

Von Flotow, Luise. "Gender in Translation". *Handbook of Translation Studies* 1 (2010): 129–133.

Von Flotow, Luise, and Farzaneh Farahzad (Eds.). *Translating Women: Different Voices and New Horizons*. Oxon/New York: Routledge, 2016.

Wainwright, Geoffrey, and Karen B. Westerfield Tucker. *The Oxford History of Christian Worship*. Oxford: Oxford University Press, 2006.

Wakabayashi, Judy, and Rita Kothari (Eds.). *Decentering Translation Studies: India and Beyond*. Vol. 86. Amsterdam/Philadelphia: John Benjamins Publishing, 2009.

Wakankar, Milind. "The Crisis in Religion: Christianity and Conversion in the Marathi Nineteenth Century". *South Asia: Journal of South Asian Studies* 41.2 (2018): 468–482.

Warf, Barney, and Santa Arias (Eds.). *The Spatial Turn: Interdisciplinary Perspectives*. London/New York: Routledge, 2009.

Washbrook, David. "Intimations of Modernity in South India". *South Asian History and Culture* 1.1 (2009): 125–148.

White, Lynn. "The Historical Roots of Our Ecological Crisis". *Science* 155.3767 (1967): 1203–1207.

Wicki, Joseph. *Documenta Indica*. Vol. XI. Rome: Institutum Historicum Soc. Iesu, 1970.

———. *Documenta Indica*. Vol. XII. Rome: Institutum Historicum Soc. Iesu, 1972.

———. *Documenta Indica*. Vol. XIV. Rome: Institutum Historicum Soc. Iesu, 1979.

Wilfred, Felix. "South Asian Christianity in Context". *The Oxford Handbook of Christianity in Asia*. (Ed.) Felix Wilfred. Oxford: Oxford University, 2014, 31–50.

Wilkins, Charles. *The Hitopadesha: A Collection of Fables and Tales in Sanscrit by Vishnusarmá, with the Bengali and the English Translations the Former by the Editor, the Latter by Sir C. Wilkins Revised. Edited by Lakshami Náráyan Nyálankár. Sansk., Beng. & Eng*. Calcutta: Sharsungro Press, 1844.

Williams, George M. *Handbook of Hindu Mythology*. New York: Oxford University Press, 2003.

Wilson, Horace Hayman. 1840. *The Vishnu Purāṇa*. London: John Murray. http://www.sacred-texts.com/hin/vp/index.htm.

———. "Essays on the Puránas. I". *The Journal of the Royal Asiatic Society of Great Britain and Ireland* 5.1 (1839a): 61–72.

———. "Essays on the Puránas. II". *Journal of the Royal Asiatic Society of Great Britain and Ireland* 5.2 (1839b): 280–313.

Woodhead, Linda. *Christianity*. Oxford: Oxford University Press, 2004.

Woodworth, Paddy. "Landscape and Literature" (2003). International Writing Program Archive of Residents' Work, University of Iowa. Web.

Wolf, Michaela. "Translation-Transculturation. Measuring the Perspectives of Transcultural Political Action". *Transversal*, 04/2008. EIPCP Multilingual Web Journal. Web.

Wolf, Michaela, and Fukari, Alexandra. *Constructing a Sociology of Translation*. Amsterdam: John Benjamins Pub. Co., 2007.

Wright, John. "The Bible's Prehistory, Purpose and Political Future" (MOOC). *Coursera*. https://www.coursera.org/.

Xavier, Ângela Barreto, and Ines G. Županov. *Catholic Orientalism: Portuguese Empire, Indian Knowledge*. New Delhi: Oxford University Press, 2015.

Zapf, Hubert. *Literature as Cultural Ecology*. London: Bloomsbury. 2017.

Zogbo, Lynell. "Bible, Jewish and Christian". *Routledge Encyclopedia of Translation Studies*. 2nd ed. (Eds.) Mona Baker, and Gabriela Saldanha. Oxon/New York: Routledge, 2009, 21–27.

Županov, Ines G. *Disputed Missions: Jesuit Experiments and Brahmanical Knowledge in Seventeenth Century India*. New Delhi: Oxford University Press, 1999.

——— "'I Am a Great Sinner': Jesuit Missionary Dialogues in Southern India (Sixteenth Century)". *Journal of the Economic and Social History of the Orient* 55.2–3 (2012): 415–446. Web.

Zwartjes, Otto. *Portuguese Missionary Grammars in Asia, Africa and Brazil, 1550–1800*. Amsterdam: John Benjamins, 2011.

APPENDIX 1
The Rise of Joseph in Egypt

(*Kristapurāṇa* 1.13.1–14)

Tãua to mhanne nrupanathu	The king then said
Aissa cauannu pã budhiyuctu	What kind of wise man is this
Pahantã nadisse Egiptantu	In all of Egypt there was never found
Iose sariqha	A man like Joseph
Maga Iosethẽ zãuallĩ bolauni	Then, calling Joseph to him
He carye tuuã quize mhannoni	He said, you take up this responsibility
Egiptacha pradhanu houni	Become the leader of Egypt
Razebharu chalauaua	And run its affairs
Yethoni sacallaiquy sthiti	From this moment I give
Meã vopily tuzã hastĩ	All matters into your hands
Egiptachy budhi samasti	All the judgement of Egypt
Tuuã chalauauy	You must pronounce
Maze sihassannicha razemanu	Except this one thing –
Ta yecu vegalla carunu	The royal glory of my throne
Yera sacallai Egiptache zanu	All else, and the people of Egypt
Tuza niropu pallity	Will do your bidding
Ratnazaddita mudrica honty	A jewel-encrusted signet
Ti didhaly Iosechã hati	He gave into Joseph's hands
Lennĩ lugaddĩ bahutĩ	Jewels and garments in abundance
Didhalĩ teya	Were presented to him
Santossuni nrupãuaru	The King being pleased with him
Gallã ghatala sauarna haru	Placed a chain of gold on his neck
Didhala apula rahũuaru	And gave him his own chariot
Baissaueya	On which to ride

Rathu hancara re hancara	Ride, O ride this chariot
Nagari petta re ddanguira	Cry around town
Egiptacha siromanny dussara	That Joseph has been proclaimed
Iose quela mhannoni	The second highest of Egypt
Iose baissauni rayachã rathĩ	Joseph was seated in the King's chariot
Sabha zana patthauile sangatĩ	The courtiers went with him
Anny pradhana dallapaty	All the chiefs and commanders
Iose sauẽ patthauile	Were sent with Joseph
Iose aruddhala ratha vari	As Joseph ascended the chariot
Vadiẽ lagalĩ nana pary	Music began to play
Bidy sinpileya paricary	The streets were sprinkled
Parimallessi	With sweet perfume
Upariyechã duarĩ	On the houses
Ballannã ttencaliya nary	Women leaned out of terraces
Puspanche ghonssa ratha vari	Look, they drop clutches of flowers
Ttanquity deqha	On the chariot
Iosechẽ suarupa deqhunu	On seeing Joseph's form
Toza patale sacallai zanu	The people were amazed
Mhanne aissa sadaiuu laqhennẽ sampurnu	And said, we have never seen
Nahĩ deqhila	Anyone so full of beauty and goodness
Saqhy saqhithẽ mhannata	Young women whispered to friends,
Dhane ya Iosechy mata	Blessed is this Joseph's mother
Anupama rupachy suarupata	She gave birth to one
Prassãualy zi	Of incomparable beauty
Nagarĩ ddanguira pettunu	A proclamation went through the city
Iosechẽ nãua praghatta carunu	Revealing Joseph's name
Rathu ala muraddunu	Then the chariot turned around
Razemandhirĩ	And returned to the royal house
Phuddã rayẽ Iose nãua palattilẽ	Then the king changed Joseph's name
Saunssarataracu nãua ttheuilẽ	And called him "Saviour of the world"
Maga Iosena cae quelẽ	Now I will tell you
Tẽ sangaina tumã	All that Joseph did thereafter

APPENDIX 2
The Fall of Angels

Kristapurāṇa 1.2.68–115

In Vaicunttha
God created angels
And placed them there
To savour all its goodness

Numerous angels were created
They had no flesh-body
Their essence was formless
Their bodies, peculiar

God showed grace to those angels
Granted them plentiful gifts
But God did not reveal himself to their sight
At that time

If they had seen God
They would not have fallen in iniquity
Yet the lord of Vaicunttha gave them power
To choose sin or be righteous

If they eschewed wickedness
To redeem them
If they followed wickedness
To punish them

Then one Christian begged
And asked the padre
There rises a doubt in my mind
Will you allay it?

When the Lord created angels
Why did he not redeem them then
Why did the Lord of Vaicunttha delay
In granting redemption?

The Guru said, You, good Christian,
Have asked me an excellent question
Now give ear to the words
That I am about to speak

Now imagine this in your mind
Look well at this knowledge
God has two qualities
Excellent ones

He is the giver of goodness and mercy
And he alone is great and righteous
Because of his goodness he created Paradise
And named it Vaicunttha

For angels and humans
To experience all goodness
He graciously created
The city of Vaicunttha

But the righteousness of God
All goodness, Vaicunttha, redemption
Is not granted to anyone
Without devotion

God purposed in his heart
To test their integrity first
According to their virtue
To give them what is good and perfect

Now the worthy angels whom God created
How they turned into transgressors
I shall narrate to you
As the saints have written it

So it happened on an occasion
Among the angels
There was a chief
By the name of Lucifer

He was the greatest of them all
Majestic and beautiful
He took pride in himself
And what did he think?

He said, In this Vaicunttha assembly
I alone have great honour
See, I alone have received
Eternal beauty

Form, glory, might, artistry
I have received wealth
None can ever
Overtake me

News has spread in heaven
That God will take human-birth
Why should angels pay obeisance
To flesh and blood?

To open the gates of redemption
Our prowess is sufficient to us
Of no help do we have need
To attain salvation

Such were Lucifer's intentions
He forgot God, the Creator
He did not consider God's gifts of any use
And was puffed up with pride

As a householder with much wealth
Is proud above all
And says I have no need of anything
Or anyone

With Lucifer there were others
Many angels
Who accepted his opinion
In futile pride

Having no thought of God in their minds
Not giving Him the honour he deserved
Not pleasing him,
Being proud

Seeing this, the other angels
Were greatly pained in their hearts
And said we must not listen to their thoughts
Saying this, they moved away

Now Miguel, among them,
Was another great angel
Immortal among angels
He was great and virtuous

He saw the proud angels
He saw their iniquity
And gathered together
The virtuous angels

In Vaicunttha there arose a murmur
As of a rising sea
And sometimes there arose thundering
If the four clouds

Or as if in the flow of the ganga
A rock had been set
The waves split and flowed in two directions
The waters rumbling thunderously

Then Miguel, gathering courage,
Said, Who is like God?
And rebuking Lucifer
He began to speak

Why did you forget the Master
Who made you chief of angels?
You become a master-hater in vain
Because of pride

God created us
And gave us Vaicunttha – mansion for our own
Why do you not remember
Your previous state?

You must consider this
Honour your Creator
Ask Him for salvation
We all must

Come with us, you all
Let us go to the feet of the Lord of Vaicunttha
And bowing our heads at his feet
Praise Him

Who is mighty like him
Whose qualities are incomparable
Perfect in all knowledge
Let His name be exalted

He spoke these things
The others rejected this friend's counsel
Then the Lord said to Miguel
And his good angels

Trample, Trample this Lucifer
Do not give him place in Vaicunttha
Throw him from heaven into hell
With his accomplices

As God was saying this
They became the evil ones
I will tell you now
How they were cast out from heaven

As in the time of rain
Lightning falls, flashing from the sky
So these enemies of righteousness
Fell from the sky

Then parting immediately
The earth swallowed them
To witness it was to see
The wondrous work of God

God created a gaping abyss
Staggering and terrible
It was kept in store
For the angels who followed sin

The sides of the abyss opened
Terrible fire danced up from it
Which climbed up to heaven
And embraced the stars

God commanded
Miguel made a chain of fire
He bound Lucifer
And tied him to the fire-abyss

All his comrades around him
In hell's fire
Were kept
To burn for ever and ever

To what shall that hell-pit be likened
Of all the places that are on earth
It is the most awful
And lies in the earth's belly

Nothing else in this world
Is deeper
Of all places
It is the deepest

The devils who became proud
To them the pit was suited
It was made most awful
To break their pride

Those who were in that great abyss
They bear uncommon pain
Forever they smoulder
In fire

INDEX

Pages followed by n refer notes.

Abbott, Justin E. 75, 77
Abhijnanashakuntalam (1789) 148
Acquaviva, Claudius 67, 131
Acquaviva, Rudolph 67
Adi Purāṇa 75
Amonkar, Suresh 76–77, 80, 105
A History of Christianity in India 1707–1858
   (1985) 45, 47
American Wilderness Philosophy (2014)
   137
amsa 91
Arte da Lingua Canarim 69

Bakhtin, M.M. 95–96
Bassnett, Susan 11–12, 88
Bastin, Georges 7
Bender, Barbara 117
Benjamin, Walter 7
Berman, Antoine 18
Beschi, Constanzo Giuseppe 43, 86
Bhabha, Homi 17
Bhagavata Purāṇa 91, 129
Bhagvad Gita 94
bhassa 73, 131
Bhavarthadeepika (1290) 94
Bhumivaincunttha 103–104
Bible translation: Serampore Mission
   46–48; Tranquebar Mission 44–46
Blanton, Casey 120
Borikar, Bhaskarabhatta 94
Buchanan, Claudius 41, 48

Carey, William 2, 46, 48
Catholic and Protestant evangelical missions
   33
Catholic Orientalism 15, 30
Catholic wave: Indian languages and
   religions 40; mission of the Jesuits 41;
   Pfarangi Christians in India 39–40;
   Portuguese Christians in India 39;
   in Portuguese colonies 49; religious
   vocabulary for Christianity in South
   Asia 41; in seventeenth-century Salsette
   54; Society of Jesus in South Asia 42;
   translation of South Asian texts to
   European languages 41
Chatterjee, Chandrani 12, 85
Christian Bible 29
Christian Inculturation in India (2007) 34
Christianities in Asia (2011) 36
Christianity 35, 40, 128; acceptance of 133;
   Biblical landscapes 131; and European
   civil life 88; local interpretations of 144
Christian writings 23, 71, 80
Clooney, Francis X. 35, 52
Collins, Paul M. 34
colonial establishments 29
colonization 13–14, 16
Concannepanni 132
contact zone 15, 26n19, 31, 34, 38, 50, 52, 54
Cosmas Indicopleustus 38
Creating a Digital Archive of Indian
   Christian Manuscripts (EAP636) 80

creative Christianity 23, 54, 100
Cronin, Michael 8, 11, 21
cultural palimpsest 48–55
cultural translation 8, 34, 143, 149; the
    borderline condition 17; definition 16,
    35; de-Westernization 19; European
    tradition of translation 19; landscapes
    146; Malayalam literary tradition
    20; of religious texts 29; role of 146;
    secondary translation 22; translating
    culture *vs.* 16–17; translation proper 21;
    vagabondage conceptuel 18
cultural turn 4, 11–15, 17–18, 24n4, 25n13

da Cunha Rivara, J.H. 72
da Gama, Vasco 39
Das, Sarala 92–93, 97–99
de Albuquerque, D. Fr. Joao 51
de Beira, Johannes 69
defective Catholicism 87
de Nobili, Roberto 40, 43, 49, 87,
    143–144
de Pedrosa, Padre Joao 79
Der Marathidichter Stephens (1957) 62
Derrida, Jacques 7, 13
de Saldanha, Antonio 77
Deshpande, Achyut Narayan 72
de S. Miguel, Gaspar 71, 79
Deva Purāṇa 75
devmandir 130
Doutrina Christa em Lingua Bramana Canarim
    69
Drago, Caridade 77
Dussarem Puranna 8, 74, 132, 147

Exploring Translation Theories (2010) 17

Fabricus, Johann Philip 45
Falcao, Nelson M 89
fetishization 8
Fitch, Ralph 63
Fitrut, Mirza 46
Frykenberg, Robert Eric 34–35

Gambier, Yves 8
Gentzler, Edwin 13, 142
Grierson, George 48

Harris, Jonathan Gil 73
Hebrew language 4
hegemonic apparatuses 13
Henderson, David 137
Henn, Alexander 133
Henriques, Henrique 43

Hi Mho Jhi Kudd 121
Hindu Catholic Encounters in Goa (2014) 133
Hinduism 2, 22, 76, 82n19, 87, 101,
    104–105, 110, 116, 128–129, 132
Hindu literary genres 109
Hindu mythology 101
History of Portugal and the Portuguese Empire
    (2009) 39–40
Hooper, J.S.M. 41, 71

inculturation: Church rites 33; definition
    33; Roman Catholic Church 34;
    transformation 34; translation–of
    written works, practices and rituals 34
Israel, Hephzibah 47, 86–87, 146
Italiano, Federico 116

Jesuit mission: in Goa 50; in Madurai 49
Jesus Christ 70, 82n16, 84, 91, 105, 109, 132
Jones, William 14, 48, 148
Joseph Wicki, S.J. 61
Judeo-Christian Bible 28

Kamparamayana 87
Kane, Pandurang 91
King, D. Joao III 42
King James Bible 5
King James Version (KJV) 70
Kothari, Rita 19
Kristapurāṇa: biblical and the purāṇic 2;
    biblical narrative in Marathi 3; changing
    landscape of 130; Christianity and
    indigenous literary practices 117;
    Christian narrative 116; corpus of South
    Asian Christian writings 30; critical
    reading of 1; as a cultural translation
    35, 89; dialogic nature of 98–100;
    "Dussarem Puranna" of 74, 132, 147;
    ecological implications 135; 11,000
    verses 148; epic genre of 2; *First Puranna*
    127; genre and cultural translation 89;
    geographical landscape and cultural
    translation in 2; Konkani translation
    of 76, 105; landscape, identity, and
    cultural translation 131–134; landscape
    writing in 119; in Marathi and Konkani
    literary-historical traditions 70; nature in
    126–127; 1907 edition of 72; Padre-
    guru 70; *Paillem Puranna* 74; purāṇic
    terms and concepts in 144; sacred-
    text translations 3; in seventeenth-
    century Goa 117; 1648 edition of 71;
    socio-cultural landscape 119; space
    and cultural translation 116; story of

the press 69; symbols, images, and landscapes in 123–127; as templates of literary and cultural transactions 150; text of 75; by Thomas Stephens 30; title page of 70; tradition of Marathi Purāṇas 31; translation of select passages of 1; work of scripture translation 31

Landscape and Literature (2009) 138
Landscape and Memory (1995) 118
Landscape and Power 117
Latin Vulgate 35
Lefevere, Andre 11–12
Liturgiam Authenticam 108
Locke, J. Courtenay 63

Malshe, S.G. 43, 61–64, 72–73, 83n24, 95, 113n20, 147
manavantara 91
Marsden Purāṇa 77, 144
Marshman, Joshua 46
metamorphosis 143
Mitchell, W.J.T. 117
Monier-Williams, Monier 61
Mosse, David 42
Mueller, Max 14
Mukherjee, Sujit 21
Mukundaraja 93
multilingualism 19, 21, 58n30, 150n1

Neill, Stephen 45
Nida, Eugene 6
Niranjana, Tejaswini 13
Nobili, Roberto de 35, 52
Nord, Christiane 8
novelization 23, 84–114, 148

Odia language 93
Orientalism (1978) 15

pañcalakṣaṇa 92
Patnaik, B.N. 92
pervasive multilingualism 19
Pfarangi Christians 39
Phan, Peter 33, 36–37
Pitaji Stephenskrut Kristapuran 77
Plutschau, Heinrich 45
Polo, Marco 15
postcolonialism 14–15, 26n22
Pounde, Thomas 61, 64
Pracheen Marathi Vangmayacha Itihas–Bhag Choutha (1977) 72
Prasad, G.J.V. 13
pratisarga 91
Priolkar, Anant Kakba 31, 43, 69, 94

Purāṇa: as Brahminic Ideology 92; deal with origins, destruction, and regeneration 90; definition 89–91; "epic" genre 90; fifth Veda 90; functionally open texts 95; genre of 95; Hazra, Rajendra Prasad 90; Hindu religious literature 97; *pañcalakṣaṇa* 91; Purāṇic tradition 97; regional "folk" narratives 96; as scripture 91; translated story of the Bible into a "sacred" tradition 97
Pym, Anthony 17

Quran 28

Ramakrishnan, E.V. 20
Ramanujan, A.K. 8
Rao, Velcheru Narayana 91, 95
Rayer, Ananda 46
Religious Transactions in Colonial South India (2011) 86
Ribeiro, Diogo 100
Rocher, Ludo 90
Roman Catholic Church 33
Rubies, Joan-Pau 88
Rukmini Swayamvara (1292) 94
Ruyl, Albert Cornelius 39

sacredness 28, 35, 87, 93, 106
sacred-text translation 1, 3, 10, 30, 87, 146
Sahyadri Varnan (1333) 94
Saldanha, J.L. 72, 76
Sarala Mahabharata 92–93, 98
Sarga 91
School of Oriental and African Studies (SOAS) 78
Schultze, Benjamin 45
Schurhammer, Georg 61–62
Sebastiao, D. 43
Second Vatican Council (1962–1965) 33
Shishupala Vadha (1292) 94
Shwartz, Christian Friedrich 46
Siddall, Stephen 138
Singh, Brijraj 88
South Asia: Apostle Thomas 38; Christianity in 36–37; Christian practices and denominations 37; complexity of Christianity in 37; context of translations in 36; expression of Christianity 38; Roman Catholic Church in 48; third wave of Christianity in 38; translation of the Bible into an Asian language 39; two-way process of intercultural transfer 39
South Asian literature 3, 14, 30, 148

spatial turn 23, 116, 139n2, 146
spiritual landscape 110, 122
Spiritu Sanctu 108, 110
Spivak, Gayatri 14
Sri Chakradhara 94
Steiner, George 6
Stephens, Richard 66
synchronicity of language 11

Tagalog society 55n6, 107, 109
Tamil ascetic 43
Tempavani 44, 86
The Bible in India (1938) 71
The First Englishman in India: Thomas
    Stephens(1995) 88
The Historical Roots of Our Ecological
    Crisis (1967) 135
The Politics of Translation 14
*The Printing Press in India: Its Beginnings and
    Early Development* (1958) 69
*The Saint in the Banyan Tree: Christianity and
    Caste Society in India* (2012) 42
*The Translator's Invisibility: A History of
    Translation* (1995) 12
Thomas Stephens, S. J. 1–2, 9–11, 22–23, 30–
    31, 35–36, 41, 43–44, 48, 50, 52; boarded
    a ship on 4 April, 1579 61; born in
    Bushton 60; crossed multiple geographical
    borders 64; cultural translation of the
    Bible 85; died in 1619 in Goa 62; as a
    European traveller 119; five letters 65–69;
    idea of Purāṇa 85; ideological struggles
    107; *Kristapurāṇa* Portuguese version 62;
    letter by Thomas Pounde S.J. 64; letters
    to his family 143; letter to his father in
    1579 120; life, and the Christian message
    121; local customs and landscapes 116;
    missionary work at Goa 62; as poet and
    translator in *Kristapurāṇa* 130; as a poet-
    priest and author of *Kristapurāṇa* 119–120;
    Purāṇa composers in Marathi 88; studied
    at Oxford 61; translation of Catholic
    literature 108; traveling and feeding in
    India 122
Thoreau, Henry David 137
Tower of Babel 3, 21, 24n2, 115–116
transculturation 15, 18
transformation 37, 40, 65, 80, 85, 107, 110,
    116–117, 121–123, 132, 143
translatability 96–97
translation: adaptation 8–9; of Christian
    texts 5; concept of deconstruction 7;
    cultural turn 4; dangers of 5, 52, 108;
    Derridean framework of 13; of English
    literature 13; history of scriptural 3;
    interlingual transaction 4; original spirit
    of Christianity 4; role of 8–13; scriptural
    7–8; South Asian approaches 19, 21,
    26n24, 142; studies 4
*Translation and Rewriting in the Age of Post-
    Translation Studies* (2017) 142
*Translation Reconsidered: Culture, Genre and
    the "Colonial Encounter" in Nineteenth
    Century Bengal* (2010) 85
translator 5–6, 10–11, 17
Travel and Ethnology in the Renaissance (2004)
    88
Travel Writing: The Self and the World (1997)
    120
Trinidad 108, 110
Trinity 74, 98, 101–102, 104, 107–109
Trivedi, Harish 16–18, 88
Tulpule, S.G. 73, 80
Tushana Tikkaram (Refutation of
    Calumnies) (1941) 44
Tymoczko, Maria 13
Tyndale, William 5

Ulee, Meer Bahadur 46
untranslatability 77, 108–110

Vaicunttha 101–104
Vaicunttha *nayeca* 104
Vaishnavism 101
vamsa 91
vamsyanucharita 91
Vatican II 35
Ved Vilakkam I (1728) 44
Vengco, Sabino 34
Vishnu Purāṇa 91–92, 98
Vivekamala 79
Vivekasindhu 93
vocabulary of geography and translation 116

Wakabayashi, Judy 19
Ward, William 46
White, Lynn 135
wilderness wanderings 142
Wilson, Horace Hayman 14, 90–91, 103
Word of God 5–6, 47–48, 106
World Council of Churches 35

Xavier, Angela Barreto 40, 48, 121
Xavier, Francis 42

Zapf, Hubert 118
Ziegenbalg, Barthelomaus 44–45, 86,
    143–144
Županov, Ines G. 40, 42–43, 48–49, 52, 65,
    100, 121

For Product Safety Concerns and Information please contact our EU
representative GPSR@taylorandfrancis.com
Taylor & Francis Verlag GmbH, Kaufingerstraße 24, 80331 München, Germany

www.ingramcontent.com/pod-product-compliance
Lightning Source LLC
Chambersburg PA
CBHW071115100726
47908CB00008B/2385